Principles of Athletic Strength & Conditioning: The Foundations of Success in Training and Developing the Complete Athlete

Published by Crew Press
1298 Ann Arbor Trail
Plymouth, MI 48170

Copyright © 2018, International Youth Conditioning Association
1298 W Ann Arbor Trail
Plymouth, MI 48170
888.366.IYCA (4922)
All rights reserved

Library of Congress Control Number: 2017947790

ISBN: 978-1-941549-26-1

Cover design, manuscript layout, and illustrations by NiTROhype Creative

www.nitrohype.com

Text photos by Paul Routon unless otherwise noted

PRINTED IN THE UNITED STATES OF AMERICA

PRINCIPLES of ATHLETIC Strength & Conditioning

The Foundations of Success in
Training and Developing
the Complete Athlete

Table of Contents

Preface

The International Youth Conditioning Association was established in 2003 as an instrument to unite and advance the knowledge base and practical skills of trainers, coaches, and allied health professionals across the globe. Today, the vision of the IYCA is to create exceptional training experiences for every young person in the world by providing training, information and certifications to the trainers and coaches working with them.

The IYCA is the only organization that proudly stands at the intersection of scientific training principles, coaching/psychological methods that help make a positive impact on young people, and sound business development education. We tackle these important areas through courses, certifications, free information, lives events, mentorships, and personal interactions with our membership.

This text and associated certification materials will provide you with an understanding of the applicable sciences with respect to human growth and development relating to middle-school and high school age athletes, but more importantly, provide you with a blueprint for working with these athletes. Bringing together the highly-regarded list of coaches/authors in this book was a tremendous undertaking, but everyone involved understands the importance of providing quality information to every coach working with athletes.

Enjoy this information and other IYCA resources, and continue to provide exceptional experiences with the athletes you work with. Together, we have an opportunity to make a positive impact on the world.

Acknowledgements

Principles of Athletic Strength & Conditioning was a tremendous undertaking that required time, energy and dedication from many people including the authors, editors, designers, and the families of everyone involved. I would like to thank every person who contributed to this project. Your hard work and effort will benefit thousands of coaches around the world, and the ripple effect will be many times larger.

Next, I would like to thank my staff, mentors and teachers who have all helped make this project possible in their own unique ways.

I would like to thank the IYCA community, and everyone who has ever been involved, for its dedication to making a difference in the world. This is an incredible organization with many outstanding people, and this book is one more step forward for everyone dedicated to exceptional training and coaching.

Finally, I would also like to thank my wife Elaina and sons Cameron, Drew, and Jack for allowing me to spend the time necessary to complete this project and encouraging me throughout the process because they also recognize the importance of the IYCA mission.

Jim Kielbaso
President & CEO
International Youth Conditioning Association

This textbook and associated material represent the culmination of countless years of education, experience, and hard work and is the tangible result of the influence of a multitude of skilled and caring fitness and health care professionals. As with any project of this magnitude, it simply would not have been possible without the contributions of the people that brought it to life.

First, to the authors, I give my deep appreciation and thanks. Your contributions are sincerely appreciated. I am also thankful to my colleagues and students at Texas Tech who have given me the time and the resources to pursue my goals like this project. Your efforts are sincerely appreciated and I look forward to the time that I can return the favor very soon. I am also immensely thankful to Jim Kielbaso, who has successfully taken over the organization and provided leadership and vision for the present and the future. It has been a pleasure to get to know you and work with you on this project, and I look forward to what the future has in store for the organization with you at the helm.

Lastly, I am forever grateful to my family who give me the freedom and support to pursue my goals. My wife Christi and my children Brynnan and Taye have sacrificed much as I spent hours behind a desk. My hope and prayer is that I will live a life the shows my gratitude and thankfulness for being a part of such a fun, supportive, and downright incredible family. You are the best and I love you all!

Toby J. Brooks, PhD, LAT, ATC, CSCS, PES, YFS-3
Associate Professor of Rehabilitation Sciences
Clinical Coordinator, Master of Athletic Training Program
Texas Tech University Health Sciences Center

CHAPTER 1

Anatomy and Exercise Physiology for the Strength & Conditioning Professional

Joe Powell

Objectives

- Utilize the appropriate anatomical terminology with respect to planes, axes, and direction
- List and describe muscles that act on the primary joints of the body, including the prime movers and their primary plane of action
- List and describe the components of the musculoskeletal system and their primary roles
- Describe the sliding filament theory and discuss how skeletal muscle functions to produce movement
- Identify the primary differences between the primary muscle fiber types
- Describe the influence of the respiratory system on human performance

Introduction

The human body is composed of several specialized systems that work to function together and provide the basis for everyday living. This network of integrated systems is responsible for maintaining homeostasis, yet also thriving when put through such rigors as intense exercise. The human body is able to achieve a remarkable range of tasks. Understanding the anatomical make-up of the body and how its systems function independently—as well as together as a unit—will provide the strength and conditioning professional (SCP) with the necessary prerequisites to provide the best possible care and training for their respective athletes.

Navigation of the Body

In order to classify direction of movement or location of structures, the human body is traditionally divided into three cardinal planes, including the sagittal, frontal or coronal, and transverse planes and movements occur about or around three axes including the lateral, the anterior/posterior, and the vertical axes. The three planes are defined when an individual is standing in anatomical position, and anatomical position is defined when one is standing erect with palms facing forward.

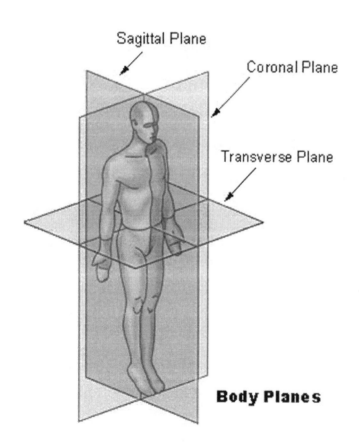

Figure 1.1: Cardinal planes of the human body. wikimedia commons photo

Each cardinal plane is always associated with the same axis. Specifically, movements in the sagittal plane occur about the lateral axis, movements in the frontal plane occur about the anterior/posterior axis, and movements in the transverse plane occur about the vertical axis. Since the majority of athletics is based upon randomized movement in all three planes as well as reacting to randomized movement in all three planes, strength coaches must program accordingly. Most strength and conditioning programs feature a variety of individual movements from all three of the planes, as well as many movements that feature a combination of two, or even all three.

The sagittal plane divides the body into right and left portions. The terms medial (closer to the midline of the body) and lateral (further from the midline of the body) are appropriate when describing location of structures in this plane. Flexion and extension typically occur within the sagittal plane and, as a result, about the lateral axis. Movements such as the back squat and forward lunges are primarily performed within the sagittal plane.

The frontal plane divides the body into front and back portions. The terms anterior (front) and posterior (back) are appropriate

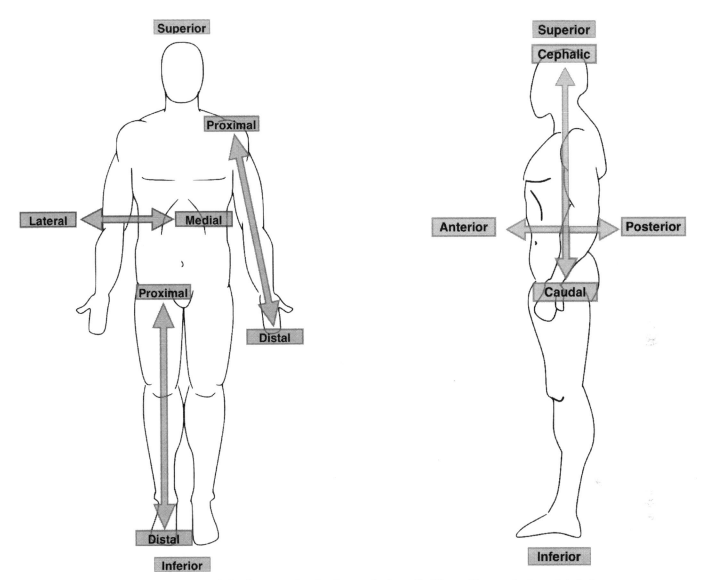

Figure 1.2: Directional terms of the human body, frontal view (left) and lateral view (right). wikimedia commons photo

when describing location of structures in the frontal plane. The joint actions of adduction and abduction occur within the frontal plane. The jumping jack and shoulder lateral raise are examples of a movement primarily taking place in the frontal plane and, as a result, the anterior/posterior axis.

The transverse plane divides the body into upper and lower portions. The terms superior (above) and inferior (below) are used to describe the location of structures in this plane. The joint action of rotation occurs within the transverse plane and about the vertical. Shoulder internal and external rotation against a resistance band as often performed four shoulder maintenance and rehabilitation is an example of a movement that takes place primarily in the transverse plane, but adding a rotation component to many skills and drills can improve function in this often-neglected plane.

All of the joints in the human body serve to perform specific functions. Skeletal, cartilaginous, and ligamentous structure are the primary determinants of the movement possible at a particular joint, but other soft tissue and neurological influences are important, as well. Most often, an inverse relationship between stability and mobility exists with regards to joint structure, with a relatively mobile articulation such as the glenohumeral joint in the shoulder being relatively unstable compared to the less mobile but more stable coxafemoral joint of the hip. Understanding the interrelationship of the muscles involved from a certain joint action, as well what a joint action looks like can help the SCP program, prevent injury, prescribe specialized exercises, and be more efficient with overall training development. Table 1.1 provides a summary of the major joints within the human body, their actions, and the prime movers involved.

Table 1.1: Major joints, Prime Movers, and Primary Planes of Action

Joint	Joint Action/ Movement	Primary Mover(s)	Primary Plane of Movement
Glenohumeral (shoulder)	flexion	anterior deltoid, pectoralis major	sagittal
	extension	latissimus dorsii, Teres major	sagittal
	adduction	latissimus dorsi, Teres major	frontal
	abduction	middle deltoid, supraspinatus	frontal
	internal rotation	subscapularis, pec major, latissimus dorsii, teres major	transverse
	external rotation	infraspinatus, teres minor	transverse
	horizontal adduction	pectoralis major, anterior deltoid	transverse
	horizontal adbduction	latissimus dorsi, teres major, teres minor, infraspinatus, posterior deltoids	transverse
Scapulothoracic (shoulder girdle)	elevation	levator scapulae, upper fibers of trapezius, rhomboids	frontal
	depression	lower fibers of trapezius, pectoralis major	frontal
	retraction	serratus anterior, pectoralis minor	sagittal
	protraction	middle fibers of trapezius, rhomboids	sagittal
	upward rotation	upper and lower fibers of trapezius, rhomboids	frontal
	downward rotation	rhomboids, pectoralis minor	frontal

Joint	Joint Action/ Movement	Primary Mover(s)	Primary Plane of Movement
Humeroradial/humeroulnar (elbow)	flexion	biceps brachii, brachialis, brachioradialis	sagittal
	extension	triceps brachii	sagittal
Proximal radioulnar (elbow)	pronation	pronator quadratus, pronator teres, brachioradialis	transverse
	supination	supinator, biceps brachii, brachioradialis	transverse
Wrist	flexion	flexor carpi ulnaris, flexor carpi radialis	sagittal
	extension	extensor carpi ulnaris, extensor carpi radialis longus and brevis	sagittal
	radial deviation	flexor carpi radialis, extensor carpi radialis longus and brevis	frontal
	ulnar deviation	flexor carpi ulnaris, extensor carpi ulnaris	frontal
Thoracic and lumbar spine	flexion	rectus abdominis, external oblique, internal oblique	sagittal
	extension	erector spinae	sagittal
	rotation	internal oblique, external oblique, erector spinae, rotatores, multifidus	transverse
	lateral flexion	internal oblique, external oblique, multifidus, quadratus lumborum, rotators	frontal
Pelvis	anterior tilt	iliopsoas	sagittal
	posterior tilt	rectus abdominis, internal oblique	sagittal

Joint	Joint Action/Movement	Primary Mover(s)	Primary Plane of Movement
Coxafemoral (hip)	flexion	iliopsoas, pectineus, rectus femoris	sagittal
	extension	gluteus maximus, biceps femoris, semitendinosus, semimembranosus	sagittal
	adduction	gracilis, adductor magnus, longus, brevis, pectineus	frontal
	abduction	gluteus maximus, medius and minimus, tensor fasciae latae, sartorius	frontal
	internal rotation	gluteus medius, minimus, tensor fascia latae, pectineus	transverse
	external rotation	gluteus maximus, piriformis, quadratus femoris, obturator internus and externus, gemellus superior and inferior	transverse
Tibiofemoral (knee)	flexion	biceps femoris, semimembranosus, semitendinosus	sagittal
	extension	rectus femoris, vastus medialis, vastus lateralis, vastus intermedius	sagittal
Tibiotalar (ankle)	plantar flexion	gastrocnemius, soleus	sagittal
	dorsiflexion	tibialis anterior, extensor digitorum longus, peroneus tertius	sagittal

Understanding biomechanics is crucial when designing and implementing a successful strength and conditioning program. Knowing which muscles are associated with a given joint action gives the SCP the ability to develop programming based on the athlete's specific needs. Exercises can be either single-joint or multi-joint in nature. Single-joint exercises are usually considered isolative and only require one working joint to perform the exercise (e.g. biceps curl), whereas a multi-joint exercise is more integrative in nature and is performed using multiple body segments together. While programming may feature a blend of multi- and single-joint exercises, optimal performance depends upon integrative strength and skill. As such, a much higher emphasis should be placed on performing multi-joint exercises. Basic athletic movements such as running, jumping, shuffling, etc. all require the body to use multiple joints and muscle groups to perform the desired action.

The principle of specificity states that the more similar training is to an actual sport movement, the higher the probability that a positive transfer to the sport movement will take place. This is also known as specific adaptation to imposed demands, or the SAID Principle. When choosing exercises to include in a program, it is important to consider the SAID principle. For example, if a strength coach is programming for a sprinter on a track team, he/she will need to focus on exercises that are explosive in nature and that would utilize the same energy system that will coincide with the athlete's event or sport. Programming long distance running for a 100-meter sprints athlete will be counterproductive in their training. By focusing on training proper energy systems as well as movements, the SCP will yield better results for their athletes.

Musculoskeletal System

The musculoskeletal system is comprised of bones, muscles, tendons, ligaments, and joints. These components are arranged in such a manner that allows an individual to achieve a great variety of movement. The following section describes how each component contributes to the overall musculoskeletal system, as well as their individual function.

Skeletal System

The human skeletal system usually contains 206 bones, with that number sometimes varying due to genetic variation. The primary function of the skeletal system is to provide the body with support, structure, protection, and to aid in movement. Bones can vary greatly in terms of size and shape, but even the largest bones in the human body remain relatively light given their impressive strength and tensile loading capabilities.

The skeletal system is most often organized into two primary divisions: the axial skeleton and the appendicular skeleton. The axial skeleton includes the skull, vertebral column, sacrum, ribs, and sternum. The bones that comprise the axial skeleton are crucial for protection of vital organs including the brain, spinal cord, heart, and lungs. Meanwhile, the appendicular skeleton is comprised of the bones of the upper and lower extremities and both the shoulder and pelvic girdles. The appendicular skeleton provides the body with more movement and greater ranges of motion than the axial skeleton.

Bony articulations, or joints, are classified into three primary categories depending on the structure and the resultant movement possible within the joint. Fibrous joints allow for virtually no movement (for example, skull sutures). Cartilaginous joints such as the intervertebral disks that separate the vertebrae in the vertebral column accommodate minimal movement but provide shock absorption. Meanwhile, synovial joints such as the knee, hip, shoulder, etc. allow for significant movement.

Joints function by rotating around on or more of the previously mentioned axes of rotation. Synovial joints that allow for greater ranges of movement are further categorized dependent on how many directions of rotation around an axis they display. Uniaxial joints rotate around one axis. Often referred to as a ginglymus or hinge joint, the elbow is one example. Biaxial articulations rotate around two perpendicular axes of rotation and the tibiotalar joint of the ankle is one example. Additionally, multiaxial joints allow for the greatest of joint movement and can move about all three of the perpendicular axes. Examples of multiaxial joints include the glenohumeral joint of the shoulder and the coxafemoral joint of the hip.

Skeletal Muscle

Movement in the human body is made possible in part by the arrangement of skeletal muscle in accordance with bone. Skeletal muscle attaches at each end via a proximal and distal attachment point, sometimes referred to as the origin and insertion respectively. The relationship between muscle and bone is what provides the ability to move. Skeletal muscle is composed of multiple long, cylindrical structures called sarcomeres, also referred to as muscle cells. These microscopic cells form tissues, and layers of skeletal muscle tissues form marcoscopic muscles that differ in location, arrangement, size, function, and even predominant fiber type. No matter what the composition of a certain skeletal muscle may be, all are composed of muscle tissue, connective tissue, vascular structures, and sensory and motor nerves that are vital for function.

Skeletal muscle is encased by a thin, sheath-like layer known as epimysium. Epimysium, also known as fascia, encapsulates the entire muscle and adjoins with tendons found at the attachment points of the structure. The muscle structure is further divided by perimysium, which serves to divide the tissue into smaller bundles of muscle fibers. These bundles are known as muscle fascicles and can consist of up to 150 individual fibers. Surrounding each individual fiber is another division of connective tissue called endomysium, surrounded by the sarcolemma of the muscle. The sarcolemma is the muscle fiber's cell membrane and plays a vital role in muscle contraction. The three connective tissue structures (epimysium, perimysium and endomysium) that surround the layers of a skeletal muscle are contiguous with tendons and it is the structural characteristics of this tissue that provides for the elastic capacity leveraged in movements like plyometrics while also transmitting the force developed through normal muscular contraction.

Understanding the function of skeletal muscle begins by examining the inside of an individual muscle fiber and learning its structural and physiological makeup. Each fiber contains sarcoplasm, which is simply the cytoplasm of a striated muscle cell. Sarcoplasm is the material within a muscle cell that houses the components necessary for a muscle fiber to function. The majority of sarcoplasm is comprised of hundreds of myofibrils that are made up of the myofilaments actin and myosin. These filaments are the basis for every skeletal muscle contraction.

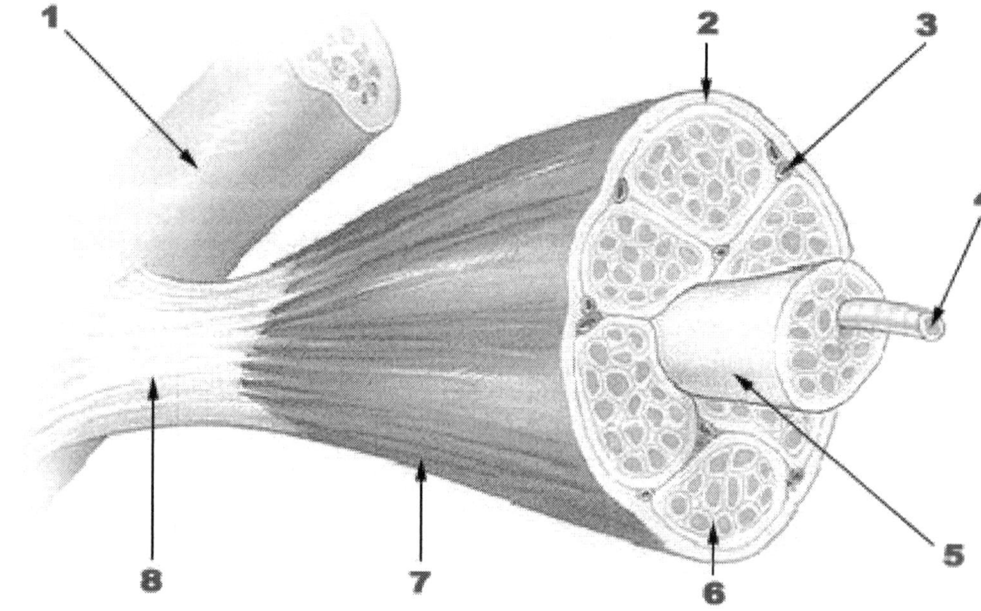

The two major filaments are classified by their structure as "thick" or "thin." Myosin is the thick myofilament and features many globular heads (which are similar in shape to a golf club) that are attached to a tail and backbone. The

Figure 1.3: Skeletal muscle structure. 1: bone; 2: perimysium; 3: blood vessel; 4: sarcomere; 5: fasicle; 6: endomysium; 7: epimysium; 8: tendon. wikimedia commons photo

IYC

heads point away from the fibrous tail-like structure and are in a position that, in the proper environment, can interact with the thin myofilament, actin. Actin is smaller in diameter than myosin and is composed of two strands that feature a double helix shape. Attached to actin and spiraling in the same helix shape between the two strands is the protein tropomyosin. The tropomyosin strand runs the entire length of the actin filament and features another protein, troponin, that is situated in intervals along its entire length. These two proteins cover the active sites on the actin filament to prevent interaction with the myosin heads except during contraction. Troponin and tropomyosin play a vital role in muscle contraction.

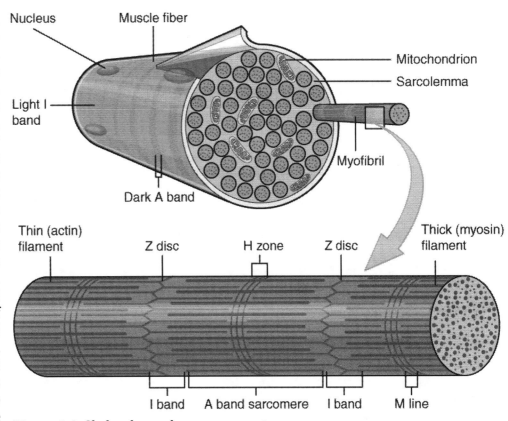

Figure 1.4: Skeletal muscle arrangement. wikimedia commons photo

Actin and myosin filaments are bundled to form the sarcomere, which is the smallest contractile unit of skeletal muscle. Many bundled formations of actin and myosin lie next to each other to give the sarcomere its length. Within the sarcomere, actin and myosin interact to cause skeletal muscle to contract. Several sarcomeres are bundled together to create an individual myofibril. Surrounding and running the length of the myofibrils is a network of tubules known as the sarcoplasmic reticulum. At the end of each stacking of actin and myosin, the sarcoplasmic reticulum features a vesicle that runs perpendicular to the rest of the structure, referred to as T-tubules. These structures are responsible for housing calcium ions, one of the catalysts in a muscular contraction.

Neuromuscular System

The nervous system allows the body to process and respond to its environment. Involvement of the nervous system is evident in every system of the body, but understanding its relationship with the musculoskeletal system in particular is paramount for those seeking to understand the human response to exercise, including strength and conditioning.

Commands sent by the brain to a working muscle are accomplished, in part, by the interaction of a nerve cell (motor neuron) and a muscle fiber. Communication between the motor neuron and the muscle fiber it innervates is accomplished through a synapse at the two sites, also known as the neuromuscular junction. An individual muscle fiber does not typically possess its own singular motor neuron. Instead, a single neuron will branch out and innervate many muscle fibers. The combination of a motor neuron and all of the muscle fibers it innervates is referred to as a motor unit. The amount of muscle fibers within a single motor unit will vary, but a typical motor unit will be comprised of hundreds of fibers. The smaller the ratio of motor neurons to muscle fiber, the more fine and precise movements of that muscle will be. For example, muscles are found around the eye or tongue are capable of much more specific and controlled movements compared to the large postural muscles of the spine. As a result, the eye muscles will have only a few muscle fibers per motor neuron, while the spinal erectors will have hundreds.

When an electrochemical signal is transmitted from a motor neuron to the motor unit, each muscle fiber belonging in the unit is stimulated and will contract at the same time and rate. Muscle fibers within a unit cannot partially contract and particular fibers are not selected to contract on an impulse-to-impulse basis. The muscle fibers either contract all at once, or not at all. This is known as *the all-or-none principle*. The electrochemical signal that a motor neuron transmits is called an action potential and it is responsible for beginning the process of muscular contraction.

Sliding Filament Theory

The basis of skeletal muscle contraction can be explained when examining what happens during the sliding filament theory. The theory states that muscle fibers are able to contract with the shortening of the myofibrils due to actin sliding over myosin. The result is a shortened muscle that has developed tension. This theory can be described by focusing on four key phases: Resting phase, excitation-contraction coupling phase, contraction phase, and relaxation phase.

- **Resting Phase**: There is minimal binding of myosin cross-bridges to actin at this point. Myosin and actin are still interacting, allowing for the bond to become strong once tension is produced
- **Excitation-Contraction Coupling Phase**: The nerve stimulates an action potential that travels down a neuron to the neuromuscular junction, which stimulates the sarcoplasmic reticulum. The sarcoplasmic reticulum releases calcium ions that bind with the protein troponin. The binding causes a shift in the protein tropomyosin that unlocks active sites on actin. Myosin cross-bridges can now attach to actin rapidly. The result is actin filaments being pulled closer to the center of the sarcomere.
- **Contraction Phase**: Contractions are stimulated by the release of calcium, but powered by the breakdown of adenosine triphosphate (ATP) into adenosine diphosphate (ADP) and phosphate (P). A contraction will continue to occur if calcium is still available and a new molecule of ATP replaces the hydrolyzed ADP molecule on the myosin cross-bridge head.
- **Relaxation Phase**: A contraction will cease when the innervating nerve is no longer stimulating. Due to the nerve no longer stimulating the sarcoplasmic reticulum, calcium is retrieved and actin and myosin return to their pre-contraction state.

Muscle Activation

Muscle Fiber Types

Skeletal muscle tissue holds a distinct difference over the other two muscle tissue types found in the human body. Skeletal muscle is unique compared to cardiac muscle and smooth muscle because it can be classified by its varying physiological differences. The most recognized classification of the muscle fibers is based on *twitch time*, which is essentially the muscle fibers' contraction speed. This qualitative trait yields the names **fast-twitch fibers** and **slow-twitch fibers**.

Fast-twitch muscle fibers are capable of rapidly developing a great amount of force, while also exhibiting the ability to relax rapidly, which results in a short overall twitch time. Conversely, slow-twitch muscle fibers develop force at a slow rate and relax slowly which results in a long twitch time. Muscle fibers are most commonly identified as:

- Type I (slow-twitch)
- Type IIa (fast-twitch)
- Type IIx (fast-twitch)

When muscle fibers within a motor unit are recruited to perform a function, they will display patterns based on the force output required to complete a task. Type I fibers are always recruited first. As the task becomes more intense, Type IIa fibers are recruited. If the task is very intense, Type IIx fibers will eventually be recruited. This means that no matter what the given exercise intensity may be, Type I fibers are always prevalent. Though Type I motor units are firing during any given action, the predominant fiber type responsible for any given action is based primarily on intensity.

An Olympic lift such as the snatch or power clean will utilize all fiber types, but a much higher percentage of Type IIx involvement compared to the other types based on the intensity of the movement. Another quality that factors into the recruitment pattern is the size of the fiber. Recruitment starts with the smaller fiber diameter and works its way up in size. Type I fibers, being the smallest in diameter, are recruited first, followed by type IIa and then IIx. This is known as the size principle of fiber recruitment.

There are many mechanical and physiological differences among Type I and Type II muscle fibers, and even several differences between the two different Type II fibers. The following chart summarizes the main differences and their characteristics.

Table 1.2: Characteristics of Muscle Fiber Types

Characteristic	Type I	Type IIa	Type IIx
Contraction time	slow	moderately fast	fast
Relaxation speed	slow	fast	fast
Fatigue resistant	high	intermediate/low	low
Endurance	high	intermediate/low	low
Force production	low	intermediate	high
Power output	low	intermediate/high	high
Capillary density	high	intermediate	low
Myoglobin density	high	low	low
Fiber size	small	intermediate	large

All three muscle fiber types are prevalent in every athlete, however the actual percentage of a certain fiber type will vary within each individual. Having a certain predominant fiber type is advantageous for different sports/activities. Aerobic athletes such as cross-country runners, long distance track athletes, marathon runners, or cross-country skiers will benefit from a greater percentage of Type I fibers. Type I fibers are incredibly efficient when compared to Type II and are fatigue resistant. While Type I fibers lack the ability to produce great force, they are ideal for long bouts of near steady state exercise.

Conversely, Type II fibers (Type IIa and Type IIx) are capable of rapid force development but are highly fatigable and relatively inefficient. They feature low aerobic power but high anaerobic power output. Athletes who benefit from a higher percentage of Type II fibers include sprinters, Olympic weightlifters and American football players.

While Type IIa and Type IIx fibers are classified under the fast-twitch fiber type, they still feature differences. The main difference between the two occurs in their capacity for aerobic-oxidative energy supply. Type IIa fibers show greater resistance to fatigue than Type IIx due to a higher concentration of surrounding capillaries as well as a greater capacity for aerobic metabolism. Type IIx fibers can gradually transition into Type IIa fibers through training.

Muscle Actions

The terms "*muscle actions*" and "*muscle contractions*" are synonymous, as both describe the process of a muscle's force development. The term "muscle contraction" does not always mean that a muscle shortens in length (as in the case of an eccentric muscular action), thus many professionals prefer the term "muscle actions." Regardless of the terminology, both define the three different contraction types a muscle can possess to generate power.

During an exercise that is static (without movement) in nature, the muscular action does not result in a change in length. This contraction type is known as **isometric**. Tension is evident throughout the muscle, but since the force produced in the muscle the resistance encountered are equal, the muscle neither shortens nor lengthens. These actions occur primarily in postural muscles throughout the body, which are help maintain static posture when seated or standing for prolonged periods. Exercises such as planks, wall sits, and hollow leg holds are examples that focus on the isometric contraction.

When movement is involved during an exercise, it is referred to as being dynamic in nature. The two primary muscle actions utilized in strength training are both dynamic. A **concentric contraction** occurs when the force produced is greater than the resistance encountered. As a result, muscle shortens and movement is created. Conversely, when a muscle is activated but the force produced is less than the resistance encountered, the muscle lengthens and (in most cases) movement is controlled or managed. This is referred to as an **eccentric contraction**. In the majority of strength training exercises, both concentric and eccentric actions occur. Manipulation of each contraction type plays an important role to the development of strength.

Proprioceptors

A proprioceptor is a specialized sensory receptor that is located within muscles, joints, tendons, and tissues. Proprioceptors are sensitive to tension and pressure, and are able to relay information to the central nervous system (CNS) regarding changes in muscle properties. When a proprioceptor sends information to the CNS, the response allows for an individual to increase their kinesthetic awareness and to perform complex and highly coordinated movements.

Muscle spindle fibers (MSFs) are an example of a proprioceptor that is embedded within the muscle tissue. MSFs are made up of modified muscle fibers enclosed within connective tissue. The modified muscle tissues are known as **intrafusal fibers** and lie parallel to the normal muscle fibers, called **extrafusal fibers**. MSFs respond to changes in length within the muscle and any stimulus that triggers an MSF response activates the muscle in which they are embedded. When a muscle lengthens due to an increased load placed upon it, the MSFs are stretched, resulting in an impulse sent to the spinal cord where it synapses with motor neurons. The additional motor neuron input accommodates a stronger contraction, allowing the athlete to combat or overcome the stressor. Manipulation of the muscle spindle for sports performance can be seen when the stretch reflex is used in plyometric training.

Another important proprioceptor is the **Golgi Tendon Organ (GTO).** GTOs are located in the tendon and are attached to extrafusal fibers. Unlike the activating nature of the MSF to accommodate greater muscular action, the GTO functions to inhibit muscular contraction and unload the muscle/tendon unit, typically to prevent injury when the unit is excessively or too rapidly loaded. When rapid and/or high levels of load are placed on a muscle, GTO activation occurs. Feedback is then sent to the spinal cord where a reflex is triggered to inhibit further muscular activation.

When the GTO inhibits muscle activation, it is protecting an individual from excessive tension brought upon by an excessive force. This mechanism can help prevent injury when placed under excessive loads. Manipulation of the GTO is done when partaking in activities such as foam rolling and certain types of stretching (i.e. Proprioceptive Neuromuscular Facilitation, or PNF). This threshold of inhibition is a trainable response, and placing an athlete under reasonably heavy loads during resistance training can help prevent this neural feedback quality, thereby allowing for adaptation to become stronger.

Cardiovascular System

The cardiovascular system, also referred to as the circulatory system, is a network of organs and vessels responsible for numerous vital functions. The major roles of the cardiovascular system include serving as a transportation system for oxygen, nutrients, and waste products and regulating the body's core temperature, pH, and fluid balance. Proper functioning of the cardiovascular system is crucial for maintaining homeostasis within the human body.

Heart

The heart serves as the pump that, in many ways, powers the cardiovascular system. The heart is a muscular organ that is divided up into two sections that allow for the pumping of blood to differing areas of the body. The left side of the heart pumps oxygenated blood to the body/periphery and the right side of the heart pumps deoxygenated blood to the lungs. Each side of the heart (or pump) features two chambers stacked on top of one another. On top is the atrium and on bottom is the ventricle. Both the right and left atria deliver blood to their respective ventricles, which then serves as the primary force for ejecting the blood into either the pulmonary (right) or peripheral (left) circulations. Between the atria and the ventricles is a specialized valve system that allows for powerful ejections of blood but inhibits backflow. The tricuspid valve separates the right chambers of the heart and the bicuspid valve separates the left chambers. Known collectively as the atrioventricular valves, they open and close passively and operate on a pressure gradient to ensure forward flow is achieved and backflow is avoided.

The heart relies on an electrical conduction system that triggers each heartbeat. Specialized cardiac muscle cells located within the walls of the heart send signals to the cardiac muscle tissue to initiate a contraction. This specialized conduction system is comprised of the sinoatrial (SA) node, the atrioventricular (AV) node, the atrioventricular (AV) bundle, the left and right bundle branches, and the Purkinje fibers. The electrical impulse that results in a heartbeat typically begins in the SA node and makes its way through the other aforementioned components of the conduction system. The timing of an impulse is incredibly systematized, and does not travel too quickly. The delays in conduction allow for the necessary contractions of the atria to preload the ventricles before they subsequently eject the blood to the corresponding vessels.

The rate at which the heart beats is dependent on many factors, but each conduction begins in the brain—specifically in the cardiovascular center of the medulla. These signals are transmitted by the autonomic nervous system, which is comprised of two components: the **sympathetic nervous system** and the **parasympathetic nervous system**. The atria are comprised of fibers from both parasympathetic and sympathetic nervous systems, whereas the ventricles are almost exclusively sympathetic. Parasympathetic and sympathetic nerves differ by the fact that stimulation of sympathetic nerves causes the heartrate to increase, whereas parasympathetic nerves decrease the heartrate.

Blood

Blood is a specialized body fluid that plays several roles vital to survival. The three major functions of blood are transportation, regulation, and protection. Blood is comprised of two components: plasma and blood cells. Plasma accounts for nearly 55% of blood and is composed almost entirely of water, whereas blood cells provide the remaining 45% and are what give blood a more viscous quality than water. The composition of blood cells is almost entirely red blood cells (RBCs), with only a fraction being white blood cells.

The most important role of blood in regards to exercise is its ability to transport oxygen and carbon dioxide. Oxygen is transported from the lungs to the cells of the body, and carbon dioxide is transported from the cells of the body and back to the lungs. Oxygen is carried by the RBCs.

Each RBC is shaped like a disc and contains no nucleus, but instead contains a protein called hemoglobin. Hemoglobin is responsible for transporting oxygen and is able to use red blood cells as the carrier to distribute oxygen from the lungs to the rest of the body. RBCs are also carriers for certain enzymes, like carbonic anhydrase, which breaks down carbon dioxide and water, allowing for carbon dioxide to be readily removed from the tissue and delivered back to the lungs. Blood is also responsible for transporting nutrients, hormones and removing waste.

Blood Vessels

Blood vessels serve as the central pathway for blood to travel through the body. This closed-circuit system is composed of two elements with opposing roles. Although similar conceptually, the anatomical make-up and function of the arterial system and venous system differ substantially. The arterial system is responsible for distributing oxygenated blood from the heart to the rest of the body, whereas the venous system returns blood from the body back to the heart.

Blood vessels display certain properties that make them unique and highly adaptable to various changes placed upon the body. Most notably, smooth muscle allows the vascular structures to vasodilate (increase in circumference) or vasoconstrict (decrease in circumference), thereby allowing the body to divert blood flow to areas, regions, or even specific organs in response to stressors. For example, exercise in a hot environment can result in hyperthermia, so the peripheral vascular structures can divert blood flow toward to the surface of the skin in order to utilize it as a radiator to cool the body.

Conversely, in a cold environment, vasoconstriction can serve to centralize blood flow in an effort to retain as much body heat as possible.

Arteries are responsible for transporting blood from the heart to all areas of the body (except for pulmonary arteries which will be addressed later in the chapter). Since the heart acts as a pumping system that drives blood away, arterial structure is somewhat different than venous structures. Arteries feature strong muscular walls that are much thicker than veins. This allows for the high pressure that is resultant with every heartbeat. The pumping system pushes blood into smaller branches in the arterial system that eventually allow for the exchange of blood from the arteriole to the venous system. Blood first passes through the arteries into the smaller arterioles before eventually making its way to the smallest of the blood vessels, the capillaries.

Capillaries are thin-walled vascular structures that accommodate diffusion and are configured into a large interweaving network referred to as the capillary bed. Capillaries are so small and thin that their walls are permeable to offload important substances like oxygen and other nutrients while also taking away carbon dioxide and other waste products. The permeable walls allow the capillaries to distribute the newly deoxygenated blood to the venous system.

Deoxygenated blood courses through venules before making its way to larger veins. The veins then return the blood to the heart. Unlike the vessels in the arterial system, venous system structures are much thinner and more pliable. Since venous return is largely a passive process and venous pressures are much lower, venous walls need not be thick and muscular like those of the arterial system. Many veins (most often in the lower extremity) have one-way valve to prevent backward flow of blood due to gravity. Lastly, veins feature thin and pliable walls that allow for great amounts of constriction and dilation. This is important since the venous system has the highest concentration of blood in the circulatory system.

Respiratory System

The respiratory system is responsible for the exchange of the two gases, oxygen and carbon dioxide, within the body. Simply put, the respiratory system allows humans to breathe. In order for this routine function to occur, the respiratory system must work in close relation with the circulatory system. The joint efforts of both the respiratory and cardiovascular systems are in place to diffuse gases to or from the blood.

Structure and Function

Structure of the respiratory system begins with a group of passages that lead into the lungs. The structures that comprise the passageways include the nose, nasal cavity, pharynx, larynx, trachea, bronchi, and bronchioles. These respiratory structures are vital for multiple reasons. During inhalation, the body goes to work by warming, filtering, and humidifying air. No matter the climate or environment, the air that is inhaled is warmed and saturated with water vapor. This serves to protect the internal temperature of the body and to prevent lung tissue from drying out. The outside air consumed during inhalation must pass through many progressively smaller stages of passages before it reaches its final destination.

First, inspired air passes through the trachea and to the large primary bronchi (both right and left). The secondary bronchi enter the lobes of the lungs and are broken down further into tertiary bronchi. After traveling through the multiple stages of bronchi, air then passes through smaller bronchioles that further divide and separate into even more smaller branches until finally reaching the alveoli. The alveoli are tiny sacs composed of thin membranes where gas exchange occurs and oxygen is transferred into the blood in exchange for carbon dioxide. This exchange is known as diffusion. Diffusion occurs because of differing concentration gradients within the capillaries and alveoli. The partial pressure of oxygen is higher in the alveoli than in the capillaries, enabling it to diffuse into the pulmonary capillary blood. Carbon dioxide diffuses in the opposite direction where it then can exit the body as an exhalation.

Mechanics of Breathing

The process of breathing is initiated when the lungs expand and recoil back to their original form. This action is not an active expansion by the lungs but rather dependent upon separate muscular actions that alter the volume of the thoracic cavity and create a pressure gradient that triggers air to either enter or exit the lungs. The diaphragm is a broad, sheet-like muscle that serves as the floor of the thoracic cavity and serves as the main driver for breathing at rest, or in a relaxed state. Upon contraction, the diaphragm increases the volume of the thoracic cavity, thereby generating a negative pressure gradient. Under such conditions, the volume of the lungs acts like a vacuum and pulls air in. When the diaphragm relaxes, the negative pressure gradient dissipates, and expiration takes place.

When the breathing rate is increased due to factors such as exercise, the mechanisms for breathing are changed. The diaphragm is not strong enough to keep up with the newly increased breathing demands, so the abdominal muscles assist by contracting. When the abdominal and intercostal muscles contract, they push against the diaphragm and expand the ribcage respectively, further increasing the negative pressure gradient in the thoracic cavity first triggered through contraction of the diaphragm. The forcing of ribcage elevation (inhalation) and depression (exhalation) via the intercostal muscles is another way to assist during times of heightened breathing rate.

Athletes are often taught certain breathing maneuvers to create the most efficient way to inhale and exhale during exercise. Proper breathing and bracing techniques can give the athlete an advantage during both sport and exercise. Three common techniques are frequently used in training to stabilize the spine. The abdominal drawing-in maneuver (ADIM) or voluntary pre-emptive abdominal contraction (VPAC) involves contracting the transversus abdominus muscles to engage the "muscular corset" that further supports the lumbar spine. Similarly, the abdominal bracing maneuver (ABM) involves also engaging the anterior core as if preparing to be punched in the stomach. During both the ADIM/VPAC and the ABM, the athlete should still be able to talk. Conversely, the Valsalva maneuver is another technique commonly performed during resistance training that involves a forceful exhalation while closing off the glottis of the respiratory pathway, suddenly increasing pressure in the thoracic cavity. This technique causes a transient spike in blood pressure and is contraindicated in older athletes or any patient who is hypertensive. Breathing and bracing techniques may not be appropriate for every athlete, so further research should be performed by a coach before teaching it in their program.

Conclusion

Proper understanding of structure and function of the human body as well as its response to exercise allows the strength and conditioning professional to understand some of the mechanisms behind different training strategies. This helps the SCP create safe and effective programs for athletes. Building a program based on scientific principles allows coaches to meet the specific needs of an athlete and help them progress to their fullest potential.

References

- Brooks T, Stodden D. *Essentials of Youth Fitness and Conditioning*. Elizabethtown, KY: International Youth Conditioning Association, 2012.
- Calais-Germain B. *Anatomy of Movement: Revised Edition*. Seattle: WA, 2003.
- Floyd R. *Manual of Structural Kinesiology*. 17th ed. New York: McGraw-Hill, 2009.
- Haff GG, Triplett NT. *Essentials of Strength Training and Conditioning*. 4th ed. Champaign, IL: Human Kinetics, 2016.
- Patton K, Thibodeau G. *Anatomy & Physiology*. 9th ed. Maryland Heights, MO: Mosby, 2016.
- Prentice W. *Principles of Athletic Training: A Competency-Based Approach*. 14th ed. New York: McGraw-Hill, 2011.
- Seeley RR, Stephens TD, Tate P. *Anatomy & Physiology*. 8th ed. New York: McGraw Hill, 2008.
- Van De Graaff KM. *Human Anatomy*. 6th ed. New York: McGraw Hill, 2002.

PRINCIPLES of ATHLETIC Strength & Conditioning

The Foundations of Success in
Training and Developing
the Complete Athlete

CHAPTER 2

Energy Systems & Conditioning

Bill Burghardt

Objectives

- List the three primary energy systems and discuss the appropriate intensity, work duration, and rest interval necessary for optimum training adaptations

- Understand the relative contributions of the three primary energy systems to most team and individual sports

- Be able to implement appropriate exercise prescriptions to best train the predominant energy system(s) associated with the specific sports being trained

INTERNATIONAL YOUTH
CONDITIONING ASSOCIATION

Introduction

Gaining an understanding of the conditioning required for optimal sport performance first requires the SCP to understand how the human body produces energy. The systems through which humans produce energy are some of the most important processes of survival. Grasping a basic knowledge will enable the SCP to understand what happens in various sports and how to best train the body for the unique demands of each. This chapter will cover both a general overview of each energy system, the fatigue experienced during activity, and the principles to follow when designing conditioning programs for sport.

Key Vocabulary

Before diving into the different ways through which the body produces energy, it is important to first take a look at some key terms that are pertinent to the functioning of the various systems. First, **energy** is a fundamental entity of nature which is transferred between parts of a system. Energy is the "currency" through which all living organisms produce and expend. It is also the product of physical change within the system and usually regarded as the capacity for doing work. **Bioenergetics** is the science of energy transformations and energy exchanges within and between living things and their environments. Metabolism involves the chemical changes in living cells by which energy is provided for vital process and activities and how new material is assimilated. Metabolism can also be viewed as the sum of the building (Anabolic) and breakdown (Catabolic) processes in the body. Lastly, **Adenosine Triphosphate** (ATP) is a molecule composed of adenosine and three phosphate groups that supplies energy for many biochemical cellular processes by undergoing enzymatic hydrolysis (breakdown) to adenosine diphosphate (meaning two phosphates, ADP).

The Three Primary Energy Systems

Every muscle contraction requires ATP. This is because the process of breaking ATP into ADP and a phosphate ion releases free energy.[1] This energy release powers every muscle contraction. ATP is stored in the muscle cells, ready for immediate use. Once depleted, replenishment of ATP can occur via one of three energy systems to allow continuing work to be performed, including the phosphagen system (also known as the alactic system or the ATP-PC system), the glycolytic system (also referred to as the lactate system, or fast or slow glycolytic system), and the oxidative system (also known as the aerobic system).

The Phosphagen System

The phosphagen system provides ATP for every movement/exercise, regardless of intensity, and is the primary energy system for activities requiring short-term, high-intensity movements such as sprinting, throwing, etc.[2] Both ATP and phosphocreatine (PCr) contain phosphates, thus the name phosphagen system (and alternatively ATP-PCr system). ATP is broken down when it reacts with water and the enzyme myosin-ATPase. This reaction causes ATP to lose a phosphate, becoming ADP. In addition to ADP, phosphate, and free energy, a hydrogen ion (aka proton, H+) is also produced. The chemical reaction equation is:

$$ATP + H_2O \xleftrightarrow{\hspace{1cm}} ADP + Pi + H^+ + \text{Free Energy (Free energy causes muscle contraction)}$$

ATP is stored within muscle cells but in very small quantities (1 Calorie); therefore, the body must rapidly replace it in order to continue to work.[3] The phosphocreatine system is the first energy system called into action.[1] Here, phosphocreatine (PCr) reacts with the now-present ADP (ATP broken down to ADP after muscle contraction), H^+, and the creatine kinase enzyme, to synthesize ATP and the waste product, creatine. Essentially the phosphate (P) bound to creatine (Cr) is moved to the ADP, forming ATP again. The chemical reaction equation is:

$$PCr + ADP + H+ \xleftrightarrow{\hspace{1cm}} ATP + Cr$$

The ATP produced in this reaction then can go through the ATP hydrolysis reaction again. Like ATP, phosphocreatine is stored in very limited amounts within the muscle cells (4 Calories).[3] A third reaction occurs as part of the ATP-PCr system when 2 ADP molecules react with each other through the myokinase enzyme to create ATP & adenosine monophosphate (AMP). AMP is important because it stimulates the glycolytic energy system (the second system called to action). Generally, the reactions in the ATP-PCr system provide enough energy needed for 5-10 seconds of very intense activity.[4]

The phosphagen system is regulated primarily by creatine kinase activity. If a cell contains a heavy concentration of ADP molecules as a result of ATP break down, creatine kinase is stimulated and the PCr system is called into action. Conversely, the presence of ATP inhibits creatine kinase and the system slows.[5] Every muscle action results in ADP production, which is why this system is the first energy system stimulated regardless of intensity. If the energy demand required to continue the exercise is low enough, the glycolytic system can take over replenishing ATP at a more efficient rate.

Glycolysis

Glycolysis involves the breakdown of carbohydrates to produce ATP. The carbohydrate source can be intra-muscular glycogen or blood glucose. Generally, all carbohydrates are broken down to pyruvate. The reaction is initiated when 2 ATP molecules are first broken down for muscle contraction, however, the resulting process generates 4 ATP, resulting in a net gain of 2 ATP. The process also produces 2 H^+ ions. From this point, one glucose (or glycogen) molecule has been converted into 2 pyruvate molecules. What happens after this process depends on the presence of oxygen molecules in the cell.

Anaerobic Glycolysis

When oxygen is not available, pyruvate is metabolized through the anaerobic glycolysis pathway. In the process, pyruvate reacts with nicotinamide adenine dinucleotide (NADH) and a hydrogen ion. The chemical equation for this process is:

$$\text{Pyruvate} + NADH + H+ \xleftrightarrow{\hspace{1cm}} \text{Lactate} + NAD+$$

This process results in the production of lactate and NAD^+. NAD^+ then goes back to help drive the glycolysis steps required earlier to produce pyruvate. There are conflicting beliefs as to what causes muscle fatigue in this energy system. Some contend that H^+ ions inhibit glycolytic reactions and inhibit muscle contractions and thus impact sport performance.[6] On the other hand, others have contended that potassium (K^+) ion build-up from the muscle contraction process is the limiting factor.[7] For practitioners, the take home point is that the production of lactate is not necessarily a bad thing. This is a common misunderstanding in strength & conditioning. After formation, lactate is shuttled to the liver and is converted to glucose through a process called the Cori cycle. All in all, anaerobic glycolysis is the primary system utilized for energy when intense effort is required for 30-120 seconds.

Aerobic Glycolysis

The other path that can be taken once pyruvate is created and oxygen is available in sufficient quantities within the cell is aerobic, or slow, glycolysis. Here, pyruvate, along with NAD^+, is shuttled into the mitochondria in muscle cells and gets converted into acetyl-coenzyme A (acetyl-CoA) and NADH. After acetyl-CoA is created, it is then utilized in the oxidative system while NADH is also utilized to allow for additional ATP creation. Slow glycolysis is really a priming step that allows for a highly efficient production of ATP in subsequent steps of metabolism.[1]

Oxidative System

The oxidative system is the third energy system for ATP re-synthesis. This system is composed of the Krebs cycle and the electron transport chain (ETC). Again, only the basics will be covered for this chapter.

Krebs Cycle

The Krebs cycle utilizes acetyl-CoA produced in slow glycolysis. Through the cycle 2 ATP are created for immediate use, as well as 6 NADH molecules and 2 flavin-adenine-dinucleotide (FADH2). These 8 molecules continue on, along with the NADH produced in aerobic glycolysis, to the electron transport chain.[1]

Electron Transport Chain

The ETC consists of a series of reactions that occur within the mitochondria. It is named the electron transport chain because electrons get passed from one molecule to another.[1] From start (glycolysis) to finish (ETC), the oxidative system yields 36-38 ATP. Compared to the 2 ATP produced in ATP-PCr system or 4 from fast glycolysis, it is clear that given adequate time, the oxidative system is far more efficient than other metabolic pathways. However, during periods of intense activity and maximal or near-maximal exertion, the time needed for the various steps in the process simply is not available. As a result, this system is predominant for long duration, low intensity, activities.[1]

Other Energy Systems

Described above were the three primary energy systems for physical activity. However, the body has other energy sources it can use for ATP synthesis, primarily fats and proteins. Fats and proteins get converted to ATP through oxidation.

Fat Oxidation

Fats may be broken down by the enzyme hormone-sensitive lipase and is circulated to the muscles via the bloodstream. Some fat can be stored in muscle tissue, as well, but only in small quantities.[8] A stored fat molecule can produce 463 ATP.

Protein Oxidation

Protein can also be converted to ATP through a process called gluconeogenesis. Protein oxidation takes place in the liver as is very similar to how lactate is converted back to glucose. The amount of ATP produced through protein oxidation is very small during short, high-intensity activities. However, protein oxidation can contribute 3% to 18% of the ATP needed for longer, lower intensity activities.[9]

The energy systems described above begin to reach a limit when their corresponding substrates are depleted. For example, the ATP-PCr system will be ineffective once most of the phosphocreatine is broken down into creatine. Each energy system in the series has more fuel at its disposal, but the time required in order to synthesize ATP takes longer. The final point to note on the conversion of protein and fat to carbohydrates relates to energy balance. Excessive carbohydrate intake above caloric needs can lead to both protein and fat synthesis. Fat synthesis above optimal levels leads to obesity, and with it, a host of health problems.

Practical Applications: Conditioning

The role of the SCP is to take this basic understanding of energy systems and apply it to the training programs for the athletes. There are numerous reasons to have athletes practice their sport or "cross-train" with other exercises including increasing muscle size and length, improvement in body composition, increased neuroendocrine function (hormones & neurotransmitters that improve health and performance), improved cardiovascular output.[10]

One primary role of conditioning is often to minimize the fatigue athletes experience in order to maximize their performance in competition. Fatigue is often the result of the depletion of the sources of energy. Table 2.1 demonstrates the various energy sources and the volumes they are stored in an average human body.

Energy Source	Major storage form	Total body Calories	Total body kilojoules	Distance covered**
ATP	Tissues	1	4.2	17.5 yards
PCr	Tissues	4	16.8	70 yards
Carbohydrate	Serum glucose	20	88	350 yards
	Liver glucose	40	1,680	4 miles
	Muscle glycogen	1,500	6,300	15 miles
Fat	Serum-free fatty acids	7	29.2	123 yards
	Serum triglycerodes	75	315	0.75 miles
	Muscle triglycerides	2,500	10,500	25 miles
	Adipose tissue triglycerides	80,000	336,000	800 miles
Protein	Muscle protein	30,000	126,000	300 miles

Table 2.1: Major energy stores in the human body with approximate total caloric value*[3]

*These values may have extreme variations depending on the size of the individual, amount of body fat, physical fitness, and diet.

**running at an energy cost of 100 Calories per mile.

Exercise & conditioning can improve the efficiency of these energy systems via numerous adaptations include increased storage of energy sources available, improved efficiency of accessing the energy stores, greater number of cells responsible for shuttling the sources to the muscles, improved oxygen uptake through respiration leading to more aerobic energy system utilization, and greater number of mitochondria available to convert the energy sources to ATP.[11]

There are several other factors a coach needs to consider when selecting the appropriate types of conditioning activities including, relatability to the demands of the sport, availability of training modalities, ability to coach the training modality in a safe environment for the athletes and coaches, and proper progression of conditioning program

Relatability to the Sport

Every coach should know the physical demands of the sport their athletes play. This knowledge will allow the coach to design conditioning programs to work the energy systems that are more predominant in the sport. This may be accomplished through a movement analysis of a game or practice situation or simply consulting a tool such as Table 2.2.

Table 2.2: Energy system contributions to select popular sports[12]

Sport / Activity	ATP-PC	Lactic Acid	Aerobic
Baseball	80	15	5
Basketball	75	15	10
Field Hockey	60	20	20
Football	90	10	0
Golf (swing)	100	0	0
Gymnastics	90	10	0
Hockey	80	20	0
Rowing	20	30	50
Soccer	60	20	20
Diving	98	2	0
Swim (50m)	95	5	0
Swim (100m)	80	20	0
Swim (200m)	30	65	5
Swim (400m)	20	40	40
Swim (1.5km)	10	20	70
Tennis	70	20	10
Field Events	90	10	0
400m	40	55	5
800m	10	60	30
3km	5	35	60
Marathon	0	2	98
Volleyball	90	10	0
Wrestling	45	55	0

While tools such as this provide a general understanding of athletic demands, some sports can have positional and play-vs-game variances. For instance, the conditioning required to play wide receiver in football is not the same as it is to play quarterback. Also, a golf swing is a pure ATP-PC activity, however, playing 18 holes requires walking almost four miles carrying a golf bag. Therefore, keep in mind the entire sport and all its variances when designing conditioning programs. With that said, there is no simpler way to condition for a sport than to play the sport at the level of intensity required on competition day. The creativity comes when the athlete either cannot play the sport (due to time of year, availability, etc.) or chooses not to participate (limit overuse injuries, etc.).

One way to increase metabolic efficiency is to utilize the interval training method. This is done by alternating periods of work with periods of rest. Which work-to-rest ratio to use is based on which energy system the athlete wants to utilize (and ultimately train) predominantly. Table 2.3 defines which work-to-rest ratios stress each system.

Table 2.3: Exercise time and work-to-rest ratios for primary energy systems[13]

% of maximum power	Primary system stressed	Typical exercise time	Range of work-to-rest ratios
90-100	Phosphagen	5-10 seconds	1:12 to 1:20
75-90	Fast glycolysis	15-30 seconds	1:3 to 1:5
30-75	Fast glycolysis and oxidative	1-3 minutes	1:3 to 1:4
20-30	Oxidative	>3 minutes	1:1 to 1:3

It is critical to consider the primary metabolic system utilized for a given sport or position in order to determine how much rest to prescribe during a conditioning session. There is some evidence that suggests doing some anaerobic conditioning can improve aerobic performance.[14,15] A high aerobic fitness capacity can also counteract fatigue in sports with numerous sprint repetitions (i.e. Football, hockey, basketball, etc.) (This chapter will not go into specifics on how to condition for each sport because there are so many variables that impact programming.

Availability of Training Modalities

Undoubtedly, both sport coaches and SCP will have to adapt their training programs to the tools they have at their disposal. For example, if inclement weather for a day prevents a cross-country team from training outside, a suitable alternative such as a treadmill, stationary bike, or elliptical jogger may be used if available. Similarly, skating for hockey may translate better from a conditioning standpoint than running. However, if ice is unavailable, the training program will have to be adapted accordingly. One suggestion is to use average shift times for hockey players and run the team for those same work-to-rest durations.

Ability to Safely Implement Training Program

The primary rule for the SCP is to minimize injury risk to athletes during training. With that in mind, if conditions are not ideal or the SCP does not feel confident in implementing certain conditioning modalities safely, then safer alternatives should be substituted. For instance, trail running is often used as a conditioning tool for runners. However, if the terrain is unfamiliar to the coach, there is a possibility of losing supervision of the athletes. If the athletes are not familiar to trail being run, it is important that the coach educate the athletes or change the training appropriately.

Proper Progression of Training Program

The SCP should consider the importance of progressing the athletes—particularly those who are untrained or undertrained—carefully to the conditioning level needed for the sport. Too much activity at too great an intensity can lead to overtraining injuries and psychological burnout. There are numerous ways to progress conditioning programs and generally these progressions should occur on a training session-to-training session or week-to-week basis. Most training programs center on increasing distance, increasing speed, increasing rate of perceived exertion, increasing intervals, decreasing rest period lengths, and/or increasing frequency of training sessions per week.

Some programs are designed to follow a linear pattern where every training session is slightly more difficult than the previous. Other programs follow an undulating pattern where training sessions are harder for a time frame, and then a modified training session is mixed in. This programing style often includes a taper to competition where some relatively lighter or easier training days are prescribed before competition to ensure optimal athlete readiness. There is no right or wrong program design so long as the demand on the athlete increases at a proper rate that limits the chances of overuse injuries. Communication with the sport coaches and athletes before, during, and after training and competitions can facilitate the development of proper conditioning programs.

Example Conditioning Programs

As mentioned previously, there are a multitude of factors that must be taken into consideration before designing and progressing a conditioning program. Following are a few sample conditioning workouts that may be of benefit when designing new programs to meet specific athlete needs.

Baseball (80/15/5 Energy Split)

- Dynamic warm-up: 15 min
- Plyometrics: 10 min
- Speed mechanics & agility training: 10 min
- Conditioning: 15 min
    - 10 reps of 30 yard runs with a goal of 5-6 seconds. Rest time should be 1 minute to mimic the pace of baseball
- Cool-down & stretch: 10 min

The program may be progressed by adding a few extra runs each session, decreasing rest, or decreasing goal time by a specified interval like 0.2 seconds. Alternative exercises include hard running outfield pole to outfield pole followed by jogging down to home plate and back, shorter sprints requiring athlete to stop suddenly to simulate playing a ball, etc.

Basketball (75/15/10 Energy Split)

- Dynamic warm-up: 15 min
- Plyometrics: 10 min
- Speed mechanics & agility training: 10 min
- Conditioning: 15 min
    - 8 reps of ladder run: Baseline to free throw, back to base, to half court, back to base, to far free throw, back to base, baseline to base line. Goal time of 45 seconds. Rest time of 3 min

- Cool-down & stretch: 10 min

Progressing this conditioning could involve decreasing the rest by 15 seconds each session, increasing the number of reps by 2, or changing distances. Alternatives include sprinting the length & jogging the width, sideline-to-sideline runs for time (with coaching changing the pace on a whistle), or a variation of running and jumping. Again, the important piece is that the athletes become acclimated to jogging & sprinting for the appropriate times to be expected in practice and games.

American Football (90/10/0 Energy Split)

- Dynamic warm-up: 15 min
- Plyometrics: 10 min
- Speed mechanics & agility training: 10 min
- Conditioning: 15 min
    - 10 reps of 110s (Full length of field from back of end zone to far goal-line)
    - Skill (WR, DB, RB): 16 seconds
    - Big skill (LB, QB, TE, FB, SP): 17 seconds
    - Power (OL, DL): 19 seconds
- Cool-down & stretch: 10 min

The times utilized in this program are representative of the capabilities of collegiate athletes. Consequently, high school and younger ages should use slower times and should NOT require all-out sprints. The rest period here should be between 45s – 1min due to the typical time from whistle to snap during normal gameplay. Each session can be progressed by increasing the reps by 1-2 or by decreasing rest time by 5 seconds. This is one of many conditioning drills that can be implemented.

Alternatives include short runs of 60 to 80 yards, half-gassers (the width of the football field and back), sprints of 10 to 20 yards, or even sled pushes. Each of these will require unique goal times and rest periods. The goal is to simulate the metabolic demands the athlete is typically exposed to during football practice and games while creating a general progression of intensity in order to safely bring players up to game/practice-ready conditioning levels.

Soccer (60/20/20 Energy Split)

- Dynamic warm-up: 15 min
- Plyometrics: 10 min
- Speed mechanics & agility training: 10 min

- Conditioning: 15 min

    o 6 laps running the length of the soccer pitch hard, slow jog the end line across. Goal is to run the length in under 20 seconds, jog the end line in 40 seconds.

- Cool-down & stretch: 10 min

Progressing this drill could be accomplished by decreasing the time allotted to cross the field by 1 second, decreasing the amount of time allotted for the jog across, or increasing the number of laps required by 1 each session. Alternative exercises include ladder runs (similar to basketball), shorter sprints with jogging, or even blowing a whistle to have athletes walk, jog, run, or sprint for times that are likely to occur in a soccer game. Again, the concept is to safely increase the load and to prepare the athletes for typical game and practice work-to-rest intervals.

Remember, the above examples are just basic conditioning drills to get started. Both the SPC and the sport coach must condition the athlete for a variety of reasons including to improve cardiovascular conditioning, muscular strength, power, and speed while also reducing the chance of overuse injuries. Planning conditioning sessions includes understanding the demands of the sport, consider the equipment available, account for the athletes' current conditioning levels, and determine what safety factors are at risk. The SPC must always be sure to provide adequate hydration and limit the increases in intensity of subsequent sessions to 15-25%. This will help mitigate the effects of overtraining and reduce the chance of injury.

It is also a good idea to include "down" weeks or de-load periods where skill instruction can emphasized and conditioning temporarily minimized in order to provide an opportunity for recovery. Typically, it is suggested to incorporate such programming every 3 to 4 weeks early. Lastly, safety is most important. The SPC must be certain all athletes are monitored for signs of distress and make communication between coaches, athletes, parents, and athletic trainers a top priority.

References

1. Baker J, McCorminck M, Robergs R. Interaction among skeletal muscle metabolic energy systems during intense exercise. *Journal of Nutition and Metabolism.* 2010:1-13.

2. Brooks G, Hittelman K, Faulkner J, Beyer R. Temperature, skeletal muscle mitochondrial functions, and oxygen debt. *American Journal of Physiology.* 1971;220:1053-1068.

3. Williams M. Human Energy. In: Williams M, Anderson D, Rawson E, eds. *Nutrition for Health, Fitness, & Sport.* New York: McGraw-Hill; 2013.

4. Berg J, Tymoczko J, Stryer L. *Biochemistry.* 5th ed. New York: WH Freeman; 2002.

5. Poortmans J. Protein turnover and amino acid oxidation during and after exercise. *Medicine and Sports Science.* 1984;17:130-147.

6. Nakamura Y, Schwartz A. The influence of hydrogen ion concentration on calcium binding and release by skeletal muscle sarcoplasmic reticulum. *The Journal of General Physiology.* 1972;59:22-32.

7. Lindinger M, Kowalchuk J, Heigenhauser G. Applying physicochemical principles to skeletal muscle acid-base status. *American Journal of Physiology.* 2005;289(3).

8. Brooks G, Fahey T. *Exercise Physiology: Human Bioenergetics and Its Applications.* New York: Wiley; 1984.

9. Brooks G. Amino acid and protein metabolism during exercise and recovery. *Medicine and Sports Science.* 1987;19:S150-S156.

10. Kraemer W, Deschenes M, Fleck S. Physiological adaptations to resistance exercise. *Sports Medicine.* 1988;6:246-256.

11. Ball D. Metabolic and endocrine response to exercise: sympathoadrenal integration with skeletal muscle. *Journal of Endocrinology.* 2014;224(2):R79-R95.

12. Fox E, Mathews D. *Interval Training: Conditioning for Sports and General Fitness.* Orlando: Saunders; 1974.

13. Herda T, Cramer J. Bioenergetics of Exercise & Training. In: Haff G, Triplett N, eds. *Essentials of Strength Training and Conditioning.* 4th ed. Champaign, IL: Human Kinetics; 2016.

14. Billat L. Interval training for performance: A scientific and empirical practice. *Sports Medicine.* 2001;31(1):13-31.

15. Hickson R, Dvorak B, Gorostiaga E, Kurowski T, Foster C. Potential for strength and endurance training to amplify endurance performance. *European Journal of Applied Physiology.* 1988;65:2285-2290.

CHAPTER 3

Testing & Evaluation

Freddie Walker

Objectives

- List and describe the reasons for testing and evaluating young athletes
- Identify several primary assessment tools used to test major components of athleticism and motor skill development in young athletes
- List and describe the Big5 Assessment tool and discuss how it can be implemented for athletes aged 6-9, 10-14, and 14+

Introduction

In the world of athletics, successes and failures are often measured by wins and losses. With stakes continuing to trend upwards, it is imperative that the strength and conditioning professional (SCP) and sport coach make efficient use of the available time and the time of their athletes. Utilizing regularly scheduled testing and evaluation methods is a means to ensure a program or team is headed in the right direction. While testing involves the processes used to determine an athlete's ability or skill, evaluation entails the SCP's or sport coach's efforts to assign significance or value to those results.

The field of strength and conditioning has been regarded by many professionals as being as much art as it is a science. With respect to testing and evaluation, it is relatively easy to see how the two constructs can complement one another very well. One could even argue that testing and evaluation are actually just two steps of the same process with neither being fully useful without the other. However, in this chapter, we will discuss the similarities and differences of the two and illustrate why they should be treated as two separate entities. To that end, it is important to analyze and discuss several issues surrounding testing and evaluation including the rationale behind the practice, the importance to a coach or athlete, the ways by which to use and apply testing data, the processes through which to communicate data (testing results) and evaluations to a coach or athlete, and identify several commonly used tests.

The goal of testing should be to gather accurate information, so the SCP should approach testing like a researcher: as merely a means of data collection. When approaching testing like data collection in research, the SCP is more likely to pursue the process with a greater attention to detail through a careful and methodical means of solving problems. More specifically, data collection should systematic, logical, empirical, reductive, and replicable.[1] For the SCP who is typically more interested in the practical rather than empirical aspects of collected data, the systematic and logical characteristics of testing are usually most important. This serves to provide the necessary structure and focus required for the testing utilized to be valid and reliable. At the same time,

Rationale for Testing

Physical testing is a critical building block in any strength and conditioning program. It allows the coach and the athlete to assess capabilities and capacities, the level to which the program is altering those capabilities and capacities, and to precisely steer the program forward. While it certainly is possible to design a training program while paying little or no attention to the athlete's current abilities, such an approach will rarely—if ever—yield optimal results.

It is important to note that while testing results will indeed determine the current level of an athlete's abilities, these findings are an intricate and complex culmination of many different factors. Physical training is one key factor, but other questions are pertinent, as well. What is the level of exertion during a training session? Is the stimulus from training such that a change in the athlete's abilities is elicited? Does the program design adequately control necessary factors to promote growth and change? Additional factors including nutrition, sleep, psychological state, current phase in training calendar, and genetic potential are relevant, too.

With so many different factors to consider when testing, it is important to focus on areas that the SCP can actually influence. Educating athletes about how to eat, sleep, and take care of themselves is one approach to help manage these factors. Genetic potential, on the other hand, is a factor most would consider unchangeable without chemical enhancement of some kind.

When testing, a coach can control the time, place, and conditions of the testing. Managing these components on a given test day can aid in the accuracy of testing results and serve to improve reliability and validity. The careful organization and administration of testing allows the SCP to replicate a similar testing environment each and every test day, giving data enhanced meaning and strength.

How to Use Testing and Evaluation

To help give direction to a program, testing can clearly define a starting point and help in developing the necessary steps to reach a goal. It can set a baseline for athletes, therefore influencing the design of their specific regimen. While testing helps define an athlete's strengths, it also allows the SCP to clearly determine weakness and areas needing improvement. Once these areas have been defined, the SCP can create a program to address them.

For instance, if a depth drop-landing test reveals a strong valgus knee pattern in a female volleyball player, we can presume she has weak musculature or central nervous system activation in her hips or core. The SCP can then tailor a plan in which the athlete has additional exercises to address these and other deficiencies. In doing so, the athlete's performance should improve while her resiliency and resistance to injury should increase, as well.

The other primary use of testing is to be able to provide the sport coach with as much objective and subjective information regarding the athletes. In an ideal situation, the sport coach and SCP would coordinate the course of action in order to develop the athlete optimally such that sport-specific skills and drills are prescribed in concert with strength and conditioning prescriptions in a global fashion. Too often, the sport coach and the SCP work independently, thereby increasing the likelihood that the practice and training prescriptions in a given week, mesocycle, or even macrocycle are not ideal. Along with a development plan, testing and evaluation could be utilized in creating potential depth charts and game plans during the competitive season.

How/What to Communicate to the Athlete

Delivering raw data to an athlete in an unedited format is haphazard and could have detrimental consequences. Communicating with athletes about their progress, how the culmination of their work has affected their development, or how their training habits need to change are important considerations when conveying testing results. The SCP must be both honest and careful in this situation. An athlete's confidence and mental state needs to be included in the thought process. Testing should not be made personal when it comes to delivering results. Instead, it should be as objective as possible. The subjectivity of a given evaluation should include a discussion as well as a plan to provide appropriate feedback and direction. Increasingly, the new generation of athlete is more knowledgeable of training and physical development than ever before. Athletes want to understand the process and often welcome an opportunity to discuss it.

Ultimately, the style in which test results are communicated to athletes is up to the coach, but it should always be clear, concise, and carefully thought out. Athletes want to know that their effort is not being wasted and they want that information to be communicated in a way that makes sense and moves them closer to their goals. With that being said, an athlete who needs to give greater effort and pay more attention to their training habits may also appreciate an honest evaluation and accept suggestions. This is an excellent opportunity to discuss important topics with an athlete and help them move in a positive direction.

Testing

Scientific & Systematic

The scientific method is used because it is systematic, logical, and proven. When an SCP evaluates athletes, he or she should have the same focus. While conditions, coaches, and athletes may change, it is critical to control as many factors as possible to ensure testing is repeatable and can be recreated by someone else at another time if necessary. This is where validity and reliability come into play.

Validity & Reliability

The role of validity is to guarantee that data is justifiable and relevant. Validity comes in two forms: internal and external. Internal validity determines the extent to which the test answers the question posed and provides the data desired. For example, the 40-yard dash does not provide a direct measure of strength. As a result, it has poor internal validity if used as a strength assessment. Conversely, the 40-yard dash possesses high internal validity when utilized as a linear speed assessment.

On the other hand, external validity refers to the relationship of one data set to another gathered in a similar manner. With that in mind, we can see how the 40-yard dash has external validity, as it is a widely accepted and utilized test of speed in various sports. External validity helps determine the extent to which one test or study conducted on a group of subjects can be applied to other similar situations and people. Continuing with the example of the 40-yard dash, since it involves a set distance and is tested in a very similar format from one trial to another, it possesses a widespread commonality.

Reliability of a test describes whether or not a test is repeatable. This is important because if a test is not repeatable time after time while using the same methods, any change observed from pre-test to post-test could potentially be a result of testing error rather than a true change due to training. For example, a max-strength squat test must be performed exactly the same each time if the SCP truly wants to evaluate strength. If the pre-test was done using a half-squat, but the post-test was done using a full ROM squat, test data will not be reliable because the procedures incorporated were inconsistent.

Schedule and Sequence of Testing

With reliability in mind, it is clear that the schedule of testing is important. For example, if a pre-test is done with lower body strength followed by speed testing, but the post-test is done with speed testing followed by lower body strength testing, the results will be skewed and erroneous. In order to ensure the most accurate assessment possible, it is also important for the SCP to establish a consistent order to the components of the test battery to be employed with all trials. At the same time, it is also important to practice the test before it is actually administered. Most tests have an element of skill and technique in order to administer accurately and tester error should not be a factor when testing physical qualities of any kind.

Evaluation

Collaboration with Sport Coach

The SCP must collaborate with the sport coach to determine the primary aims of testing and what qualities should be subject to interpretation of the resultant data. By doing this, the SCP can be better prepared to thoroughly discuss the data with the sport coach. Testing data could potentially influence depth charts, allocation of resources, use of eligibility, etc. With that in mind, it is important to take time to accurately assess each athlete given all the information available. Simply put, we need the complete picture. Collaboration with the sport coach is essential because he or she is chiefly responsible for the success and failure of the team, which includes the athletes' physical development.

Sport-Specific Evaluation & Correlation with Sport Requirements

To assume that an athlete will perform better in a given sport solely because test results are favorable is highly inaccurate. While there is most likely a relationship between improved test performance on valid tests and actual game performance, it is not considered a direct correlation. For example, while a fast time on a 40-yard dash test demonstrates speed and speed is certainly advantageous in football, the best football players do not always have the fastest 40-yard dash times. Although there is a relationship, it does not imply causation—an important point to understand. This simply means that improvement on a test does not necessarily equal improvement in the sport. The athlete still needs to apply that physical trait to their sport and specific skill-set.

Types of Testing

Speed

Speed testing usually consists of linear running drills. An athlete is tracked for time over a set distance with no change of direction or impedance of any kind. Common tests include the 5, 10, 20, 40, or 60-yard dash.

Figure 3.1: 20-yard dash testing Toby Brooks photo

5-, 10-, 20-, 40-, or 60-Yard Dash (also commonly measured in meters)

On the subject of a dash, a given distance is marked along a straight path or lane. The athlete being tested is given a specific starting line at the beginning of that lane.

For a starting position, the athlete can assume any number of stances. Ultimately whether the athlete utilizes a two-point, three-point, staggered, parallel, or any other type of stance depends on the nature of the athlete's sport and position as well as the wishes of the SCP. Two of the most frequent starting positions are a three-point stance or a two-point speed stance. In a three-point stance, the athlete staggers the feet front to back and also places a single hand on the ground. This hand is typically positioned opposite of whichever foot is placed in front.

With the two-point speed stance, the athlete similarly staggers their feet front to back. The only change is that they do not place a hand on the ground; instead they simply bend their knees and ready themselves to propel off of the start line.

Regardless of stance, timing usually starts at the athlete's first movement and ends when the chest breaks the finish line.

Agility

Agility testing is focused on assessing the repetitive acceleration, deceleration, and change of direction skill of an individual. In agility testing, the athlete is given a determined course that must be navigated as quickly as possible while timed from a starting point to a finish line. Common assessments include the pro-agility, L-drill, and arrowhead agility tests.

Pro-Agility (5-10-5) Shuttle

The athlete should begin at the 5-yard point in a ten-yard segment and straddles the center line, facing the coach while placing one hand on the ground. The athlete should then sprint five yards to the right, touch the yard line with the right hand, turn and sprint 10 yards to the left, touch the yard line with the left hand, turn and sprint back five yards to the right, and finish by sprinting through the original starting line.

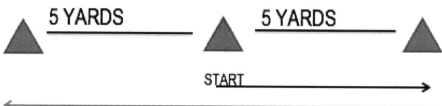

Figure 3.2: Pro Agility Shuttle

L-Drill

The SPC begins by establishing a course consisting of three cones spaced five yards apart in an upside down "L" configuration. The athlete then starts from a three-point stance and sprints to the first cone/line and touches the line with the right hand. The athlete then turns and sprints back to the starting line, touching with the right hand again. The athlete completes the drill by turning and running around the second cone to the third while weaving inside it then back around the second cone and through the start.

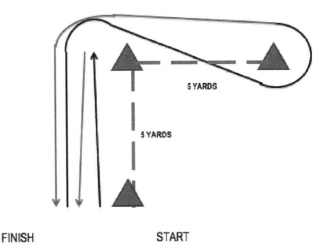

Figure 3.3: L-Drill

Arrowhead Agility Test

The arrowhead agility test includes both linear speed and change of direction in one test. The athlete begins from a pre-determined starting position at the designated start line. A cone is placed 10 yards directly ahead with a second cone placed five yards beyond in and five yards to the right and left are a third and fourth cone, creating an arrowhead shape.

To begin the test, the athlete sprints forward and to the left of the cone at the 10-yard mark, turning right at that cone. The athlete should proceed to the cone 5 yards ahead, and to the right of that cone. Once reaching that cone, the athlete should turn left to the cone that was placed 15 yards from the starting line at the top of the arrowhead. After reaching that cone and going around it to the right, the athlete should turn left and sprint back through the finish line. The drill should be repeated to the opposite side. While sprinting was used in the previous description, it may be performed using various patterns of movement including shuffling, sprinting, backpedaling, crossover running, and other movement skills.

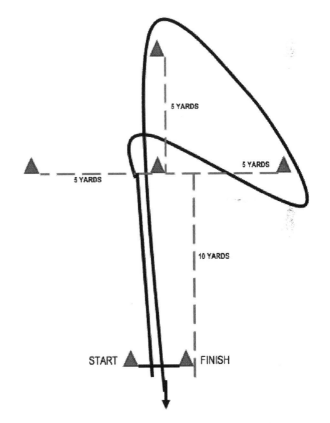

Figure 3.4: Arrowhead Agility Test

Conditioning/Aerobic Capacity

Conditioning tests come in a number of various distances, formats, and other variants. These tests are used to determine the aerobic capacity or maximal oxygen uptake capabilities of an athlete.

To determine this, the SCP can use either a field setting – the field, court, track, etc. – where the athlete would be tested primarily in an applied/functional setting or in a laboratory setting, providing more accurate but more costly results.

The laboratory setting can be more research-oriented but may not be as practical. For example, a soccer player could be tested for aerobic fitness while playing in a game. Although the tools used to measure or estimate aerobic fitness may be less sensitive than lab-based measures, they are likely be more representative of actual game play than lab-based measures that are usually performed on a treadmill or stationary cycle. Conversely, while a lab-based measure such as a VO2max test may be more sensitive since oxygen consumption is determined directly as expired gases are collected during a controlled bout of maximal cardiovascular output, it is impossible to conduct in an actual game play environment.

Strength

When assessing strength, it may be beneficial to examine upper body, lower body, and total body strength independently. Maximal strength refers to an individual's ability to apply force to a given object within a particular lift/exercise in order to determine maximal force output. Strength testing is widely considered as one of the most inherently dangerous things we must do as strength and conditioning professionals, but it is often necessary for evaluation purposes. Testing maximal strength directly ensues much more risk than submaximal testing, so both methods will be discussed.

Maximal Strength Testing

Maximal strength testing consists of the athlete's attempt to lift a given load for a single repetition without being able to complete a subsequent second rep. This is often referred to as a 1-RM or one repetition maximum. This form of testing determines the highest load an athlete can lift in a given exercise. The choice of exercise is up to the SCP, although a good deal of maximal strength testing research/field testing has been conducted utilizing barbell exercises.

This form of testing directly demonstrates the athlete's maximal capabilities on a particular exercise. Unfortunately, the risk of injury is high because predicting the appropriate load can be difficult and inherently includes some amount of estimation. If the estimate is wrong, the athlete's technique can break down, which can be very dangerous. Also, a maximal load will impose an incredible demand on the muscular and skeletal systems of the body. One should choose this type of testing with a healthy dose of preparation and caution.

Sub-Maximal Strength Testing

Sub-maximal strength testing is similar to maximal testing, except instead of determining a maximal load ability of an athlete, it establishes a maximal effort with a particular exercise. For instance, instead of completing a 1-RM test, the athlete could complete a 5-RM (five repetition max) test. With this strategy, the target is to load the exercise such that the athlete can complete five repetitions but due to fatigue will not be able to complete a sixth. The actual repetitions performed are then used to calculate an estimated 1-RM using an established multiplier chart.

The similarity is that the athlete is pushed to their maximal capacity, yet the load used in a 5-RM is considerably less than the load used with a 1-RM test. The lighter load can reduce the risk of injury and alleviate some of the concerns associated with the 1-RM test. The major drawback with this type of test is that it does not give you a direct measurement of an athlete's strength capabilities. However, it is very easy to predict a 1-RM based on the results of a sub-maximal test.

Power

Vertical Jump

The vertical jump test is a great test for lower body power development. As the athlete attempts to propel themselves upward as high as possible in a controlled fashion, requiring both force production and speed of movement. This test can be completed using various methods, most commonly the Vertec, whole body motion capture, or the digital jump mat. While the Vertec is commonly used in considered a field-based gold standard, it does require the SPC to measure the athlete's standing reach prior to testing. Vertec testing should be completed using a standard testing protocol.

Figure 3.5: Vertical leap testing Toby Brooks photo

1. The athlete begins with the feet positioned shoulder-width apart

2. The athlete should then reach both arms up as high as possible

3. From this position, the athlete should then forcefully swing the arms downward while squatting down with the lower body

4. As soon as the athlete reaches a quarter to half-squat position, he or she should drive the feet into the ground, extend the hips vertically, and reach as high as possible with the dominant hand while propelling the entire body upward

5. The measurement is taken from the highest point touched. When the standing reach is subtracted, the SPC can then determine the athlete's vertical leap

Standing Long Jump

The standing long jump is also a great test for lower body power development. It is very similar to the vertical jump with regard to recruitment, utilizing both strength and speed qualities. The main difference is that athletes propel themselves horizontally rather than vertically. A simple tape measure can be used to measure the distance of the jump. Similar to the vertical jump testing, proper long jump testing should be performed using a standardized approach.

1. The athlete begins with the feet positioned shoulder-width apart

2. The athlete should then reach both arms up as high as possible for the initial vertical stretch

3. From this position, the athlete should then forcefully swing the arms downward while hinging the hips and pushing the glutes back

4. As soon as the athlete reaches the downward position with hips back and shoulders forward, he or she should attempt to drive the feet into the ground, extend the hips forward, and extend the entire body out in front of the line

Figure 3.6: Standing long jump testing Toby Brooks photo

5. Once the athlete jumps from the line, the hips are forcefully flexed and the feet are accelerated under their body to prepare to absorb the force of the landing

6. The athlete must land cleanly without falling back or touching the floor behind

7. The measurement is taken from the back of the heel closest to the starting line

Medicine Ball Throw

The medicine ball throw is utilized to test for total body power development. The major differences are that the medicine ball throw entails the use of a medicine ball of a designated weight, and does not require the athlete to land and maintain a given distance with their feet at the conclusion of the throw. In this test, the athlete uses upper and lower body power to launch the medicine ball from a given start line.

1. The athlete holds the medicine ball under their chin, against their chest.

2. With feet shoulder width apart, the athlete forcefully drives their hips back into a hinge position.

3. As soon as they reach the downward position with hips back and shoulders forward – and the medicine ball still against their chest – they must attempt to drive their feet into the ground, extend their hips thru and forward, and finish by extending their arms and entire body out in front of the line.

4. At this point, the medicine ball should be released and launched forward.

5. The measurement is taken from the spot at which the center of the ball strikes the ground.

Body Composition

Body composition refers to the athlete's physical make-up in reference to fat-free mass (i.e. muscle, organs, bone, connective tissue) and body fat – both subcutaneous (under the skin) and visceral (in the abdomen surrounding the organs).

Testing body composition can give a clear picture of the affect training and nutritional practices are having on an athlete. There are various methods in which to assess body composition. A broad overview of each will be covered in this section.

Skinfold Testing

Skinfold testing is a method where skinfold calipers are used to measure the dimensions of a skinfold at a specific site on the body. Depending on the equations used, one may have to measure three to seven different sites on the body to calculate body fat percentages.

This method is very common due to its ease of testing since one would only need a pair of skinfold caliper to conduct the test. The drawback is it can be highly variable.

Hydrostatic Weighing

With hydrostatic weighing, an individual is submerged in water, and measurement of water displacement is measured. Body fat can then be calculated from this displacement. Other factors include determining lung volume so the amount of air in the body can be accounted for, as well as race-specific equations.

Hydrostatic weighing was once considered the "gold standard" of body composition testing, but the difficulty of testing – determining a person's residual lung volume and the actual methods of testing in a water tank – makes this method rather inconvenient.

Air Plethysmography

A rather new method in the field of body composition testing, air plethysmography is very similar to hydrostatic weighing. The main difference is it uses displaced air in a determined space to calculate percent body fat rather than water. Again, it is also has race-dependent equations.

The ease of testing body composition with air plethysmography has made this a very popular method in current day research; however, it can be quite costly or difficult to get access to a Bod Pod, the most popular device utilizing this method.

DEXA (Dual-energy X-ray Absorptiometry)

The new gold standard in body composition, Dual-energy X-ray Absorptiometry uses a specific form of x-ray to scan the body. DEXA can give the SCP a breakdown of the body composition with very accurate reports. DEXA has been tagged as the gold standard due to its accuracy of measurement; however, it is extremely difficult to get access to this form due to its financial cost and the time it takes to carry out a full body scan.

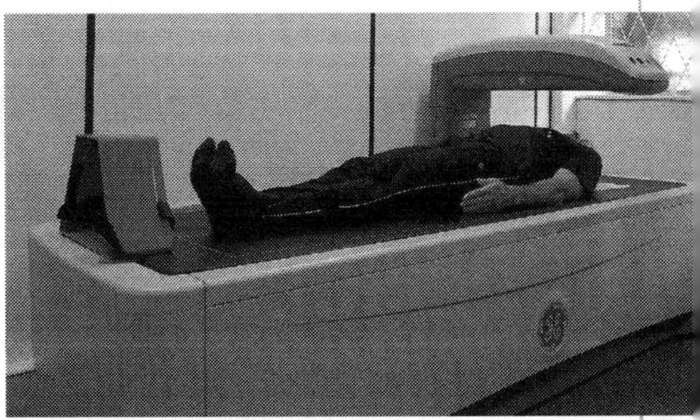

Figure 3.7: DEXA scan wikimedia commons photo

Score	Descriptor
0	No ability, aptitude, control, mobility, flexibility, strength, endurance or skill
1	Less than average ability, aptitude, control, mobility, flexibility, strength, endurance or skill
2	Average or good ability, aptitude, control, mobility, flexibility, strength, endurance or skill
3	Above average ability, aptitude, control, mobility, flexibility, strength, endurance or skill
4	Ideal ability, aptitude, control, mobility, flexibility, strength, endurance or skill

Figure 3.8: Grading criteria for the IYCA's Big 5 Assessment

Functional and Integrative Assessment: The Big 5

Although several commercially available functional assessment strategies exist, the IYCA developed a new system designed specifically for the IYCA's often-cited three developmental periods, Guided Discovery (ages 6-9), Learning Exploration (ages 10-13), and Train with Application (14+).[2] With many young athletes lacking the strength, stability, mobility, and/or motor control required to perform other functional assessments, the "Big 5" was crafted as a developmentally appropriate functional test battery that could be quickly and consistently administered to an individual athlete or an entire team. Additionally, the system was devised to grow with the athlete as he or she developed and acquired additional motor skill and component biomotor abilities. As a result, a specific Big 5 Assessment has been developed for each of the three developmental periods.

While the three versions of the Big 5 vary with respect to the specific component tests that make up the entire battery, the scoring system and instructions are consistent throughout. Specifically, each test within the battery is graded using a series of sub-criteria assessed on a 0-4 scale as outlined in Figure 3.8.

The SCP is encouraged to write notes/comments on each young athlete during assessment. This qualitative component is at least as important as any quantitative measure, as the discovery of "why" an athlete moves in a particular pattern is paramount. Experience level, dysfunction and competency are all critical factors to keep consider while administering the assessment.

The vague, non-descript character of the component tests is subjective by nature for two primary reasons. First, every athlete—regardless of developmental level—moves in a unique way, so it is difficult to apply rigid numerical standards to all athletes. The term "ideal" is what may be optimal for any particular athlete. Secondly, every coach will see or interpret what they see in a slightly different manner.

The goal with the Big 5 scoring system is to be as detailed as possible with each individual athlete to ascertain proper class placement in lieu of chronological age. Additionally, the mission of the IYCA serial athletic assessment system moving forward is to collect as much valid, specific, data on each athlete. In application in many coaching settings, this data collection should occur on a quarterly basis.

This information is critical for several reasons. First, developing a well-rounded and comprehensive understanding of each new athlete allows the SCP to better serve each individual's unique needs through programming. It is also highly beneficial to utilizing findings to educate the individual athletes and parent(s) as to how the program will be of benefit in reaching identified goals. Furthermore, as discussed previously, serial athletic assessment creates a baseline or "starting point" for the athletes that can be compared to subsequent findings, recommended to be collected in three-month intervals. Such information can provide invaluable talking points when the SCP is attempting to convince athletes or parents regarding the importance of persisting in the training system. Lastly, collecting all scores assists the SCP in developing standards and facilitating internal review regarding the efficacy of testing and programming.

Each of the three variants of the Big 5 Assessment System has been developed to best fit the needs of the majority of athletes who fall within that particular chronological age group. It is critical to point out the fact that these divisions are "loosely held" and that a strict adherence to their cut points is not suggested. Development of a young athlete is a highly individualized process. For example, a 9-year-old athlete who is an early developer may be better assessed using the Learning Exploration (10-13) assessment. It is no less common for a slower developing athlete to best be assessed using the assessment intended for a younger age group, either. In all instances, the SCP should utilize sound clinical judgment in determining the test that best meets the needs of each athlete.

Guided Discovery (6-9)

As children enter elementary school, increased opportunities are available for youth physical development in the form of physical education, youth sport, and after-school programs. Taking advantage of these options to further promote fundamental movement patterns is critical as the developmental status of children is highly variable. Many children are not provided with adequate movement experiences between the ages of 2-5 to appropriately develop fundamental movement patterns or even promote adequate physical activity. Thus, the SCP should be cognizant of each individual's developmental status and tailor movement experiences at the individual level to optimize progression.

Many children who lack basic proficiency in fundamental movement patterns can "catch-up" to normally developing children if they are identified at this early age, as many children still have not developed the cognitive capacity to accurately compare themselves to peers. Many children still relate "effort" to "success" and positive feedback and encouragement will promote and enhance self-efficacy and intrinsic motivation. In addition, children in middle childhood can be introduced to the basic fitness concepts that will serve to augment skill development.

Name: _____   **Date:** _____

Overhead Squats (5)   Points   Comments

Spinal posture	0	1	2	3	4
Shoulder mobility	0	1	2	3	4
Movement sequencing	0	1	2	3	4
Knee alignment	0	1	2	3	4
Heels loaded	0	1	2	3	4

Lunge (3/leg)   Points

Front knee alignment	0	1	2	3	4
Depth	0	1	2	3	4
Vertical pillar	0	1	2	3	4
Balance/control	0	1	2	3	4

Balance   Errors   Points

Lifting hands off hips		
Opening eyes		
Stepping, stumbling, falling		
Moving hips more than 30 degrees		
Lifting forefoot or heels		
Out of position for more than 5 sec		

Pushup Hold (5 sec)   Points

Pillar posture	0	1	2	3	4
Neutral pelvis	0	1	2	3	4
Scapular positioning	0	1	2	3	4
Endurance	0	1	2	3	4

Prone Extension (3)   Points

Thoracic mobility	0	1	2	3	4
Upper back strength	0	1	2	3	4
Lower back strength	0	1	2	3	4
Strength endurance	0	1	2	3	4

Figure 3.9: Guided Discovery (6-9) Big 5 Assessment score sheet

Many 4-7 year-old children cannot complete one push-up, pull-up, or even a sit-up if they have not had experiences with these types of activities. Initially performing these types of skills also demands a certain amount of coordination to coordinate and control multiple joints and complex muscle firing patterns to complete these tasks.

The Big 5 test battery for Guided Discovery includes overhead squats (5), inline lunges (3 each leg), static balance (20 seconds each stance), pushup hold (5 seconds), and prone extensions (3). Figure 3.9 represents the score sheet for the Guided Discovery Big 5 test battery.

Criteria to watch with the overhead squats include neutral spine, shoulder mobility, appropriate movement sequencing and fluidity, neutral knee alignment in the frontal plane (no varus or valgus) with minimal travel in the sagittal plane ("knees behind the toes") and loading through the heels. With the inclusion of multiple repetitions, the SCP can assess the athlete's local anaerobic endurance and resistance to fatigue and its influence on motor expression as well,

For lunges, the athlete should perform three repetitions with the left leg leading, then reverse stance and perform three repetitions with the right leg leading. Criteria to consider include alignment through the stride leg knee, overall depth of the lunge attained, vertical alignment demonstrating good trunk control, and overall balance and control during dynamic movement.

For balance assessment, the athlete is instructed to perform a modified Balance Error Scoring System assessment in which he or she attempts to maintain a balanced positioning despite varying stances.[3-5] The athlete is instructed to stand with the hands on the hips and the eyes closed and is monitored for any of the following errors during a 20 second trial: 1.) lifting hands off hips; 2.) opening eyes; 3.) stepping, stumbling, or falling; 4.) abducting hips greater than 30 degrees; 5.) lifting the forefoot or heels; 6.) or remaining out of the test position for more than 5 seconds. The test is performed in a hip-width bipedal stance, single leg (non-dominant) stance, and again in a heel-to-toe tandem stance with the dominant foot in front.[3-5] The maximum number of errors per trial is 10, with an overall maximum for all three stances of 30. Following total scoring of the modified BESS, athletes are assigned a 0-4 value for balance based upon the following scale:
0-6 total errors=4; 7-12 total errors=3; 13-18 total errors=2; 19-24 total errors=1; 24+ total errors=0.

The pushup hold is intended to assess upper body strength and core stability. The athlete should assume a prone bridge/plank position and maintain the static hold for 5 seconds. During that time, the SCP should assess the linearity of the body ("pillar posture") and the athlete's ability to maintain a neutral pelvis. Additionally, establishment and maintenance of stable, non-winging scapulae and the ability to maintain the posture for the duration of the test should also be evaluated.

Lastly, the athlete should perform three repetitions of prone extensions to assess posterior chain strength, endurance, and spinal mobility. Thoracic mobility, thoracic and lumbar spine strength, and strength endurance should all be evaluated.

Learning Exploration (10-13)

As children transition into adolescence, their developmental status (both for maturation and skill levels) becomes increasingly important in further advancing their overall development and athletic potential. Specifically, a lack of coordination and control displayed in fundamental movement skills and foundational strength and agility performance necessitates a continued focus on foundational concepts rather than attempting to push these underdeveloped youth to more complex training. As previously noted, the concept of "age-related, not age-determined" programming speaks to the understanding of individual progression based on an individual's developmental status. Recent cross sectional and longitudinal research also has demonstrated that the relationship strengths among fundamental movement skills and aspects of physical fitness (i.e., muscular strength, muscular endurance, and cardiorespiratory endurance), physical activity, and body composition (inverse relationship) increase over time. Thus, an emphasis on motor skill development in early, middle, and late childhood is paramount to adequately preparing the young athlete physically and mentally for more complex, high level progressions of athletic development.[6]

Name: _____   **Date:** _____

Overhead Squats (12)   Points   Comments

Spinal posture	0	1	2	3	4	
Shoulder mobility	0	1	2	3	4	
Movement sequencing	0	1	2	3	4	
Knee alignment	0	1	2	3	4	
Heels loaded	0	1	2	3	4	

Lunge (10/leg)   Points

Front knee alignment	0	1	2	3	4	
Depth	0	1	2	3	4	
Vertical pillar	0	1	2	3	4	
Balance/control	0	1	2	3	4	

Balance   Errors   Points

	Errors	Points
Lifting hands off hips		
Opening eyes		
Stepping, stumbling, falling		
Moving hips more than 30 degrees		
Lifting forefoot or heels		
Out of position for more than 5 sec		

Pushup Hold (10 sec/2 pushups x 3)   Points

Pillar posture	0	1	2	3	4	
Neutral pelvis	0	1	2	3	4	
Scapular positioning	0	1	2	3	4	
Endurance	0	1	2	3	4	

Prone Extension (10)   Points

Thoracic mobility	0	1	2	3	4	
Upper back strength	0	1	2	3	4	
Lower back strength	0	1	2	3	4	
Strength endurance	0	1	2	3	4	

Figure 3.10: Learning Exploration (10-14) Big 5 Assessment score sheet

Early maturing young athletes also may have an advantage over late maturing individuals in their capability to develop strength and their capability to improve skill performance. Thus, the SCP needs to be sensitive to each individual's developmental background and current physical status to optimize progression and continued physical development.

With respect to upper extremity physical development, many girls and boys continue to participate in multiple youth sports that involve upper extremity throwing and striking skills (e.g., softball, baseball, tennis, volleyball). Throwing and striking, in addition to demanding high levels of coordination and power, also place extremely high demands on shoulder and elbow joint structures. Thus, the SCP needs to be continually cognizant of sport participation demands, as such information is critical in determining appropriate volume and mode of upper extremity training exercises.

The Big 5 test battery for Learning Exploration includes overhead squats (12), inline lunges (10 each leg), static balance (20 seconds each stance), pushup hold (10 second hold/2 pushups x 3), and prone extensions (10). Figure 3.10 represents a score sheet for the Learning Exploration Big 5 test battery.

Criteria to watch with the overhead squats include neutral spine, shoulder mobility, appropriate movement sequencing and fluidity, neutral knee alignment in the frontal plane (no varus or valgus) with minimal travel in the sagittal plane ("knees behind the toes") and loading through the heels. With the inclusion of 12 total repetitions, the SCP can assess the athlete's local anaerobic endurance and resistance to fatigue and its influence on motor expression as well,

For lunges, the athlete should perform 10 repetitions with the left leg leading, then reverse stance and perform three repetitions with the right leg leading. Criteria to consider include alignment through the stride leg knee, overall depth of the lunge attained, vertical alignment demonstrating good trunk control, and overall balance and control during dynamic movement.

For balance assessment, the athlete is instructed to perform a modified Balance Error Scoring System assessment in which he or she attempts to maintain a balanced positioning despite varying stances. The athlete is instructed to stand with the hands on the hips and the eyes closed and is monitored for any of the following errors during a 20 second trial: 1.) lifting hands off hips; 2.) opening eyes; 3.) stepping, stumbling, or falling; 4.) abducting hips greater than 30 degrees; 5.) lifting the forefoot or heels; 6.) or remaining out of the test position for more than 5 seconds. The test is performed in a hip-width bipedal stance, single leg (non-dominant) stance, and again in a heel-to-toe tandem stance with the dominant foot in front. The maximum number of errors per trial is 10, with an overall maximum for all three stances of 30. Following total scoring of the modified BESS, athletes are assigned a 0-4 value for balance based upon the following scale: 0-6 total errors=4; 7-12 total errors=3; 13-18 total errors=2; 19-24 total errors=1; 24+ total errors=0.

The pushup hold is intended to assess upper body strength and core stability. The athlete should assume a prone bridge/plank position and maintain the static hold for 10 seconds, then perform two pushups, then repeat the static hold and two pushups again. During that time, the SCP should assess the linearity of the body ("pillar posture") and the athlete's ability to maintain a neutral pelvis. Additionally, establishment and maintenance of stable, non-winging scapulae and the ability to maintain the posture for the duration of the test should also be evaluated.

Lastly, the athlete should perform 10 repetitions of prone extensions to assess posterior chain strength, endurance, and spinal mobility. Thoracic mobility, thoracic and lumbar spine strength, and strength endurance should all be evaluated.

Train with Application (14+)

The application of more complex training regimens for adolescents is critically dependent on the SCP possessing a thorough understanding of the young athlete's training history, current developmental status, and volume of current sport participation and practice. As most individuals will be in the later stages of their transition into adolescence, the increased ability to develop muscle mass at an increased pace (especially in boys) will be an added benefit to continued optimal progression and performance. If a young athlete is adequately prepared in his or her physical development (i.e., coordination, skill, foundational muscle strength, muscle endurance, and agility), then he or she will be able to better adapt to increased training intensities and progress in training complexity.

Name: _____   **Date:** _____

Overhead Squats (18)

						Points
Spinal posture	0	1	2	3	4	
Shoulder mobility	0	1	2	3	4	
Movement sequencing	0	1	2	3	4	
Knee alignment	0	1	2	3	4	
Heels loaded	0	1	2	3	4	

Lunge (15/leg)

						Points
Front knee alignment	0	1	2	3	4	
Depth	0	1	2	3	4	
Vertical pillar	0	1	2	3	4	
Balance/control	0	1	2	3	4	

Lateral Lunge (8/leg)

						Points
Outside knee alignment	0	1	2	3	4	
Depth	0	1	2	3	4	
Spinal posture	0	1	2	3	4	
Balance/control	0	1	2	3	4	

Balance

	Errors	Points
Lifting hands off hips		
Opening eyes		
Stepping, stumbling, falling		
Moving hips more than 30 degrees		
Lifting forefoot or heels		
Out of position for more than 5 sec		

Pushup Hold (15 sec/4 pushups x 3)

						Points
Pillar posture	0	1	2	3	4	
Neutral pelvis	0	1	2	3	4	
Scapular positioning	0	1	2	3	4	
Endurance	0	1	2	3	4	

Prone Extension (15)

						Points
Thoracic mobility	0	1	2	3	4	
Upper back strength	0	1	2	3	4	
Lower back strength	0	1	2	3	4	
Strength endurance	0	1	2	3	4	

Comments

Figure 3.11: Train with Application (14+) Big 5 Assessment score sheet

One caveat related to increased training intensity and complexity must be acknowledged. Individuals lacking a strong foundation in physical development should not be progressed quickly in an attempt to "catch-up" to more adequately prepared athletes. Youth physical development takes years to promote and training progression levels cannot be "skipped" in order to promote success in the short-term. Athletic successes and failures can usually be tracked back to their physical (i.e., skill and strength, endurance, power and agility) development trajectories from childhood through adolescence. In addition, injury history may also be tracked in the same manner.

The Big 5 test battery for Train with Application includes overhead squats (18), inline lunges (15 each leg), lateral lunges (8 each leg), static balance (20 seconds each stance), pushup hold (15 second hold/4 pushups x 3), and prone extensions (15). Figure 3.11 represents a score sheet for the Train with Application Big 5 test battery.

Criteria to watch with the overhead squats include neutral spine, shoulder mobility, appropriate movement sequencing and fluidity, neutral knee alignment in the frontal plane (no varus or valgus) with minimal travel in the sagittal plane ("knees behind the toes") and loading through the heels. With the inclusion of 18 total repetitions, the SCP can assess the athlete's local anaerobic endurance and resistance to fatigue and its influence on motor expression as well,

For inline lunges, the athlete should perform 15 repetitions with the left leg leading, then reverse stance and perform 15 repetitions with the right leg leading. Criteria to consider include alignment through the stride leg knee, overall depth of the lunge attained, vertical alignment demonstrating good trunk control, and overall balance and control during dynamic movement.

For lateral lunges, the athlete should perform 8 repetitions with the left leg leading, then reverse stance and perform 8 repetitions with the right leg leading. Criteria to consider include alignment through the stride leg knee, overall depth of the lunge attained, spinal posture, and overall balance and control during dynamic movement.

For balance assessment, the athlete is instructed to perform a modified Balance Error Scoring System assessment in which he or she attempts to maintain a balanced positioning despite varying stances. The athlete is instructed to stand with the hands on the hips and the eyes closed and is monitored for any of the following errors during a 20 second trial: 1.) lifting hands off hips; 2.) opening eyes; 3.) stepping, stumbling, or falling; 4.) abducting hips greater than 30 degrees; 5.) lifting the forefoot or heels; 6.) or remaining out of the test position for more than 5 seconds. The test is performed in a hip-width bipedal stance, single leg (non-dominant) stance, and again in a heel-to-toe tandem stance with the dominant foot in front. The maximum number of errors per trial is 10, with an overall maximum for all three stances of 30. Following total scoring of the modified BESS, athletes are assigned a 0-4 value for balance based upon the following scale: 0-6 total errors=4; 7-12 total errors=3; 13-18 total errors=2; 19-24 total errors=1; 24+ total errors=0.

The pushup hold is intended to assess upper body strength and core stability. The athlete should assume a prone bridge/plank position and maintain the static hold for 15 seconds, then perform four pushups, then repeat the static hold and four pushups again. During that time, the YAAS should assess the linearity of the body ("pillar posture") and the athlete's ability to maintain a neutral pelvis. Additionally, establishment and maintenance of stable, non-winging scapulae and the ability to maintain the posture for the duration of the test should also be evaluated.

Lastly, the athlete should perform 15 repetitions of prone extensions to assess posterior chain strength, endurance, and spinal mobility. Thoracic mobility, thoracic and lumbar spine strength, and strength endurance should all be evaluated.

Big 5 Scoring

For all Big 5 assessments with sub-part or component subscores, it is best for the SCP to consider the true message conveyed by the subscore values, then assign a single rating value (again using the 0-4 point scale). This will then provide a ready representation of overall ability with respect to lower extremity strength, stability, and mobility, upper extremity strength, stability, and mobility, core strength, and overall balance. Lower scored tests would then be specifically addressed through strategic training and corrective exercise prescription in the coming weeks, days and months.

Other Isolative Assessment Tests and Measures

While the Big 5 Assessment variants provide excellent functional and integrative assessment data, the SCP may also wish to add selected other global non-sport specific testing in order to further broaden the scope of information gathered during testing. Most frequently, such additional testing may be impractical for use in large team settings but may prove valuable in personal or small group training settings as time permits. Most frequently, this additional isolative testing involves grip strength and manual muscle testing of isolated muscles or muscle groups. Additionally, information such as basic biometric measures (standing height, sitting height, arm length, leg length, biacromial (shoulder) width, and bicristal (hip) width) can also prove to be a valuable additional component of a thorough serial athletic assessment.

Summary

Functional and integrative assessment through the use of one of the three available variants of the IYCA's Big 5 Assessment system can serve to objectify an inherently subjective process of athletic movement assessment. Additionally, through the use of developmentally appropriate and age-related modifications, the Big 5 can serve to avoid the disappointment and demotivation that might tend to occur when an assessment originally intended for an adult population is employed.

With the introduction of a regular (quarterly) serial assessment system built around the Big 5 and supplemented with other measures of isolative strength and biometrics as indicated, the SCP can ensure that the development of every athlete under his or her charge is thoroughly tracked and optimal for informing current and future training prescriptions.

References

1. Tuckman B, Harper B. *Conducting Educational Research.* 6th ed. Estover Road, Plymouth, United Kingdom: Rowman & Littlefield Publishers, Inc.; 2012.

2. Brooks T, Stodden D. *Essentials of Youth Conditioning and Fitness.* Louisville, KY: International Youth Conditioning Association; 2012.

3. Susco T, Valovich McLeod T, Gansneder B, Shultz S. Balance recovers within 20 minutes after exertion as measured by the Blance Error Scoring System. *Journal of Athletic Training.* 2004;39(3):241-246.

4. Valovich McLeod T, Perrin D, Gansneder B. Repeat administration elicits a practice effect with the Balance Error Scoring System but not with the Standardized Assessment of Concussion in high school athletes. *Journal of Athletic Training.* 2003;38(1):51-56.

5. Valovich McLeod T, Perrin D, Guskiewicz K, Shultz S, Diamond R, B G. Serial administration of clinical concussion assessments and learning effects in healthy young athletes. *Clinical Journal of Sports Medicine.* 2004;14(5):287-295.

6. Myer G, Faigenbaum A, Ford K, Best T, Bergeron M, Hewett T. When to initiate integrative neuromuscular training to reduce sports-related injuries and enhance health in youth? *Curr Sports Med Rep.* 2011;10(3):157-166.

PRINCIPLES of
ATHLETIC
Strength &
Conditioning

The Foundations of Success in
Training and Developing
the Complete Athlete

CHAPTER 4

Warm-Up, Flexibility, and Mobility

Brian Clarke

Objectives

- List and describe the concepts behind the four-point warm-up system

- Develop and implement a General Warm-Up (GWU) appropriate for a particular sport and/or athlete

- Describe and be able to implement common self-myofascial release/foam roller mobility techniques

- List and describe the differences, indications, and specific uses of static flexibility, dynamic flexibility, and proprioceptive neuromuscular facilitation techniques

Introduction

Athletes of all ages need to properly prepare their bodies for activity by means of a well-planned warm-up. Teaching young athletes the importance and application of this process is vital early in their athletic journey. Warming-up prepares both the muscular and cardiovascular systems for training and competition. A comprehensive warm-up routine provides countless benefits for the athlete, as it helps the individual mentally prepare for training and competition, increases core temperature, enhances lubrication of many of the joints by increasing synovial fluid distribution within the joint capsules, and it can reduce injuries by increasing the elasticity of muscles. Furthermore, a proper warm-up can increase joint range of motion, increase metabolic rate, improve the rate of force development, reduce reaction time, and improve oxygen delivery to the musculature.

Warm-Up System

The strength & conditioning professional (SCP) should utilize systems and principles to help guide their programming. The following is a four-point warm-up system that can be used in most training sessions. These points do not necessarily need to occur in the following order and each section can be combined with or integrated into another section or phase of the warm-up.

1. Mental focus

2. General warm-up

3. Deep breathing

4. Activation/specific warm-up

Mental Focus

Frequently, an under-utilized element of the warm-up period is the opportunity for the SCP to help the athlete enter a training or competitive mindset. Effectively communicating expectations and daily objectives can help the athlete mentally prepare for the upcoming session. Lessons can be taught/reviewed during the warm-up and points of emphasis can be introduced. Some coaches may want to create an environment that mimics a typical practice or game atmosphere, while others will use more of a relaxed routine that calms the athlete's mind. The SCP should use the warm-up period to engage the athlete and help prepare for practice or competition.

General Warm-Up (GWU)

The purpose of the GWU is to increase the athlete's heart rate, improve synovial fluid distribution within the joints, and to increase core temperature. Athletes will usually break a light sweat as a result of the GWU. The GWU can be completed by using a variety of rhythmic movements such as jumping rope, jogging, calisthenics, complexes, low-intensity cardio, etc. The GWU should take approximately 5-10 minutes and may include aspects of the other warm-up phases such as dynamic flexibility movements. The following general warm-up sample has been provided to serve as a template depending on the time and space available as well as the specific athletes to be trained.

	Noblesville GWU		
1	**Movement**	**Cues**	**Time**
	Jog in place	Lift feet off ground	x20's
		Start driving knees	
		Start rotating arms at the shoulders	
2	**Movement**	**Cues**	**Time**
	Rt. Ft. Skip Rope	Bounce on right leg	x20's
		Toes come off ground	
		Create a lot of foot contacts	
3	**Movement**	**Cues**	**Time**
	Lt Ft Skip Rope	Bounce on left leg	x20's
		Toes come off ground	
		Create a lot of foot contacts	
4	**Movement**	**Cues**	**Time**
	Both Ft Skip Rope	Bounce on both legs	x20's
		Toes come off ground	
		Create a lot of foot contacts	
5	**Movement**	**Cues**	**Time**
	High Knees	Knees to hip	x15's
		Arms ear to hip	
6	**Movement**	**Cues**	**Time**
	Glute Kicks	Knees to hip	x15's
		Heelt to glute	
		Arms ear to hip	
7	**Movement**	**Cues**	**Time**
	Sprint	Fast knee drive	x15's
		Create a lot foot contacts	
		Violent arms	

Figure 4.1: Sample general warm-up

8	Movement	Cues	Time
	Power Sprint	Fast knee drive, Knees to hip	x15's
		Violent (Fast) arms, Ear to hip	

9	Movement	Cues	Time
	Wave Squats	Feet outside shoulders	x15's
		Shoulder behind knees, knees behind toes	
		Glide back and forth	
		Hips 24" of ground	

10	Movement	Cues	Time
	C-Skips	Knee to hip	x15's
		Etrenal rotate hip, knee to hip	
		Internal rotate hip, knee to hip	
		Repeat with other leg	

11	Movement	Cues	Time
	Pistol Squat Rt	Pop hips back	x10 Reps
		Heel flat	
		Drop hips 1-2" below hips	
		Drive through heel	

12	Movement	Cues	Time
	Pistol Squat Lt	Pop hips back	x10 Reps
		Heel flat	
		Drop hips 1-2" below hips	
		Drive through heel	

13	Movement	Cues	Time
	Tuck Jumps	Hands even with belly button	x15's
		Jump, Knees to hands	
		Land athletic	

14	Movement	Cues	Time
	SLR TJ	Hands even with belly button	x10's
		Jump, Right knees to hands	
		Land athletic	

15	Movement	Cues	Time
	SLL TJ	Hands even with belly button	x10's

Figure 4.1: Sample general warm-up (cont.)

		Jump, Left knees to hands	
		Land athletic	
16	**Movement**	**Cues**	**Time**
	Push-ups	Hands shoulder width distance	x25 Reps
		Fingers point forward	
		Chest to ground	
		Complete arm extension at elbows	
17	**Movement**	**Cues**	**Time**
	Air Squats	Arms locked in a "Y" or "V"	x25 Reps
		Pop hips back	
		Drop Hips 1-2" below knees	
		Drive through heels, stand up	

Figure 4.1: Sample general warm-up (cont.)

Deep Breathing

The diaphragm's role in warm-up is frequently under-estimated and often forgotten compared to other muscles in the body. Implementing deep-breathing exercises into the warm-up period will provide the athlete with more control over breathing and assist in core stabilization. Deep breathing techniques are also used to relax the mind, improve mental focus, increase oxygen levels in the bloodstream, and lower blood pressure. One such diaphragmatic breathing exercise is "90/90" breathing.

Figure 4.2: 90/90 Deep breathing

To perform this technique, the athlete should begin in supine with the back flat on the floor with the feet on a wall and the knees and hips flexed to 90 degrees. The athlete's neck and spine should be comfortably positioned in neutral. The athlete should place one hand on the upper chest and the other on the lower abdomen while slowly moving through the following sequence: 1) Inhale slowly through the nose (3-4 seconds); 2) Hold the inhalation for one second; 3) Exhale slowly through the nose or mouth (4-6 seconds); 4) Hold the exhalation for 2-3 seconds; 5) Begin the next breathing cycle. The air movement should expand the lateral portion of the stomach, pushing the hands out.

Activation/Specific Warm-up

The final phase of the warm-up should be to perform multiple sub-maximal repetitions of drills or exercises that are about to be performed. This is intended to activate the nervous system and more completely prepare the body for performance. The CNS is the processing center for the entire nervous system and includes the brain and spinal cord. Performing sub-maximal repetitions of an exercise stimulates the nervous system and bridges the gap between warm-up and actual training of competition. This phase should not be overlooked as it can have a large impact on performance in injury prevention.

For example, when training for speed, the athlete should perform two or three build-up sprints, gradually increasing the intensity of each rep, before a maximal effort sprint is performed. When performing a strength/power exercise like the squat, bench press or clean, perform several sets with sub-maximal weights before beginning "working sets."

Additional Warm-up Considerations

Every athlete, sport, and training program will have unique needs. Whether it is an injured athlete, lack of equipment, or shortage of time, the SCP must find a way to adapt and adjust programming as needed in order to enhance effectiveness and efficiency. The warm-up period offers the SCP a time to assess the group, provide instructions, and set the tone for the training session. It is also a time to include specific exercises to correct deficiencies or improve sport-specific skills.

While the warm-up should be concise, it serves many functions and lays the foundation of each training session. The system described in this chapter provides a template that can be modified by the SCP to meet the needs of each athlete or team. Utilizing this system will ensure the SCP addresses all aspects of preparing the body for optimal performance.

Mobility Training

Although warm-up programming is critical for preparing the athlete for participation in practice or competition, it is not the ideal time to work on enhancing range of motion, mobility, or flexibility. In years past, many coaches would require athletes to perform static stretching as a part of the warm-up, erroneously believing that static stretching is helpful in preventing injury before activity. However, decades of study have conclusively supported the notion that static stretching immediately prior to performance compromises peak force output by exposing the contractile units to plastic deformity and transiently compromising peak power output.[1,2]

At the same time, mobility training certainly can be beneficial to the athlete, as compromised range of motion can alter mechanics and undermine peak performance. However, its placement in the training session is better located at the conclusion of the practice, workout, or competition rather than with the warm-up. As a result, the SCP who wishes to help his or her athletes improve mobility should typically place mobility training at the conclusion of activity, as the athlete's muscles and connective tissues will already be warm and extensibility will be optimized. At the same time, and potential transient deficits will not hamper performance, as activity will already be concluded.

Mobility training can take several forms, including self-myofascial release, dynamic flexibility, static flexibility, and proprioceptive neuromuscular facilitation (PNF). With that said, some mobility drills or exercises that are more ballistic in nature may be appropriate for some athletes as a part of the warm-up, especially for highly trained individuals who consistently use good form and are aware of the differences in techniques between more dynamic warm-up drills and more static mobility techniques. However, any technique that incorporates prolonged static stretching is most often better utilized in a stand-alone mobility session at the conclusion of activity rather than as part of the structured warm-up.

Self-Myofascial Release (SMFR)

The use of implements such as foam rollers, trigger sticks, and lacrosse balls can be a helpful strategy to increase mobility. These tools massage and create neuro-physiological responses to "triggers" in myofascial connective tissues that can cause discomfort and reduce mobility.[3-6] SMFR stretches any overly-tight fascia to ease the pain and discomfort in the surrounding bodily structures. Each initial technique should be performed for 90-120 seconds, then a deeper application can follow to help create a greater relaxation of the fascia allowing for greater dynamic movements.[3-6]

Figure 4.3: IT Band SMFR

Sample SMFR Routine

Iliotibial Tract (IT Band)

The athlete should begin in sidelying with the involved hip on the foam roller and the non-involved leg crossed over and the non-involved foot flat on the floor for stability or off the ground for additional pressure. The athlete should maintain a neutral/linear posture while rolling just inferior to the hip to the lateral thigh and to the lateral knee.

Piriformis

The athlete should begin positioned in seated on the foam roller with the involved leg crossed over into a "figure-four" position with the non-involved foot flat on the floor for support. The athlete should support the involved leg with the contralateral hand and support the trunk with the

Figure 4.4: Piriformis SMFR

ipsilateral hand. The athlete should then roll into the stretch, deepening hip flexion while feeling the stretch deep to the gluteal on the involved side.

Hamstring

The athlete should begin in seated with both hands on the floor for support and both posterior thighs on the foal roller. The athlete may cross the feet to provide additional force to one side. The athlete should then roll from the posterior aspect of the knee proximally up to the gluteals while keeping the quadriceps contracted.

Quadriceps

The athlete should begin in prone with both forearms on the floor and both quadriceps positioned on the foam roller. The athlete should maintain good neutral/ linear posture by engaging the core, spinal erectors, and gluteals while rolling from the groin inferiorly down to the knees.

Adductor

The athlete should begin in prone with the medial thigh of the involved leg positioned on the foam roller while supporting the upper body on the forearms and the non-involved leg flat on the floor. The athlete should then roll from the proximal medial groin down to the distal medial thigh just above the knee.

Latissimus Dorsi

The athlete should begin in sidelying with the foam roller positioned beneath the lateral chest with the involved arm extended overhead with the thumb "up" toward the ceiling and the foot of the contralateral leg

Figure 4.5: Hamstring SMFR

Figure 4.6: Quadriceps SMFR

Figure 4.7: Adductor SMFR

Figure 4.8: Latissimus dorsi SMFR

Figure 4.9: Rhomboid SMFR

	DYNAMIC		
1	**Movement**	**Cues**	**Distance**
	HIGH KNEES	KNEES TO HIP	15 yards
		DORSIFLEX FOOT (TOE TO SKY)	
		ROTATE AT SHOULDER	
		HANDS "EAR TO HIP"	
2	**Movement**	**Cues**	**Distance**
	GLUTE KICKS	KNEES TO HIP	15 yards
		DORSIFLEX FOOT - HEEL TO GLUTE	
		ROTATE AT SHOULDER	
		HANDS "EAR TO HIP"	
3	**Movement**	**Cues**	**Distance**
	FORWARD LUNGE	RIP KNEE	15 yards
		STEP OUT	
		KNEE BEHIND TOES	
		BACK KNEE OFF GROUND	
4	**Movement**	**Cues**	**Distance**
	A-SKIP	TOES TO SKY	15 yards
		RIP KNEE TO HIP	
		HANDS "EAR TO HIP"	
5	**Movement**	**Cues**	**Distance**
	C-SKIP	TOES TO SKY	15 yards
		RIP KNEE TO HIP	
		ROTATE LEG OUTWARD	
		RIP KNEE TO HIP	
6	**Movement**	**Cues**	**Distance**
	SIDE SHUFFLE	CHEST UP, BACK FLAT	15 yards
		DROP HIPS	
		DON'T CROSS FEET	
7	**Movement**	**Cues**	**Distance**
	CARIOCA	RIP KNEE UP	15 yards
		STEP OVER OUTSIDE LEG	
8	**Movement**	**Cues**	**Distance**
	SIDE LUNGE	HIPS LOW	15 yards
		BRING LEG IN	
		REACH LEG OUT	
		SLIDE / SHIFT WEIGHT	
9	**Movement**	**Cues**	**Distance**
	INCH WORM	HANDS TO TOES	15 yards
		WALK TO PUSH-UP POSITION	
		KEEP KNEES STRAIGHT	
		WALK FEET TO HANDS	
10	**Movement**	**Cues**	**Distance**
	WALKING MARCH W/ "RDL"	SWING LEG UP	15 yards
		RAISE PLANTAR LEG TO TOES	
		SWING LEG BACK BEHIND	
		LAND EVEN	

Figure 4.10: Sample dynamic flexibility routine

	GBF – GROUND BASED FLEXIBILITY		
1	Movement	Cues	Time
	FIRE HYDRANTS	START ON ALL 4'S	x10s
	(RIGHT)	LIFT LEG AWAY FROM BODY	
	(LEFT)	HEEL TO GLUTE	
		LOWER LEG START POSITION	
2	Movement	Cues	Time
	CIRCLES	START ON ALL 4'S	x10s
	(RIGHT CW/CCW)	LIFT LEG AWAY FROM BODY	
	(LEFT CW/CCW)	ROTATE LEG AROUND AT HIP	
		KEEP HEEL TO GLUTE	
3	Movement	Cues	Time
	KICKBACKS	START ON ALL 4'S	x10s
	(RIGHT)	HIPS SQUARE TO GROUND	
	(LEFT)	DORSIFLEX FOOT	
		KICK LEG BACK AND UP 45*	
4	Movement	Cues	Time
	INVERT - BICYCLE	LAYING ON SHOULDER BLADES AND TRICEPS	x10s
	(REGULAR)	PEDAL LEGS AS IF ON A BIKE	
	(REVERSE)	LEG MUST STRAIGHTEN AT TOP	
5	Movement	Cues	Time
	INVERT - SCISSOR	LAYING ON SHOULDER BLADES AND TRICEPS	x10s
		ONE LEG STRAIGHT IN AIR	
		OTHER LEG PULLED TOWARD GROUND	
		SWITCH	
6	Movement	Cues	Time
	INVERT - SPLIT	LAYING ON SHOULDER BLADES AND TRICEPS	x10s
		OPEN INTO LARGE V	
		CLOSE	
		OPEN INTO LARGE V	

Figure 4.11: Sample ground-based flexibility (GBF) routine

flat on the floor for support. The athlete should then roll from the axilla (armpit) inferiorly. Movement during this technique is minimal.

Rhomboids

The athlete should begin in supine with the foam roller positioned beneath the scapulae and the feet flat on the floor and both knees flexed to 90 degrees. With the arms crossed and held tightly to the chest, the athlete should roll from the upper back inferiorly to the thoracic spine/mid-back region while holding the core tight.

Dynamic Flexibility

		Static Stretching	
1	**Movement**	**Cues**	**Time**
	Head to Knee	Right leg straight out, left leg tucked in to the inside of thigh	x10s right
	(Hamstring)	Slowly bend forward from hips keeping back straight	x10s left
		Hold	
		Repeat with other leg	
2	**Movement**	**Cues**	**Time**
	Knee to Chest	Lay on back	x10s right
	(Extensors/Gluteal)	Bring knee to chest, hold	x10s left
		For additoinal Stretch, Bring head to knee, hold	
		Repeat with other leg	
3	**Movement**	**Cues**	**Time**
	Knee Overs	Lay on Back, Keep back flat and Knees together	x10s right
	(Lumbar Rotators)	Rotate knees to one side	x10s left
		Hold	
		Repeat for other side	
4	**Movement**	**Cues**	**Time**
	Leg Overs	Lay on back, keep shoulders flat on the floor	x10s Right
	(External Rotators)	Pull leg across body to the floor until stretch is felt	x10s Left
		Hold	
		Repeat for other leg	

Figure 4.12: Sample static flexibility routine

5	Movement	Cues	Time
	Hip Cradle	Lay on back, Gently pull foot and knee toward shoulders	x10s Right
	(Internal Rotators)	Rotate leg at hip	x10s Left
		Hold	
		Repeat for other side	

6	Movement	Cues	Time
	Lunge	Move right leg forward until knee is over right ankle	x10s Right
	(Hip Flexor)	Keep the back leg straight and gently lower hips	x10s Left
		Create an easy stretch in the front of your hip	
		Repeat for other leg	

7	Movement	Cues	Time
	Lunge - Leg Pull	Kneel down, place chest on front leg	x10s Right
	(Quadricep)	Hold left foot with right hand, Pull foot toward glutes	x10s Left
		Hold	
		Repeat with other leg and hand	

8	Movement	Cues	Time
	Side Lunge	Start in a side lunge	x10s Right
	(Thigh Adductors)	Slide foot further to side until stretch is felt	x10s Left
		Hold	
		Repeat with other side	

9	Movement	Cues	Time
	Deep Squat	Start in a squat position	x10s
	(Thigh Adductors)	Place elbows inside knees and thumbs inside feet	
		Gently push knees outward until a stretch is felt	
		Hold	

Figure 4.12: Sample static flexibility routine (cont.)

Dynamic stretching requires the athlete to actively perform movements through a range of motion that elicits a stretch sensation, but the movement is not necessarily held in the end position. Examples of these include high knees, glute kicks, skipping variations, inchworms, walking marches, trunk rotations, lunge variations, ankle rolls, and neck rolls. Dynamic warm-up movements should take the athlete through safe and complete ranges of motion and through multiple planes of movement. Since these movements do not require long static holds, they do not typically compromise performance and are also appropriate prior to training and competition.

Static Flexibility

Static flexibility requires the athlete to hold a joint or series of joints in a fixed position for a pre-determined amount of time—typically between 15-45 seconds. As discussed previously in this chapter, static stretching can increase ROM but has consistently demonstrated a temporary decrease in power and strength for as much as 3-4 hours following the stretch. That said, static stretching still persists in the warm-up phase of many sports, most notably those requiring extremes of flexibility such as gymnastics, diving, and taekwondo. However, athletes in most other traditional individual and team sports should usually confine heavy static flexibility work to the end of the practice, workout, or competition.

Proprioceptive Neuromuscular Facilitation (PNF)

Proprioceptive neuromuscular facilitation (PNF) is a technique intended to temporarily alter the resting length of a given muscle or muscles by altering the inputs into the Golgi Tendon Organ (GTO), the muscle spindle fiber (MSF) or both.[7] The GTO are found embedded in the tendons that attach muscles to bone, and when activated they serve to inhibit muscular action, thereby triggering

	PNF		
1	**Movement**	**Cues**	**Time**
	Forward Bend With Partner	Pull trunk forward over leg until stretch is felt	hold x10s
	(Hamstring)	Partner gently apply pressure to increase stretch	Relax x10s
		Hold, Relax, Hold	hold x10s
		Repeat for other leg	
2	**Movement**	**Cues**	**Time**
	Leg Raise With Partner	Keeping leg straight, Partner slowly raise leg until stretch is felt	hold x10s
	(Hamstring)	Hold, Relax, Hold	Relax x10s
		After relax, raise leg further for a greater stretch	hold x10s
		Repeat for other leg	
3	**Movement**	**Cues**	**Time**
	Supine Betterfly	Feet together, Partner gently push knees toward floor until stretch is felt	hold x10s
	(Thigh Adductors)	Hold, Relax, Hold	Relax x10s
		After Relax, press legs further towards floor	hold x10s
		Repeat	

Figure 4.13: Sample proprioceptive neuromuscular facilitation routine

4	Movement	Cues	Time
	Reverse Arm Raise	Place arms behind back	hold x10s
	(Biceps)	Partner should then raise arms until stretch is felt	Relax x10s
		Hold, Relax, Hold	hold x10s
		After relax, have partner raise arms further	

5	Movement	Cues	Time
	Reverse Arm Pull	Clasp hands behind head	hold x10s
	(Pectorals)	Have partner pull arms back until stretch is felt	Relax x10s
		Hold, Relax, Hold	hold x10s
		Repeat	

6	Movement	Cues	Time
	Prone Leg Lift with partner	From lying position, have partner raise leg until stretch is felt	hold x10s
	(Rectus Femoris)	Hold, Relax, Hold	Relax x10s
		After relax, have partner raise leg further	hold x10s
		Repeat with other leg	

7	Movement	Cues	Time
	Self Neck Pull	Gently grasp side of head with one hand, with other hand behind back	hold x10s
	(Side Benders)	Tilt head away until a gentle stretch is felt	Relax x10s
		Hold, Relax, Hold	hold x10s
		Repeat for other side	

8	Movement	Cues	Time
	Side Lunge	With hands on wall, have partner push chest toward wall	hold x10s
	(Shoulder Extensors)	Push until a stretch is felt	Relax x10s
		Hold, Relax, Hold	hold x10s
		Repeat	

Figure 4.14: Sample proprioceptive neuromuscular facilitation routine (cont.)

relaxation and facilitating a greater range of motion. Conversely, the MSF are found embedded within the muscle tissus itself and when activated, the muscle is facilitated. Due to the principle of reciprocal inhibition, if a muscle is activated, its antagonist is inhibited to help prevent injury.

This phenomena of facilitation or inhibition can be utilized by the SCP to manipulate the threshold at which the athlete senses a stretch sensation. As such, it is helpful in significantly altering range of motion at a joint or series of joints without altering the structure of the muscle or connective tissue at all. PNF mobility techniques consist of a combination of active and passive movements intended to trigger the change in threshold.[7]

In addition, PNF techniques can also be used to increase strength and coordination in areas that may be lacking. Before deciding which PNF techniques are going to be used, the SCP must consider the end goal. Once the goal has been established and communicated, then a series of techniques can be selected to aid in reaching the end result. For optimal results, the athlete should start from the most distal or weakest point of the limb and work up the chain. Most techniques require the assistance of a partner to resist the movement of the performer as they contract, however, there are tools available to accommodate the technique without a partner. While beyond the scope of this text, PNF techniques include hold-relax (isometric action with passive stretch), contract-relax concentric action with passive stretch), and hold-relax with agonist contraction (HRAC)(isometric action with passive stretch and resisted return to starting position).

Summary

Warm-up and mobility have long been recognized as important components of peak athletic performance. However, until relatively recently, coaches have somewhat sloppily intermingled the techniques one with another and thereby potentially hindered performance, mitigated improvements in range of motion, or both. By incorporating a multi-component warm-up system that prepares the athlete for practice, workout, or competition and a dedicated mobility training period near the activity's conclusion, the SCP can best prepare the athlete for participation while also minimizing risk of injury and maximizing athletic performance.

References

1. Behm D, Chaouachi A. A review of the acute effects of static and dynamic stretching on performance. *European Journal of Applied Physiology.* 2011;111(11):2633-2651.

2. Kubo K, Kanehisa H, Kawakami Y, Fukunaga T. Influence of static stretching on viscoelastic properties of human tendon structures in vivo. *Journal of Applied Physiology.* 1985;90(2):520-527.

3. Barnes M. The basic science of myofascial release. *Journal of Bodywork and Movement Therapies.* 1997;1(4):231-238.

4. Mohr A, Long B, Goad C. Effect of foam rolling and static stretching on passive hip-flexion range of motion. *Journal of Sport Rehabilitation.* 2014;23(4):296-299.

5. Pearcey G, Bradbury-Squires D, Kawamoto J, Drinkwater E, Behm D, Button D. Foam rolling for delayed-onset muscle soreness and recovery of dynamic performance measures. *Journal of Athletic Training.* 2015;50(1):5-13.

6. Clark M, Russell A. *Self Myofascial Release Techniques.* Calabasas, CA: National Academy of Sports Medicine; 2015.

7. Hindle K, Whitcomb T, WO B, Hong J. Proprioceptive Neuromuscular Facilitation (PNF): Its mechanisms and effects on range of motion and muscular function. *Journal of Human Kinetics.* 2012;31:105-113.

CHAPTER 5

Program Design

Mark Naylor

Objectives

- Identify the multi-faceted nature of effective program design

- Describe and discuss the primary differences between the novice, intermediate, and advanced lifter and identify the implications for training

- Describe and discuss the phases of program design and the varied approaches to devoping the annual conditioning plan

- Understand the relationship between intensity and volume as well as the influence of loading parameters on meeting the goals of training

Introduction

When designing a strength training program there are many important factors to consider. Before anything else, the strength & conditioning professional (SCP) must consider some basic questions including the demands of the sport, the number of athletes to be trained, equipment availability, and the time available to train. The goal of this chapter is to provide a foundation for writing a safe, well-organized, and efficient strength program based on sound, age-appropriate principles. We will also discuss how to organize the program in a sequential manner that will maximize results. While the main emphasis of this chapter will be the off-season strength program, the principles can be applied to programming at any time during the year.

Program design is a widely-debated topic by many SCPs, and it's a topic that is ever-changing and constantly evolving. As you grow as a strength coach, you will see that there are multiple ways through which to accomplish a singular goal, so it is highly recommended to keep an open mind when viewing different programs. Different coaches have different ways of doing things. Enhancing your skill set or "filling up your tool box" with multiple ideas, experiences, and sound scientific principles is the best approach to this topic. The bottom line is this: if a program is safe, comprehensive, well-supervised, and the athletes are progressively overloaded with excellent technique, it is probably a high-quality program.

The principles discussed in this chapter have stood the test of time and have been implemented successfully by many SCPs. Yet, like anything in strength and conditioning, this is not a "one-size-fits-all" approach. As time passes and your experience grows, your strength and conditioning program will organically adapt and evolve to fit your style and the needs of the athletes you train.

Basic Principles of Program Design

While many differences can be found, there are basic principles of program design that are present in all well-written strength training programs. They are principles that, regardless of training philosophy, are necessary for overall strength development in the most efficient and safe manner. These principles guide the decision making and planning of any well written strength program and include safety, technique, overload, progression, balanced development, de-loading periods, needs analysis, and training age.

Safety

It is the SCP's responsibility to facilitate an environment that is safe for the trainee. The SCP is not doing his/her job if the athletes are getting hurt while lifting, conditioning, and preparing for the demands of the sport itself. The strength training program should never predispose an athlete to injury due to poor teaching of technique. A well-organized, clean, and clutter-free weight room with well-maintained equipment is also a must to maximize safety. Additionally, supervision by coaches who have the ability to teach proper lifting technique should be a priority when starting a strength program. In addition to qualified coaches, experienced spotters should be present at all times during lifting. Each lift is different and spotting the lifts is a critical skill. The techniques and principles are specific to the lifting modality being performed and should be taught to all involved. It is recommended that only individuals who have demonstrated the necessary spotting skills be allowed to spot during lifting sessions. More on proper spotting techniques can be found in chapter 13.

Technique

Proper technique should never be sacrificed for the sake of achieving a desired result (i.e. specific load in a given lift). Before any athlete can progress in strength training, it is important that all technical skills be instructed, learned, and demonstrated before introducing significant load. As a SCP, it is important to place a premium on rep replication. This means the lifter can replicate perfect reps of exercise for each set, regardless of fatigue level. This is easier said than done, and oftentimes overlooked. Doing this will yield improved results and enhance safety.

Overload

The concept of overload means stressing a system beyond its current state. Over time, there must be an increase in the amount of work that is done. This must occur for overload to take place. Overload can come in the form of increased weight, an increase in the number of sets and reps, an increase it time spent under tension, or an increase in total workout volume. More stress must be placed on the system in order for adaptation to occur. The muscular system will adapt specifically to the level of stress placed on it. Adaptation is the end goal; thus overload is vital to the long-term success of the strength program.

Progression

Progression is closely related to overload and can be defined as a steady increase of the 'stressor' over time. Progression can be conceptualized as *"anti-steady state,"* and the goal of progression is to avoid the developmental plateaus often attributed to the body's ever-present preference for homeostasis. As such, the construct can involve altering exercise selection, strength emphasis, number of sets, or number of reps over an extended period of time to optimize adaptation.

Balanced Development

The concept of balanced development involves an understanding that integrative rather than isolative exercises are critical to help the body develop as a whole. A complete strength program must not be focused on any particular muscle or region, but rather address the system equally with regards to upper/lower body and all aspects of a joint. Over the course of the training week, each body part should be stressed appropriately. This will aid in injury prevention and produce greater overall results in performance.

Typically, the body will resist imbalance. For example, if you only exclusively use the bench press for chest size and strength, then strength will be limited to a degree. Just by adding upper back work to the routine, the bench press strength and chest size will increase without adding to the bench press routine. A well-written program always takes balanced muscular development into account. The SCP should ensure the program has equal numbers of pushing and pulling movements for each joint. In some cases, due to the repetitive nature of some sports, it may be necessary to combat the demands of the sport. For example, a football offensive lineman pushes on nearly every play. Incorporating extra upper body pulling movements in a routine is one way to help achieve balance and improve posture, thereby reducing the risk of injury.

De-load Periods

Although the beginning (novice) lifter has the ability to recover quickly between workouts, it is still important to monitor fatigue levels and plan for recovery through de-loading periods or "back off" days from training. Depending on the level of the trainee, a de-load period of 4-6 days is recommended after 4-6 weeks of progressive training. This approach produces a supercompensation and a permanent adaptation to strength training.

A de-load period does not always have to involve complete cessation of activity. Instead, it can consist of the same lifts at a reduced intensity (load) and volume (sets and reps) as previous weeks. However, a short period of days involving no training activity will also do the lifter well in terms of adaptation to strength training. Fortunately, academic calendars often create de-load periods naturally. Breaks for holidays and vacation time usually do this in a school setting.

Needs Analysis

The needs of each sport must be taken into account when developing a strength training plan. This means analyzing specific movements and demands during actual sport play and practice. This also means collaboration with the sport coach. Strength training alone (for non-strength sports like powerlifting or weightlifting) is general and not specific to the competition itself, but can complement sport skills by improving strength levels in the involved muscles and making the body more resilient to the specific demands of the activity. Because of this, it is important to know what muscle groups play the largest role in the sport.

While added strength can certainly compliment sports skill, getting stronger plays an even larger role in keeping an athlete healthy and more resilient to the rigors of everyday practice and competition. A specific sport and/or position analysis that includes an assessment of commonly injured muscles and joint structures should occur when developing the program. If the commonly injured body part or region of the body is a result of a lack of strength, then a major improvement can be made by a well-written progressive strength program.

Training Age

Many high school coaches make statements like "I got this program from..." or, "We are doing the same program as (insert popular collegiate program)." This alone proves they are missing a fundamental principle of strength training. By not training within the boundaries of one's training age, we risk putting the athlete at a disadvantage in their overall development. As a SCP, it makes more sense to program in a way that maximizes the athlete's time through the appropriate number of sets, reps and loading parameters.

Understanding the concept of training age might be one of the most overlooked principles in writing an appropriate strength program. This topic was first introduced to the masses by Mark Rippetoe in his book *Practical Programming*.[1] Understanding training age has a large impact on not only writing a strength program but in the long term results of the program.

Training age is not the biological age of the individual. Training age is determined by two major factors: 1) the duration (in months) one has been in a continuous, progressive training program, and 2) the rate at which the individual recovers and adapts from one workout to the next. The interplay between training experience, and the duration, rate of adaptation, and training complexity will be the focus of much of the remaining content in this chapter.

As demonstrated in Figure 5.1, there is large difference in terms of adaptation rate and the need for complexity in program design based on the time an individual has trained. Therefore, the way each trainee addresses their specific needs is quite different. Here is a quick overview of each 'level' of training age and how to best plan and create a program for each. These are not complete explanations but rather a quick overview of each level to demonstrate the differences between them.

Now that we understand the different levels of a trainee, let's go back to the statement described previously: *"We are doing the same program as (plug in popular University here)."*

The obvious problem is that those programs are designed for athletes who have been training for a number

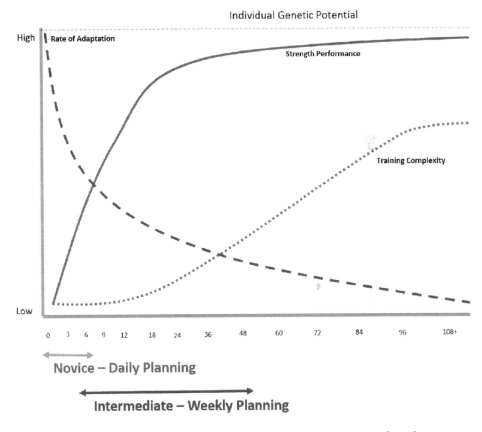

Figure 5.1: Relationship between individual gentic potential and training status over time

of semesters and years in a well-organized and well thought out college strength and conditioning program. These programs were also designed for their specific program's demands. A college athlete can handle—and sometimes needs—this higher level of change in exercise selection and intensities. It would not be a good idea to hit "copy and paste" on other coaches' programs. Every program is different for different reasons, especially comparing programs of individuals whose training age and demands are different.

NOVICE WHAT

- Has a high recovery & adaptation rate (24-72 hours)
- Lacks proficient technique. Is unable to consistently replicate reps over the duration of a set.
- Lacks basic motor skills.
- Has NOT progressively trained for more than 9 months of continuous strength training using the basic barbell lifts.
- Lacks basic levels of strength.
- Need for overall muscular size.

NOVICE HOW

- Can progressively train 2-3 times per week.
- Full body workouts.
- Progression is from workout to workout.
- Use linear progression (increasing wt. after achieving desired reps).
- Use few basic lifts. Teach proficiency first. Repeat from workout to workout.
- End of the novice level occurs when a plateau is reached in performance. After 3-9 months of continuous training.

INTERMEDIATE WHAT

- Increased strength levels.
- Increased muscular body mass.
- Proficient execution of basic lifts.
- Trained progressively for more than 8 months.
- Adaptation takes a week worth of training and recovery.
- Heavier loads cause more stress on the body resulting in longer recovery between workouts.
- Training becomes specific to the needs of the sport.

INTERMEDIATE HOW

- Allow approximately 4-7 days to recover from heavy lifting.
- Higher Intensity work must be varied.
- Utilize weekly periodization using heavy/moderate/light (of 1 RM) workouts per week on basic barbell lifts.
- Exercise selection, sets, reps and speed of movement become more sport specific.
- More reliance on assistance exercises to improve core lifts. 2-5 sets of 8-15 reps.
- 3-5 sets of 1-5 reps on primary exercises.
- 4-8 sets of 1-4 reps on power exercises.
- Weeks of deloading might be necessary.

ADVANCED WHAT

- Has progressively strength trained for more than 28 months.

- Does not recover and adapt from weekly periodization anymore.

- Plans for a peak in strength and weight room performance within the monthly plan.

- Must adjust volume down as intensity rises.

ADVANCED HOW

- Plan for recovery and adaptation to take 2 weeks or more to occur with workouts of lower volume.

- Workouts in between heavy days are backed off to keep skill and conditioning levels high.

- Adjust volume down as intensity rises during the duration of a monthly plan.

- Higher reliance on assistance exercises.

NOTE:

- *There is an overlap of time between each phase of trainee. These phases are individually-based and should be determined not solely on time, but more by the parameters outlined.*

At the high school level, each athlete starts out at the novice level and, at best, bounces in and out of the beginning phases of the intermediate level towards the end of their high school career. This is often due to the transition periods typical at the start and end of competitive sports seasons where strength training is not the primary focus. It is important to understand that, when weight training is not the primary activity (in-season), a step back in training age and program complexity is appropriate when returning to an off-season strength training program.

When writing the strength program, remember that training age is predicated not only by years of weight training, but more so on how quickly the individual can recover from workout to workout. If a younger, more inexperienced trainee can recover quickly, it usually makes sense to use a program that maximizes both short and long-term results rather than waste time with inappropriate programing.

At the high school level, trainees will respond best to sound technique, rep replication, daily progressions, and few exercises. By engraining great technique, the SCP can ensure that the initial learning of technique will be retained and improper technique—that can frequently take months to "unlearn"—can be avoided altogether. Rep replication is important, as each rep should look the same throughout sets regardless of fatigue level. The athlete should not advance until this occurs. Progressions should occur daily, as 1-2 days off should be enough to recover and adapt from workout to workout. Lastly, minimizing the total number of exercises is beneficial. The SCP should typically keep programming relatively basic, especially early on in training development. Only teaching basic barbell movements will lead to mastery of fundamentals.

The Blueprint to Daily Program Design

Whether you are training with a full body, an upper/lower split, or a body part routine, daily program design and order of exercise is vital for overall strength development and safety. Each training day should start with a complete warm-up. Warm-up activities should consist of general activities to increase body temperature before moving to mobility and muscle activation work which addresses joints and muscles that will be worked on that particular day. The warm-up should end with specific movements that the athlete will see during the training day. The warm-up should be concise and not take up too much of the total training time allowed for the day. For a complete description of proper warm-up system, see Chapter 4.

After the warm-up, strength training should be completed in a systematic order. As stated previously, this order of exercise should increase performance as well as prevent any training induced injury. The first exercise performed should be the one that requires the highest degree of technical proficiency and/or speed of movement. If you incorporate Olympic movements into your program or have traditional barbell exercises performed at a high rate of speed, the beginning of the training session is the appropriate place for these exercises. The SCP should have the athlete complete a few warm-up sets, gradually increasing load until he or she is ready to complete the first working set.

If no explosive movements are included in that training day, the next lift should be the primary multi-joint movements of the day. These exercises typically include squats, deadlifts, and multi-joint upper body pressing. Additional warm-up sets may be needed, gradually increasing in weight to the working sets.

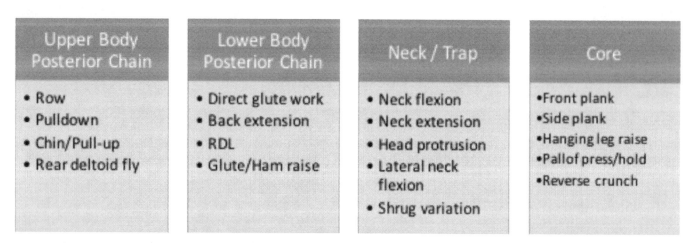

Upper Body Posterior Chain	Lower Body Posterior Chain	Neck / Trap	Core
• Row	• Direct glute work	• Neck flexion	•Front plank
• Pulldown	• Back extension	• Neck extension	•Side plank
• Chin/Pull-up	• RDL	• Head protrusion	•Hanging leg raise
• Rear deltoid fly	• Glute/Ham raise	• Lateral neck flexion	•Pallof press/hold
		• Shrug variation	•Reverse crunch

Figure 5.2: Body part regions and sample exercises for each

After the explosive or primary movements are completed, supplemental or assistance movements should be performed. There are many ways to organize these lifts, from a push/pull fashion to setting up a circuit or stations. There is not a wrong way to set up the rest of the training day as long as supervision, technique, and effort are monitored and coached. This being said, many supplemental exercises are important for athletic development and this is where many individual and sport-specific needs will be addressed. For example, exercises that address the posterior chain, the neck/trap region, and the core are necessary and should be included each day of training. Areas of concern such as the rotator cuff, grip, and hip work should also be addressed here.

Table 5.1 is an example of a full body template with exercises plugged in. Notice there are no sets and reps included. This is provided only to show order of exercise.

Table 5.1: Full body exercise template with exercise examples

FULL BODY TEMPLATE	EXERCISE
General warm-up activity	1 lap / jump rope
Specific mobility/flexibility	Hip flexor stretching/shoulder mobility
Specific activation	Glute bridging/scapular retraction
Specific warm-up movements	Hip hinge/goblet squat/push-up
Olympic movement	Hang clean pull/weighted squat jump
Multi-joint exercise (lower body)	Barbell back squat/trap bar squat
Multi-joint exercise (upper body)	Barbell bench press/dumbbell press
Posterior chain (lower body)	Barbell RDL/hyperextension
Posterior chain (upper body)	Chin up/pulldown
Neck work	4-way neck/dumbbell shrug
Posterior chain (lower body)	Barbell hip thrust/Nordic hamstring lean
Posterior chain (upper body)	Dumbbell row/chest-supported row
Core work	Front plank/side plank
Injury prevention (upper body)	Rotator cuff work
Core work	Hanging leg raise/med ball twist

Phases of Program Design

The goal of this section is to give principle-based programing *ideas*, and discuss how to implement them most effectively. Keep the principles outlined previously in mind as we dive deeper into program design. Also, remember that these recommendations for program design are for athletes involved in a field/court sports outside of the realm of weightlifting and/or power lifting. If weightlifting or power lifting is the goal, then programming will be different.

The two most common approaches are a ***traditional sequential program***, meaning each specific physical characteristic is developed in a sequential order and a ***traditional concurrent program***, meaning several physical qualities are developed 'concurrently' or simultaneously. These two approaches are equally effective but are not the only strategies used by SCPs. They are, however, two approaches that are commonly used and will fit well with athletes participating in off-season strength programs. Both of these approaches can be easily adjusted to individuals of different training ages by a simple alteration in volume *(sets x reps)*, intensities *(load)*, exercise selection, and de-load days. Also, each training approach can be modified to fit most weekly schedules that an athlete and coach will encounter.

A number of other factors should be considered before choosing any particular approach. The SCP should build programming based upon the time available each day for training as well as the time available within the given training cycle (how many weeks or months can be devoted to a continuous strength program?). Additionally, factors such as sport demands, goals and/or number of training goals, facilities and equipment available, and total number of participants should also be taken into account.

Traditional Sequential Model

A sequential program develops physical qualities in a sequential order by means of different training phases. It is used most often when an athlete has a longer off-season time frame (4-6 months) to train continuously. The sequential method allows the strength coach to take the individual(s) from a detrained state into a period of intense training and preparedness for the sport demands. The traditional phases include introduction, anatomical adaptation, basic strength, max strength, and power phase.

Introduction Phase

Because a basic goal of a strength program is to improve strength (represented by weight on the bar), this is a phase that is often overlooked, or even skipped altogether. This has been proven over and over again to be a mistake, and should only be skipped in experienced lifters. As a SCP, it is your job to start at the foundation and begin with the fundamentals. This will not only lead to long-term health and immediate safety, but also a stronger athlete in the long run. The introduction phase is used primarily for individuals who are new to training and/or who need to reintroduce technique after a long break in focused training (where strength training was not the primary focus) such as a sport season.

During this brief phase, the athlete will focus on the fundamentals. Although the duration may vary, typically it consists of a few weeks (at most) depending on the learning curve of the trainee. The SCP should use this time to teach the primary multi-joint exercises that will be used for the remainder of the off-season program and implement mobility/corrective exercises to help improve these lifts. Multiple sets of higher reps should be used, keeping the load relatively light.

The teaching and refinement of movement patterns is critical during this phase and should never be overlooked. This requires constant coaching. Ingraining proper patterns and positions will lead to improved physical gains, while ensuring safety in the weight room. The athlete should never load a lift before he/she is able

INTRODUCTION

- *Goal: Technique*

- *Approximate duration: 2 weeks*

- *Sets x reps: Many (higher volume)*

- *Load: Very light to none*

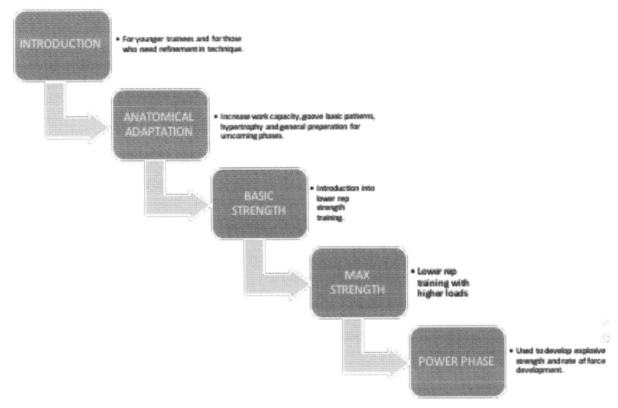

Figure 5.3: Traditional sequential model

to consistently demonstrate great technique. The basic movements that should be taught and mastered in the Introduction Phase include planks, hip hinges, squats, lunges, and push-ups.

During the introduction phase, the SCP can spend plenty of time on supplemental and assistance exercises that do not require as much teaching. These exercises will help increase muscular body mass, improve strength in the muscles used in the basic barbell exercises, and also improve deficient regions of the body. Examples of these exercises include back extensions, machine pulls, various neck work, bodyweight exercises, single-joint shoulder movements, and direct glute work.

Bodyweight exercises work very well in this phase. Increasing the athlete's relative strength has proven to be very beneficial to athletic performance. A simple series of pull-ups and push-ups is beneficial for both the coach and the athlete in terms of the athlete's strength and fitness level. Bodyweight exercises will demonstrate how important body composition is to athletic performance and movement. These routines can be very difficult but usually pay off in terms of teaching *'grit'* in any population.

Anatomical Adaptation Phase

Starting any new training program will likely be accompanied by general fatigue and soreness. This is normal and will subside as the body adapts to the new stimulus. The Anatomical Adaptation Phase will help minimize this, limit the chance of injury, and maximize the training effect. Essentially, this phase prepares the body for the stress that is to come. Think of the Anatomical Adaptation Phase as "gliding" into subsequent strength training phases where volume and intensity will increase.

In addition to providing general preparedness to the overall system (muscles, tendons, nervous system, etc.), this phase is also an opportunity to make progress toward several other training goals such as grooving basic movements, developing muscle mass, and improving overall work capacity. Improvement in all these characteristics is possible during this phase because loads will be relatively low, with a relatively high training volume. An increase in overall volume will provide an opportunity to practice and rehearse *(groove)* perfect rep replication in all basic movements. The increased volume can also stimulate hypertrophy and increase overall work capacity. Because the benefits are essential to sports performance training, the Anatomical Adaptation Phase should not be overlooked.

Organizing the Anatomical Adaptation Phase

Keeping in mind the idea of including higher volume and lower intensities in this phase, writing the program becomes simple. First, choose the major lifts to train in later phases. These should be the same exercises introduced in the previous introduction phase.

Example: Squat, deadlift, bench press

Next choose the supplemental exercises that facilitate a balanced strength throughout the body, and around each joint.

Example: Neck, back extension, lunge, pull-up, dumbbell row, shrug, overhead press

Lastly, choose additional exercises and/or activities that can be used to increase overall work capacity.

Example: Sled pushing, stair run, kettlebell swing, loaded carry, calisthenics

Because intensity (load) is relatively low, the order of exercise is not as critical as it will be in later phases. To stay consistent with our principles, however, it is still important to place more technique-intensive exercises, such as squats and deadlifts, at the beginning of the training day. Conversely, exercises intended to increase work capacity produce a tremendous amount of fatigue, and should be done at the end of the routine.

During this phase, it is important to ramp up the effort that is given by each athlete. We are "gliding in" to heavier loads, but a critical part of this phase is teaching the athlete how to exert higher levels of effort. Coaches who have worked with younger athletes understand this concept well. Most young athletes simply have not yet learned how to dig down and exert maximal effort. This phase offers many opportunities to teach this important trait.

Over the course of this phase, the SCP should continue to build on total volume by adding sets and/or increasing the effort required, while keeping training safe for all involved. Workouts should only take about 60 minutes to complete. The main lift(s) will be programmed in a slightly different way than the other exercises. While reps on most exercises will increase throughout this phase, a slow progression toward heavier weights is recommended for the main lifts. This means a slight reduction in the number of reps so heavier weights can be used. This will set up success for the next phase when loads will increase.

By the end of the Anatomical Adaptation Phase, athletes should be in great shape, able to demonstrate high effort and have the ability to replicate excellent technique in the required tasks. Table

5.2 provides an example of one day of a three-week anatomical adaptation program.

Table 5.2: Sample anatomical adaptation program

DAY 1	Week 1	Week 2	Week 3
General warm up, activation, mobility activities	10 minutes	10 minutes	10 minutes
(Main Lift) Barbell squat	4 x 12	4 x 10	4 x 8
Circuit:	2x's Through	3x's Through	4x's Through
Pull-up	Max effort	Beat last week	Beat last week
Dumbbell walking lunge	10 steps each	12 steps each	15 steps each
Overhead press	10	2x10	3x10
Back extension	10	2x10	3x10
Barbell shrug	15	2x15	3x15
4-way neck	10 each way	10 each way	10 each way
Front plank	30 sec.	60 sec.	90 sec.
Farmer's walk	Max distance	Beat last week	Beat last week

Creating 2-4 different workouts based on the above principles and repeating for 2-4 weeks will set the foundation needed for more specialized work for your athletes in coming phases. Middle-school and high-school aged athletes will spend most of their time in the Anatomical Adaptation Phase before moving to an in-season program. This is because many young athletes are only able to dedicate a few weeks to training before the next sports season begins. Because this type of program elicits many benefits, it is totally appropriate for young athletes to spend a lot of time in this phase.

> **Anatomical Adaptation Phase**
>
> - **Goal: Groove technique, increase work capacity & hypertrophy**
> - **Approximate duration: 2-4 weeks**
> - **Sets x reps: Many (higher volume)**
> - **Load: Light**

Basic Strength Phase (BSP)

Following the Anatomical Adaptation Phase are the Basic Strength and Max Strength phases. These two phases are very similar, where building maximal strength is the primary goal. The main differences between these phases are the intensity and volume used in the primary lifts. It is important to understand that the training age of the individual should determine the amount of time spent in each phase. The novice trainee should spend much more time in the 'basic' strength phase, as this phase will produce plenty of benefit in a safer manner.

As the pendulum swings to the end ranges of intermediate lifting, more time can be spent in a maximum strength phase due to technical proficiency and adaptation to training. On the other hand, the Basic Strength Phase serves to bridge the gap from 'higher' rep strength work into 'lower' rep strength training. Traditionally, this strength work is done for the basic primary movements like the squat, deadlift, bench press, and overhead press variations. Due to the complexity and stress placed on the body, it is critical to perform these lifts early in the workout.

The duration of the BSP is dependent on two factors, including how long the individual has been training (train age and recoverability) and how much time can be devoted to the strength phase. For individuals of a younger training age, more time should be spent in this higher rep phase of strength development. These individuals can spend several weeks performing multiple sets of 5-8 reps. As long as progression in weight is taking place, there is no need to change the routine. If there is a strong need to move closer to max strength work, then a pyramid down in sets and reps such as week 1: 4x6, week 2: 4x5, and week 3: 4x4 would be appropriate.

The intensities or loads used in the BSP become critical to match the sets and reps selected. Loads in the moderate range (70-85%) are appropriate for these sets. That being said, it is not absolutely necessary to establish a one rep max (1RM) for the athlete and load the lift to the exact percentages yet, especially if the lifter is at a young (adolescent) age. Determining a weight for a prescribed rep scheme is easy and can/should be completed in a matter of a few sets. It is important to understand that although load is important, the athlete can be within the rep ranges and still achieve the desired results as long as progressive overload is present. More on load parameters will be outlined later in the chapter.

After completion of the primary lifts, the athlete can move to the supplemental exercises. These exercises should have been taught and practiced in earlier phases and should be beneficial to the sport. They should also help in the performance of the primary lifts. In this phase, the supplemental exercises will greatly assist in the development of maximal strength. For example, strengthening the glutes will help to improve squat strength and extra triceps work will help pressing movements.

BASIC STRENGTH PHASE

- *Goal: Build a foundation of strength*
- *Approximate duration: 4-6 weeks*
- *Sets x reps: 3-6 sets/4-8 reps*
- *Load: Moderate to heavy (70%-85%)*

Table 5.3 provides an example of one total-body workout in a 5-week Basic Strength Phase.

Table 5.3: Sample total-body workout in a 5-week Basic Strength program

DAY 1	Week 1	Week 2	Week 3	Week 4	Week 5
General warm up, activation & mobility	10 min	10 min	10 min	10 min	10 min
Hang clean	3x3	3x3	3x3	3x3	3x3
Barbell back squat	4x8 (70%)	4x6 (75%)	5x5 (75-80%)	5x4 (80-82%)	4x4 (82-85%)
Barbell bench press	4x8 (70%)	4x6 (75%)	5x5 (75-80%)	5x4 (80-82%)	4x4 (82-85%)
Bodyweight chin-up	3x8	3x10	4x8	3x10	3x12
Dumbbell shoulder press	3x8	3x8	3x8	3x8	3x8
Back extension	2x8	2x8	2x8	2x8	2x8
1-leg dumbbell squat	3x5	3x5	3x5	3x5	3x5
4-way neck work	10	10	10	10	10
Barbell shrug	2x12	2x12	2x12	2x12	2x12
Upright row	15	15	15	15	15
Core work	50 total reps	60 total reps	75 total reps	100 total reps	100 total reps
Shoulder external rotation	12	12	12	12	12
1-arm farmer's walk	50 yds	50 yds *	50 yds *	50 yds *	50 yds *

*Increase weight used each week.

As indicated previously, percentages (%) used are approximate based on predicted maxes or a coach selecting appropriate weights.

Max Strength Phase (MSP)

The max strength phase is essentially a continuation of the basic strength phase. In this phase, the lifter(s) will now train at lower rep ranges and closer to their true 1RM. It is import to understand that this phase is reserved for those who have mastered the basic barbell lifts and have progressively moved through the previous phases of training. Because loads/intensity go up in the MSP, overall volume must be adjusted. In the BSP, the athlete performed as many as 5-6 sets of multi-joint barbell lifts. This is due to the moderate loads. Because the loads/lifting intensities are higher, the number of working sets should decrease slightly in this phase.

During the MSP, a specific adaptation is made to the neuromuscular system due to the high loads being used. That is what separates the BSP and the MSP. Sets of 1-4 reps at a lifting intensity of 85-95% are typical in this phase. Because of the specific neuromuscular involvement, it is critical to monitor and track the weight lifted, the volume handled (number of sets) and the rest time given.

Multi-joint barbell lifts with heavy loads are stressful to the system. These will result in the athlete needing longer rest periods between sets and consistency in those rest periods is key. An active rest of 2-4 minutes (depending on load) is sufficient. This active rest can consist of light mobility work or exercise that has zero interference with the lift being performed. These rest intervals are very important, so it is critical to allow full recovery between sets and not worry about keeping everyone active.

The supplemental lifting in the MSP is basically the same as in the BSP. Of course, it is fine to change exercises due to technique progression or to simply add variety to the program. The SCP should be certain to choose supplemental exercises that are safe, create balanced development, and meet the needs of the sport.

Table 5.4 provides an example of one day of a 4-week Max Strength Phase program.

MAX STRENGTH PHASE

- *Goal: Develop max levels of strength*
- *Approximate duration: 4-6 weeks*
- *Sets x reps: 3-4 sets/1-4 reps*
- *Load: Heavy (>85%)*

Table 5.4: Sample workout in a 4-week Max Strength Phase program

DAY 1	Week 1	Week 2	Week 3	Week 4
General warm up, activation & mobility	10 min	10 min	10 min	10 min
Hang clean	3x3	3x3	3x3	3x3
Barbell back squat	4x4 (85%)	3x4 (87%)	4x3 (87-90%)	3x2 (95%)
Barbell bench press	4x4 (85%)	3x4 (87%)	4x3 (87-90%)	3x2 (95%)
Weighted chin up	3x6	3x6	4x5	4x4
Dumbbell shoulder press	3x6	3x8	3x6	3x8
Glute/ham raise	2x4	2x6	3x6	3x8
Barbell lunge	3x5	3x5	3x5	3x5

4-way neck work	10	10	10	10
Barbell shrug	2x12	2x12	2x12	2x12
Rear deltoid raise	2x15	2x15	2x15	2x15
Front bridge	1 min.	75 sec.	90 sec.	2 min.
Shoulder external rotation	12	12	12	12

The Duration of Strength Phases

In reference to the basic strength phase and the max strength phase, it is important to note that strength is a "use it or lose it" characteristic. If strength is not developed or at least maintained, it will gradually diminish over time. The BSP and MSP can be used both for developing and maintaining strength, but neither is intended to be sped through. The SCP should encourage the athlete to take their time and not feel the need to "max out" every week. Each week, making small incremental jumps in load will lead to significant strength increases over the longer training phases. As a coach, the SCP should develop a plan that starts with moderate intensity and volume and slowly intensifies over the course of weeks and months. Prescribe training loads in this phase that the athlete can successfully complete without making large increases in load from workout to workout.

Maximal Power Phase (MPP)

The Maximal Power Phase focuses on applying force in the shortest amount of time possible. To accomplish this, it is important to understand that power is the product of the force *(F)* being produced multiplied by the velocity *(V)* of the movement, and is typically expressed in *Watts. F x V= Power*

With this in mind, we can see that each variable (force & velocity) contribute to the production of power. The amount of force applied to an exercise depends on the amount of weight used, and force increases as the weight/load increases. Velocity, on the other hand, has an inverse relationship to load. Lighter loads can be moved faster than heavier loads, so velocity decreases as load increases. Therefore, the key to demonstrating maximal power production is to choose the heaviest weights possible that can still be moved quickly. Loads in the 50-75% range of maximal strength typically produce the highest power outputs.

Because strength has such a large impact on overall power, it is important to clarify that any lifter who has not yet developed a high level of strength need not participate in the MPP. The MPP is not appropriate for under-developed athletes. Similarly, this is not a phase to jump into without proper technique training and adequate levels of strength. At the high school level, the power phase might only be reserved for upper classmen who have been progressively strength training for 2-3 years. Younger trainees will improve their power production simply by increasing the force side of the power equation through the steps outlined previously.

A common question in regards to the MPP is exercise selection. Training in this manner should only be conducted with exercises that have been well-coached and mastered by the athlete. It is not the intent of the chapter to determine what exercises fit best with any particular program. Some programs utilize Olympic movements and their variations while others use traditional lifts performed at higher velocities. Others do not perform any dynamic lifting and strictly use jumps and explosive medicine ball throwing as a means to develop power. All are acceptable, as long as they are coached very precisely.

The SCP should never prescribe an exercise he/she is not comfortable coaching or cannot instruct correctly, as an increased velocity of movement demands proper technique. It is good professional practice to never have an athlete perform any ballistic exercise that the coach is unable to perform proficiently. If the coach is unable to perform due to injury, then providing supplementary coaching and demonstration through other coaches, proficient athletes, or video instruction may be acceptable.

It is important to understand that any lifts or exercises for the development of power should not result in fatigue to the lifter. At the completion of power work, the lifter should feel good and in a state of readiness for any subsequent work. This means the power portion of the program should have lower volume (generally 2-5 sets), performing fewer than six repetitions per set. This is because power production drops dramatically after approximately six reps. A complete rest interval is necessary between each set, and athletes should not perform power exercises in a state of fatigue.

Another common way to develop power is to combine maximal strength work with explosive exercises between sets. This is commonly referred to as Post-Activation Potentiation (PAP). Basically, the lifter is training maximally on both sides of the power equation (force and velocity). In this scenario, the lifter would perform a high force/low velocity movement immediately followed by a low force/high velocity movement. For example, the athlete could first perform a heavy barbell squat followed by a max height vertical jump for a lower extremity combination. Similarly, a heavy barbell bench press followed by a kneeling medicine ball chest pass would serve as an upper extremity dominant example. This method allows the lifter to train with familiar lifts and still have the ability to develop power by training both high force and high velocity movements.

During the MPP, much of the workout template stays the same with regards to supplemental lifting. It is important to perform the dynamic/ballistic work at the very beginning of the workout when the athlete is fresh, as these are exercises that require focus and attention to detail. The overall workout volume that is performed on the training day needs to be evaluated during the MPP. Because these exercises require such high neuromuscular synchronization, it is important to take a step back in the amount of total workout volume. Reducing the volume of other exercises—both strength lifts and the supplemental exercises—is recommended in the MPP.

Table 5.5 is an example training day using the same Max Strength Phase workout with a slight reduction in volume to account for the power work that has been added.

POWER PHASE

- Goal: Develop power and rate of force production
- Approximate duration: 4-6 weeks
- Sets x reps: 3-4 sets/1-4 reps
- Load: Moderate (50%-75%)

Table 5.5: Sample Max Strength program

DAY 1	Week 1	Week 2	Week 3	Week 4
General warm up, activation & mobility	10 min	10 min	10 min	10 min
Hang clean	3x2	3x2	2x1	3x1
Barbell back squat	4x4 (85%)	3x4 (87%)	4x3 (87-90%)	3x2 (95%)
*Vertical jump	X2	X2	X2	X2
Barbell bench press	4x4 (85%)	3x4 (87%)	4x3 (87-90%)	3x2 (95%)
*Lying med ball chest pass	X3	X3	X3	X3

Weighted chin-up	3x6	3x6	3x6	3x6
Dumbbell shoulder press	2x6	2x6	3x6	3x6
Glute/ham raise	2x4	2x6	2x6	2x6
Barbell lunge	2x5	2x5	2x5	2x5
4-way neck work	10	10	10	10
Barbell shrug	2x12	2x12	2x12	2x12
Rear deltoid raise	2x15	2x15	2x15	2x15
Front bridge	1 min.	75 sec.	90 sec.	2 min.
Shoulder external rotation	12	12	12	12

Traditional Concurrent Model

Training for athletic performance usually requires the SCP to address multiple physical quali-ties during off-season preparation. Work capacity, hypertrophy/body size, strength levels, power, and rate of force development are all necessary qualities to develop. Concurrent programing is a way to address multiple qualities simultaneously as opposed to focusing on one quality at a time like the Sequential Programming Model.

In the Sequential Model, each physical quality is met sequentially because there is enough time available for each phase of the program. If time (in training weeks) is a limiting factor, the Concurrent Model may be the most appropriate choice for programming. As a result, the Concurrent Model works very well in the high school setting where most athletes are novice or intermediate lifters and/or time is often limited. Typically, this group of athletes tends to adapt quickly to different stimuli and there is a multitude of needs to be addressed. If the SCP chooses to utilize a Concurrent Model, it would still be appropriate to begin with an Anatomical Adaptation Phase and an Introduction Phase prior to start-ing specific strength training.

A concurrent approach can be structured several different ways depending on the number of days committed to training within the training week. Most commonly, coaches structure a concurrent approach with either multiple characteristics trained each day, or with each day having a singular training focus, while meeting all desired training qualities and goals throughout the training week.

With a daily approach, multiple non-conflicting qualities can be addressed in one workout, but exercise order remains important. The SCP should always place power development exercises first in the training day. Heavy strength work in the multi-joint lifts should be performed next. Once both of those lifts are completed, hypertrophy work, auxiliary exercises or specialty lifts would be placed third, followed by core and work-capacity exercises.

Table 5.6 provides an example of exercise order using the Concurrent Model.

Table 5.6: Exercise order using the Concurrent Model

Quality	Exercise	Sets x Reps
Power/RFD	Med ball squat/throw	2x3
Power/RFD	Hang clean	4x2
Max strength	Barbell squat	4x3
Max strength	Barbell bench press	4x3
Basic strength/hypertrophy	4-way neck	10
Basic strength/hypertrophy	Dumbbell shrug	2x15
Basic strength	Barbell RDL	3x6
Basic strength/hypertrophy	Dumbbell row	3x8
Basic strength/hypertrophy	Shoulder press	2x10
Core	Front bridge	1 min
Core	Hanging leg raise	2x12
Work capacity	Weighted sled push	3x29 yds

Table 5.7: Sample week using the Concurrent Model

Day 1		Day 2		Day 3	
Power Day		Strength Day		Hypertrophy / Work Capacity / Basic Strength	
Exercise	sets x rep	Exercise	sets x rep	Exercise	sets x rep
Box Jumps (Up to Box)	3x3	Trap Bar Deadlift	1x4, 3x2	Barbell Back Squat	2x8 , 2x6
Med Ball Rotation Throws	2x3	Barbell Bench Press	4x3	DB Split Squat	3x8 ea.
Speed Box Squat	4x3	Barbell Front Squat	3x4	Stability Ball Leg Curl	3x10
Barbell Incline	3x6	Glute/Ham Raise	2x6	Seated DB Shouldr Press	4x10
*Med Ball Chest Pass	3x3	Rowing Machines	4x6	Pull Up	4x8-10
DB Row	3x8	4 Way Neck	10	Push Up	4x8-10
Barbell Hip Thrust	3x10	Barbell Shurgs	3x6	4 Way Neck	12 ea. Way
DB Shoulder Lateral Raise	3x8	Ft. Bridge / Side Bridge	1 min / 30 s	Sled Dragging	3x50yd
Hanging Leg Raise	2x12				

With weekly concurrent planning, each day of the training week has a specific focus. An example of this would include Day 1 devoted to power and rate of force development, Day 2 devoted to max strength, and Day 3 devoted to overall work capacity and hypertrophy.

Considerations should be made to the weekly planning in term of the athlete's overall state of fatigue during the week. While it may not always be obvious to the coach or athlete, the cumulative effects of training tend to set in during the week. Therefore, the SCP is advised to schedule power development days early in the week followed by the strength day next and the most fatigue-inducing routines last before taking the weekend to recover.

Table 5.7 provides an example of a week using the Concurrent Model (not including warm-up).

Loading Parameters

It is important to understand that each physical quality—max strength, hypertrophy, work capacity, power, etc.—responds specifically to the demands being placed upon it. Referred to as the Specific Adaptations to Imposed Demands (SAID) principle, this means that in order to develop a specific strength characteristic, the SCP must program the exact intensity and volumes they intend to develop. For example, if the goal is maximal strength in the bench press, time must be spent not only on the bench press, but training in the exact intensities and reps of the intended strength quality. The loading intensities should always match the intended physical characteristics and quality.

Generally speaking, maximal strength is developed through heavier loads, and hypertrophy/work capacity responds better to moderate or high volume with reduced loads relative to the lifter. With this in mind, it is important for the SCP to understand the relationship between intensity and volume, and the different ways to modify them in order to achieve the desired goals. Before we go any further, it is important to define two relevant terms: intensity and volume.

Intensity

With regard to strength training, intensity typically refers to the load or weight that the athlete is using in any particular exercise. Intensity can also be expressed by the percent (%) of 1-repetition maximum (1RM) that a athlete is using. Intensity is a term that gets used in different ways by different coaches. Many coaches use intensity to refer to how hard something is or how much effort is being expressed in a given task. Oftentimes, athletes will describe intensity as how hard work is *perceived*. While that definition can be useful when monitoring fatigue, it is not the definition we will use moving forward in this chapter.

Volume

Volume is the quantity of work completed and can be defined as the number of sets and/or reps performed in a specific workout, as well as the total number of sets/reps performed over a series of workouts. Volume can also be represented in total workout volume where the amount of load is taken into account. The *total workout volume* can be expressed by the following equation:

Total number of sets (x) reps per set (x) weight used = total workout volume

This total workout volume is represented in pounds. For example, an athlete who performs 4 sets of 5 reps with 225 lbs. has a total workout volume of 4,500 lbs.

4 x 5 x 225 = 4,500

This shows that each variable has a direct effect on the other. Tracking total workout volume allows the coach to monitor training loads and is a quantifiable way to track overload.

The Intensity/Volume Relationship

Workout intensity and volume are variables the SCP should monitor over the course of a training day, as well as an entire training phase. When a spike in either or both occurs, the risk of injury increases if the athlete is not properly prepared. Intensities should be programmed to increase gradually to facilitate an overload effect without exposing the athlete to unnecessary risk due to an inappropriate spike in training loads.

Intensity and volume are inversely related, therefore as intensity rises (as in most pre-season programming), volume should typically decrease. Balancing this will guard against spikes in total workout volume that may lead to a state of over-reaching. Over-reaching for too long will eventually lead to a significant increased risk of a training injury. Similarly, as volume increases (as in most off-season programming), intensity should decrease. The SCP should always track and be aware of training volumes and intensities. A gradual increase is the only appropriate progression when training athletes, especially younger, less-experienced trainees.

Selecting Appropriate Set and Rep Schemes

Many athletes have a difficult time choosing appropriate weights for various set/rep schemes. They simply do not have the experience to know which weights to choose on each exercise. Therefore, it is critical that the SCP be very involved in this process to ensure both safety and effectiveness. It is absolutely critical to select weights that can be handled with excellent technique for the prescribed number of reps, yet are heavy enough to stimulate the desired training effect. The effectiveness of the program is reduced when this does not occur.

For example, if an athlete in the Maximal Power Phase chooses a weight that is too heavy to move quickly, the wrong physical quality is being trained, and technique may be compromised. Conversely, if the goal is hypertrophy, and the program calls for 10-12 reps, choosing a weight that can only be lifted 4-5 times will not elicit the desired effect. Table 5.8 gives a general outlook of the intensity and reps used for each specific training characteristic used in the programming templates previously outlined.

Table 5.8: Intensity and rep range relationship

Physical Quality	Intensity	Rep Range Per Set
Power	50-75%	1 - 4
Max Strength	87 - 100%	1 - 3
Basic Strength	70 - 87%	4 - 8
Hypertrophy	50 - 70%	8 - 20

Selecting Appropriate Volume

Since determining training volume is a critical aspect of program design, it is important to have an understanding of this process. Training volumes are somewhat individual in nature as people respond differently to different volumes of work. Nonetheless, the SCP should understand general volume guidelines in order to achieve safe and effective results.

In the 1960s, A.S. Prilepin collected extensive data regarding volumes used by thousands of world class weightlifters from around the world. He compiled his data into a

Table 5.9: Prilepin's Table

Intensity (% of 1RM)	Rep Range	Total Reps	Optimal Reps
< 70%	3-6	18-30	24
70 - 79%	3-6	12-24	18
80 - 89%	2-4	10-20	15
> 89%	1-2	4-10	7

widely recognized chart for determining volumes for basic barbell lifts known as the "Prilepin's Table for Determining Volume."[2] This table is used by many strength coaches as a guideline for determining the total number of sets and reps to perform for basic barbell movements. This table should only be used as a guide for selecting appropriate volumes. The further the SCP moves away from max intensities (<70%), the more volume can be added to the desired rep ranges.

It is important to remember that this resource was created by data from world-class Olympic weightlifters, not young and/or novice field/court sport athletes. Nevertheless, the guidelines outlined can serve to optimize performance, and more importantly, maintain a safe training environment.

Determining 1RM

Many SCPs like to create programs using percentages of the athlete's maximal strength or one rep maximum. In this case, it is necessary to first determine the 1RM so that appropriate load can be assigned. It is not recommended to perform 1RM testing until the athlete has completed both the Introductory Phase and Anatomical Adaptation Phase of the program. This will ensure technique proficiency as well as the specific conditioning needed to perform the task. In addition, it is not recommended to perform any maximum effort testing on Olympic or ballistic lifts for the novice lifter. Doing so will place the lifter at a risk of injury that is not worth the result.

Testing the 1RM may be performed using either a single rep/actual 1RM or a predicted max test. Both tests require a lengthy warm up by the athlete consisting of approximately two warm up sets of very light weight for approximately 5-8 reps with approximately 90 seconds between sets. Then the athlete should complete two sets of moderate to heavy sets for approximately 2-3 reps with 2 minutes between sets. Finally, the athlete should complete one heavier set of 1-2 reps to complete the warm-up. After a 2-3 minute break, the athlete should be primed for a test, and a weight should be chosen for testing based upon working loads used in warm-up and how the athlete performed.

In performing an actual 1RM test, the goal is to select the highest load possible that can be lifted just one time with a failure to complete the second rep. If the load selected is successfully lifted, the athlete should take another break and perform another set with a slightly heavier weight. The SCP should have the athlete continue this sequence until the athlete can no longer increase the weight. The final weight successfully lifted is the athlete's 1RM.

While the actual 1RM is more accurate, it does increase the athlete's risk for injury compared to predicted max testing.[3] To combat this risk, the predicted max test can be used, although it does introduce the possibility of error since the athlete's capability is not measured directly. When using the predicted max method, the athlete should begin by using a load that he or she can lift approximately 2-5 times. This will provide more accuracy when predicting the 1RM than when loads selected are lighter and rep ranges higher. In other words, the closer the predicted max text load is to the actual 1RM load, the less likely it is for error to occur. Once the appropriate load is selected, the athlete should perform as many reps as possible. The load used and the number of repetitions completed are then referenced to the chart provided to determine a predicted 1RM.

Table 5.10: Estimated 1-repetition maximum chart

1	2	3	4	5	6	7	8	9	10
135	143	147	151	156	159	163	167	171	176
140	148	153	157	161	165	169	174	178	182
145	154	158	162	167	171	175	180	184	189
150	159	163	168	172	177	181	186	190	195
155	164	169	174	183	188	192	197	202	207
160	170	174	179	184	189	194	198	203	208
165	175	180	185	190	195	200	205	210	215
170	180	185	190	195	201	206	211	216	221
175	186	191	196	201	207	212	217	222	228
180	191	196	203	207	212	218	223	229	234
185	196	202	207	213	218	224	229	235	241
190	201	207	213	218	224	230	237	241	247
195	207	213	218	224	230	236	242	248	254
200	212	218	224	230	236	242	248	254	260
205	217	223	230	236	242	248	254	260	267
210	223	229	235	241	248	254	260	267	273
215	228	234	241	247	254	260	267	273	280
220	233	240	246	253	260	266	273	279	286
225	239	245	252	259	266	272	279	286	293
230	244	251	258	264	271	278	285	292	299
235	249	256	263	270	277	284	291	298	306
240	254	262	269	276	283	290	298	305	312
245	260	267	274	282	289	296	304	311	319
250	265	272	280	287	295	302	310	317	325
255	270	278	286	293	301	308	316	324	332
260	276	283	291	299	307	315	322	330	338
265	281	289	297	305	313	321	329	337	345
270	286	294	302	310	319	327	335	343	351
275	292	300	308	316	325	333	341	349	358
280	297	305	314	322	330	339	347	356	364
285	302	311	319	328	336	345	353	362	371
290	307	316	325	333	342	351	360	368	377
295	313	322	330	339	348	357	366	374	384
300	318	327	336	345	354	363	372	381	390
305	323	332	342	351	360	369	378	387	397
310	329	338	347	356	366	375	384	394	403
315	334	343	353	362	372	381	391	400	410
320	339	349	358	368	378	387	397	406	416
325	345	354	364	373	384	393	403	413	423
330	350	360	370	379	389	399	409	419	429
335	355	365	375	385	395	405	415	425	436
340	360	371	381	391	401	411	422	432	442
345	366	376	386	397	407	417	428	438	449
350	371	381	392	402	413	423	434	444	455
355	376	387	398	408	419	430	440	451	462
360	382	392	403	414	425	436	446	457	468
365	387	398	409	420	431	442	453	464	478
370	392	403	414	425	437	448	459	470	481
375	398	409	420	431	443	454	465	476	488
380	403	414	426	437	448	460	471	483	494
385	408	420	431	443	454	466	477	489	501
390	413	425	437	448	460	472	484	495	507
395	419	431	442	454	466	478	490	502	514
400	424	436	448	460	472	484	496	508	520
405	429	441	454	466	478	490	502	514	527
410	435	447	459	471	484	496	508	521	553
415	440	452	465	477	490	502	514	527	539
420	445	458	470	483	496	508	521	533	546
425	450	463	476	489	501	514	527	540	552

Progressive Set and Rep Schemes

Table 5.11 provides examples of different set/reps schemes for each training phase. These are just principle-based examples and can be used and/or adjusted to fit any desired training goal.

Limitations with Percentage Based Programs

Loading strictly based on a percentage (%) of 1RM has several limitations in its accuracy and should be constantly evaluated by the coach and athlete. There are two reasons for this inaccuracy. First, is the constant change in the individual's 1RM. The second is the individual's level of training readiness on the actual training day.

Changes in 1RM

Percentage-based training works very well with those individuals who have established maxes and train for competition purposes. The majority of percentage-based plans were (and are) established for those individuals whose training has hit a point where periods of training must either be backed off or intensity must adjust over the course of a prolonged training phase. These are individuals with an elevated training age who no longer sufficiently respond to a linear approach.

Most field/count sport athletes have a training max that is constantly changing. This is due to the fact that weight training is not the only priority to the athlete. The athlete has other obligations to the actual sport which may conflict with weight training. Obligations like practices, film study, academics, and conditioning for the sport all have a cost and can negatively impact an athlete's weight training progress.

Take, for example, a powerlifter training the squat. When he or she enters the weight room, this is their arena of competition. This athlete will usually know exactly what their squat max is at almost any given time of the year. Their training and success depend on it. Therefore, a percentage-based, periodized plan is more appropriate for them.

On the other hand, consider a high school football player who is consistently participating in other activities related to football. During the course of the week, he may have conditioning, 7-on-7, and skill work. All of these activities will have a cost to his overall training and must be accounted for by both the coach and athlete. This cost to training could have a slight effect on the training max at any given time.

Another reason for changes in the 1RM is a rapid jump in strength and skill acquisition, especially in the novice lifter. These changes can make his initial evaluation inaccurate after just a few weeks of training. Additionally, yet another reason for fluctuations in training maxes is the daily readiness of the lifter. Athletes 12-22 years old experience drastic emotional highs and lows. A bad academic report or social situation can have a dramatic impact on a young athlete. Suddenly, 100 lbs. on the bar feels like 300 lbs. and the athlete is not mentally engaged in weight training.

All of these factors make it difficult to accurately create long-term programs using percentages of a 1RM for young athletes. When using percentage-based programs, the SCP will need to take the aforementioned factors into account and reassess frequently. While best-laid plans are encouraged and can certainly help the SCP plan for the future, with young athletes especially, building flexibility

Table 5.11: Progressive set & rep schemes

Training Phase	Scheme Description	Set Rep Scheme			
		Week 1	Week 2	Week 3	Week 4
Anatomical Adaptation	Constant Volume Increased Load	3x10 (62%)	3x10 (65%)	3x10 (67%)	3x10 (70%)
	Incerased volume Constant Load	3x8 (67%)	3x10 (67%)	3x12 (67%)	3x15 (67%)
	Increased Volume and Load	3x10 (65%)	3x12 (65%)	4x10 (67%)	4x12 (67%)
		3x10 (65%)	3x12 (65%)	4x10 (67%)	4x8 (70%)
		3x8 (65%)	3x8 (67%)	4x8 (67%)	4x8 (70%)
Basic Strength	Constant Volume Increased Load	3x6 (77%)	3x6 (80%)	3x6 (82%)	3x6 (85%)
	Decreased Volume Increased Load	4x6 (75%)	4x6 (77%)	3x5 (82%)	3x4 (85%)
		4x6 (75%)	5x5 (77%)	4x4 (85%)	3x4 (87%)
		4x8 (70%)	4x6 (75%)	4x5 (80%)	5x4 (85%)
		3x8·6·4 (72·75·77%)	3x8·6·4 (75·77·80%)	3x6·4·2 (80·82·85%)	3x6·4·2 (82·85·87%)
		6x4 (77%)	5x4 (80%)	4x4 (82%)	3x4 (85%)
Max Strength	Decreased Volume Increased Load	4x4 (85%)	3x4 (87%)	4x3 (90%)	3x2 (95%)
		4x4 (85%)	3x4 (87%)	3x2 (95%)	4x1 (97%)
		3x3 (87%)	3x3 (90%)	3x2 (95%)	4x1 (97%)
		4x4·3·2·2 (85·87·90·90%)	4x4·3·2·2 (87·90·92·92%)	4x3·2·1·1 (90·92·95·95%)	4x3·2·1·1 (92·95·97·97%)
		5x4 (80%)	4x4 (85%)	3x3 (90%)	2x2 (95%)
Power*	Post-Activation Potentiation	4x4 (85%)	3x4 (87%)	4x3 (90%)	3x2 (95%)
	Decreased Volume Increased Load	4x5 (55%)	4x4 (60%)	4x3 (65%)	4x2 (70%)

into such programming is critical in order to best meet the needs of the athlete when, where, and how they are each day.

Basic Linear Progression

With the novice and de-trained lifter, progressive overload with a simple linear progression is the most effective way to get the lifter stronger in the most efficient way. This progression is simply selecting a desired weight for the lift and assigning a goal number of repetitions to perform. Once the lifter has completed the goal number of repetitions for the particular lift, the load is then increased for the next workout. This method is not only simple in its design, but equally simple in its implementation. It can be done using just one set per exercise or multiple sets.

For example, the workout could call for 3 x 10 on dumbbell incline press. This means the athlete would attempt to perform 3 sets of 10 reps with the **same weight** on each set. When he/she can perform all three sets with the same weight, the SCP should increase the weight for the next workout.

If the athlete gets 10 reps on his first set, 8 on his second set and 6 on the third, he would record his performance and stick with the same weight on the next workout. The next time he performs this workout, he would attempt to do one more rep on the second and third set. The athlete would continue in this fashion until he can perform all three sets of 10, at which time load would be increased and the whole process would start over again.

These are all great ways to help younger/inexperienced athletes understand the concept of progression and the following are examples of linear progression using both a single set and multiple sets.

Table 5.12: Sample basic linear progression program

GOAL: 1 Set x 10 Reps						
Week 1:	Week 2:	Week 3:	Week 4:	Week 5:	Week 6:	Week 7:
155 x 10	160 x 10	165 x 8	165 x 10	170 x 10	175 x 9	175 x 10

GOAL: 3 Sets x 6 Reps						
Week 1:	Week 2:	Week 3:	Week 4:	Week 5:	Week 6:	Week 7:
155 x 6	160 x 6	165 x 6	165 x 6	165 x 6	170 x 6	170 x 6
155 x 6	160 x 6	165 x 5	165 x 6	165 x 6	170 x 6	170 x 6
155 x 6	160 x 6	165 x 4	165 x 5	165 x 6	170 x 4	170 x 6

Loading Based on Rate of Perceived Exertion (RPE)

The American College of Sports Medicine (ACSM) defines a rating of perceived exertion (RPE) as "A psychophysiological scale, meaning it calls on the mind and body to rate one's perception of effort. The RPE scale measures feelings of effort, strain discomfort, and/or fatigue experienced during both aerobic and resistance training."[4] The RPE scale is rated differently by many different coaches and for many different situations. Most commonly it is rated on a scale of 1-10 with 10 being the hardest. However, other measurement scales can range from 1-20.

The RPE method is intended to assign a subjective measure of how hard something *feels* at the time, and it has become a very popular and effective way of individualizing strength training with advanced lifters who understand their bodies. Because percentage-based programs do possess the previously-described inherent limitations, this method of training is a way to systematically make more individualized adjustments. In the current world of sports performance and the constant monitoring of loads, research has shown that a perceived exertion rate is a very accurate representation of one's actual fatigue levels.[5-7] This means that perceived exertion is real exertion even if the quantifiable training intensity is low at the moment. This makes training with a RPE scale very useful in terms of strength development and determining training intensities by the use of individual readiness. Training based on RPE is more appropriate for an experienced lifter, however, this method that can be used by any coach or athlete.

Rest Periods

The rest interval between sets allows the athlete to recover so he/she is able to perform subsequent sets. Rest intervals between sets can be a complicated topic, with many different ranges to follow dependent on the goal(s) of the athlete. In general, as the intensity (load) of the lift increases, the amount of rest between sets needs to increase, as well. In hypertrophy/work capacity workouts, rest between sets can be relatively low (30-90 sec.) compared to strength and power work. In a Basic Strength Phase, the athlete should take approximately two minutes between sets on the major barbell movements. In a Max Strength or Max Power Phase, rest between sets should increase to approximately 2.5-3 minutes. This is due to the increase in demands placed on the lifter to complete each repetition.

It is important that rest intervals are kept constant from workout to workout. This ensures that consistency is present, which is vital when it comes to tracking data and comparing one workout to the next. During sub-max lifting, rest intervals can be used to accomplish other objectives and increase the productivity of the workout. Mobility or non-competing exercises are a common use of time within rest intervals. An example would be performing heavy sets of bench press and pairing it with lower body stretching and/or neck work during the rest interval. Both will add value to the workout and not influence performance of the bench press. Of course, spotting other lifters is always a good way to spend a rest period, too.

If the athlete is still so fatigued after a rest period that he does not feel ready to safely perform the next set, a longer rest period is needed. Safety should never be compromised.

Table 5.13: Suggested rest intervals

General Guidelines for Rest Intervals Between Sets	
Goal:	Time Between Sets:
Power	2 - 5 min.
Strength	90s - 5 min.
Hypertrophy/ Work Capacity	30s - 90s

Constructing the Strength Program

Annual Planning

"Failure to plan is planning to fail."

The annual plan allows the coach to look at the entire year of training to ensure proper progression and avoidance of competing demands. It is an outline of the training year. A comprehensive annual plan will take a number of factors into consideration, including the number of weeks in the training year, the phases of training, the time required and scope of testing and evaluation periods, game/competitions schedules, sport practice schedules, conditioning demands, speed work performed, and a number of other influences.

This outline allows the SCP to plan training phases accordingly and identify the best times for intense weight training. Without this advanced planning, the coach becomes reactive rather than proactive. Traditionally, annual plans are created with three distinct phases, including the macrocycle, mesocycle, and microcycle. The macrocycle is a period of several months to a year of training and is built around a few broad annual goals. On the other hand, the mesocycle is a period of 2-6 weeks and the microcycle is typically a single week. Both the mesocycle and microcycle are built around training goals that ultimately will contribute to the attainment of the broader goals of the macrocycle.

The annual plan should represent distinct phases of pre-season training, in-season training, and off-season training, all of which have specific training goals and desired outcomes. Before finalizing an annual training plan, it is advised to consult with the sport coach, as he/she will have a major impact on scheduling.

Table 5.14: Sample annual plan

Blank Annual Plan Template for Football

TIME OF YEAR:	EARLY OFF SEASON	GENERAL OFF SEASON	GENERAL OFF SEASON	GENNERAL OFF SEASON	LATE OFF SEASON	PRE SEASON	COMPETITION	BOWL GAME PREP.
	WINTER CONDITIONING		SPRING BALL	POST SP BALL	SUMMER CONDITIONING	CAMP	IN SEASON	
WEEK:	1 2 3 4 5	6 7 8 9 10 11	12 13 14 15 16	17 18 19 20 21 22 23 24	25 26 27 28	29 30 31 32	33 34 35 36 37 38 39 40 41 42 43 44 45 46	47 48 49 50 51 52
LIFTING DAYS PER WEEK								
RUNNING DAYS PER WEEK								
TESTING / EVALUATION								
PHASE (BLOCK)								
UB CORE LIFT/ INTENSITY (%)								
LB CORE LIFT/ INTENSITY (%)								
SPEED								
CONDITIONING								
PLYOMETRICS								

Creating an Exercise Menu

Every SCP should have a menu of lifts and exercises commonly used in the program. There are hundreds of exercises available, so working from an exercise menu provides a variety of choices without becoming too random. Cycling through a few exercises is much better then performing a totally new lift every other training cycle. This eliminates the learning curve and allows the athlete to start progressively training and overloading upon adding the new stimulus.

The following charts are commonly used lifts for each major movement and/or region of the body. This exercise menu is not complete, but gives you a place to start.

Creating a Training Template

Like an exercise menu, a training template is something a coach can always reference when writing a program. The training template can be used much like the annual plan by keeping the coach and program on task. A training template is a nonspecific outline of the goals and objectives of each individual day, of each day or week.

This daily template should include the specific region of the body, movement, and/or physical quality to be addressed each day. Also outlined should be intensity, generally listed as high, moderate, or low as well as time allotted per training day. Doing all of this gives direction when developing the training plan. Creating a well thought-out training template will guard against overlooking qualities in training intended on developing.

Table 5.15: Sample exercise menu

Example Exercise Menu:

Lower Body - Quadriceps Dominate:	
Primary: Squat Variation	*Assistance*
Back Squat Variations	Single Leg Squat
Front Squat	DB Squat
Leg Press	Step Ups
	Leg Extension
	Forward Lunge

Lower Body - Posterior Chain Dominate:	
Primary : Deadlift Variation	*Assistance*
Deadlift Variations	Hip Thrust
Romanian Deadlift	Back Extension
	Glute/Ham Raise
	Leg Curl
	Reverse Hyper
	Reverse Lunge

Upper Body - Press:	
Primary	*Assistance*
Bench Press Variations	Push Ups
Incline Press Variations	Shoulder Lateral Raise
Overhead Press Variations	Shoulder Front Raise
	Chest Fly

Upper Body - Pull:	
Primary	*Assistance*
Pull Ups	Rear Delt Raises
Rowing	Pulldown Machine
	Inverted Body Row

Neck/Traps:
Neck Flexion
Neck Extension
Neck Forward Nod
Neck Backward Tilt
Lateral Neck Extension
Neck/Head Protrusion
Shrug Variations

Olympic Lifts:
Clean Variations
Jerk
Snach

Explosive Exercises:
Med Ball Throws (Horizontal)
Med Ball Throws (Vertical)
Box Jumps
Vertical Jumps
Broad Jumps
Split Jumps

Example Weekly Training Templates:

Table 5.16: Example training templates

Lifting 3 Days Per Week:

Full Body / Full Body / Full Body

Day 1:	Day 2:	Day 3:
Intesity: Heavy	*Intesity: Light*	*Intesity: Moderate*
Squat Variation	Explosive Exercise/ Oly Lift	Deadlift Variation
Posterior Chain - *Assistance*	Single Leg Squat Variation	Squat Variation- *Assistance*
UB Horizontal Press- *Primary*	Upper Body Vertical Pressing	UB Press- *Assistance*
Horizontal Pulling- *Primary*	Upper Body Vertical Pulling	Body Weight Pulling
Shrug Variation	Neck	Neck
	Core	Core

Full Body / Upper Body / Lower Body

Day 1:	Day 2:	Day 3:
Intesity: Heavy Upper / Light Lower	*Intesity: Moderate Upper*	*Intesity: Heavy Lower*
UB Horizontal Press- *Primary*	Explosive Exercise/Oly Lift	Explosive Exercise
UB Horizontal Pulling- *Primary*	Upper Body Vertical Pressing	Squat Variation- *Primary*
Shrug Variation	Upper Body Vertical Pulling	Posterior Chain- *Primary*
Squat Variation- *Assistance*	Neck	Posterior Chain- *Assistance*
Posterior Chain- *Assistance*	Arms	Core
	Core	

Power / Strength / Hypertrophy

Day 1:	Day 2:	Day 3:
Intesity: Power-Moderate	*Intesity: Heavy*	*Intesity: Light/Moderate*
Explosive Exercise/Oly Lift	UB Horizontal Press- *Primary*	Explosive Exercise
Explosive Exercise/Oly Lift	Deadlift Variation	Single Leg Squat Variation
Explosive Exercise/Oly Lift	Upper Body Vertical Pulling	UB Horizontal Press- *Assistance*
Squat Variation- *Primary*	Shrug Variation	UB Horizontal Pull- *Assistance*
UB Horizontal Press- *Assistance*	Neck	Posterior Chain- *Assistance*
Neck	Core	UB Horizontal Press- Assistance
Core		UB Horizontal Pull- *Assistance*
		Posterior Chain- *Assistance*

Lifting 4 Days Per Week:

Upper Body / Lower Body / Upper Body / Lower Body

Day 1:	Day 2:	Day 3:	Day 4:
Intesity: Heavy	*Intesity: Light*	*Intesity: Moderate*	*Intesity: Heavy*
UB Horizontal Press- *Primary*	Explosive Exercise/Oly Lift	Explosive Exercise/Oly Lift	Squat Variation- *Primary*
UB Horizontal Pulling- *Primary*	Explosive Exercise	Shrugs	Posterior Chain- *Primary*
UB Horizontal Pulling- *Primary*	Single Leg Squat Variation	Neck	Squat Variation- *Assistance*
UB Horizontal Press- *Assistance*	Squat Variation- *Primary*	UB Horizontal Press- *Primary*	Posterior Chain- *Assistance*
UB Horizontal Pull- *Assistance*	Posterior Chain- *Assistance*	UB Horizontal Pull- *Assistance*	Posterior Chain- *Assistance*
Arms	Posterior Chain- *Assistance*	UB Horizontal Press- Assistance	Core
Neck	Core	UB Horizontal Pull- *Assistance*	Core
Shrug	Core	Upper Body Vertical Pulling	

Strength / Power / Strength / Power

Day 1:	Day 2:	Day 3:	Day 4:
Intesity: Heavy	*Intesity: Light*	*Intesity: Moderate/Light*	*Intesity: Heavy/Moderate*
Squat Variation- *Primary*	Explosive Exercise/ Oly Lift	Posterior Chain- *Primary*	Explosive Exercise/ Oly Lift
Posterior Chain- *Primary*	Explosive Exercise/ Oly Lift	Squat Variation- *Primary*	Explosive Exercise/ Oly Lift
UB Horizontal Press- *Primary*	Single Leg Squat Variation	UB Horizontal Press- *Primary*	Explosive Exercise/ Oly Lift
UB Horizontal Pulling- *Primary*	Posterior Chain- *Assistance*	UB Horizontal Pulling- *Primary*	Single Leg Squat Variation
Neck	UB Horizontal Press- *Assistance*	Neck	Posterior Chain- *Assistance*
Shrug	Upper Body Vertical Pulling	Shrug	Upper Body Vertical Pressing
	Core		Upper Body Vertical Pulling
			Core

Body Part: Press Dominate (UB) / Post Chain Dominate (LB) / Pull Dominate (UB) / Quad Dominte (LB)

Day 1:	Day 2:	Day 3:	Day 4:
Intesity: Heavy (wk 1)	*Intesity: Light (wk 1)*	*Intesity: Light (wk 1)*	*Intesity: Heavy/Moderate (wk 1)*
Intesity: Light (wk 2)	*Intesity: Heavy (wk 2)*	*Intesity: Moderate (wk 2)*	*Intesity:Light/Moderate (wk 2)*
UB Horizontal Press- *Primary*	Explosive Exercise/ Oly Lift	UB Horizontal Pulling- *Primary*	Explosive Exercise/ Oly Lift
UB Horizontal Pull- *Assistance*	Posterior Chain- *Primary*	UB Horizontal Press- *Assistance*	Squat Variation- *Primary*
UB Horizontal Press- *Primary*	Squat Variation- *Assistance*	UB Horizontal Pulling- *Primary*	Posterior Chain- *Assistance*
UB Horizontal Pull- *Assistance*	Posterior Chain- *Primary*	UB Horizontal Press- *Assistance*	Squat Variation- *Primary*
Upper Body Vertical Pressing	Squat Variation- *Assistance*	Upper Body Vertical Pulling	Posterior Chain- *Assistance*
Shrug	Single Leg Squat Variation	Shrug	Single Leg Squat Variation
Neck	Core	Neck	Core

The Middle School/Beginner Lifting Program

Strength training for the middle school athlete has grown so much that it is now normal to start an organized strength training program for a 6th or 7th grader. This is cause for a deeper understanding of the proper training of athletes of this age range. One of the first questions asked regarding strength training for young athletes is *"Will a strength training program have a negative effect on the adolescent's growth?"*

This is a question that has been asked for decades and with good concern. At this time, there is no evidence that a properly designed and supervised strength program will have any impact on growth.[8,9] In the early adolescent ages, using relatively heavy weights is not recommended and progress should be made in the relatively high rep ranges (10-20 reps) with an emphasis on mastering correct technique with relatively light loads.

Much progress can also be made increasing the adolescent's *relative strength,* which is the amount of strength an athlete has in relation to his/her own bodyweight. One way to increase relative strength is to train with classic bodyweight exercises involving chin-ups, pull-ups, push-ups, dips, body weight squats, and bodyweight lunges. Progressively increasing the athlete's performance in just these exercises (without even touching a barbell) will have a dramatic impact on a young athlete's overall strength, body control, and athleticism.

If the SCP decides to use additional resistance, ample time should be devoted to engraining perfect technique with zero loads. As proficiency in technique increases, the ceiling for overall strength and size later in training will increase. These are skills that, when learned correctly, will carry over for years of training. If learned incorrectly, it will be necessary to spend more time overcoming and training out the poor habits created.

It is critical to note that loading a movement is only appropriate when a young athlete displays consistent technical proficiency without load first. After movement proficiency is attained, it is recommended to start with relatively high rep ranges (10-20 reps) using the double progression method. In the double progression method, the SCP begins by picking a rep range such as 10-15, 15-20 or 10-12. If the range is 10-15 reps, the goal is to choose a weight that can be lifted at least 10 times but not more than 15. Each workout, the athlete should attempt to do more reps than the last workout until he/she hits the top of the rep range. When that occurs, the weight should be increased, and the athlete starts the process all over again from the bottom of the rep range.

If the load is selected appropriately, it will take the athlete multiple workouts to achieve the end range goal. Progressing in this fashion allows the athlete to maintain appropriate loads, yet continue to progress.

The double progression method is often used with a single set of an exercise, having the athlete perform as many reps as possible (AMRAP) on each exercise. If an athlete chooses a weight that is too light, he/she may be able to go well past the assigned range. That is totally acceptable in the early phases of training because it shows the athlete that it is time to increase the weight. Many young athletes get nervous about increasing weights, so this slow progression helps establish confidence and gradually works up to more appropriate loads. Volume can be increased by adding sets, but the SCP will generally only record the first set.

The double progression method can be used for many weeks or even months with new lifters. Some SCPs even use this method with more advanced lifters during certain times of the year. Continue using this method as long as progress is being made.

Table 5.17 provides an example of how the double progression method would be recorded on a workout card.

Table 5.17: Double progression method sample

Machine Bench Press:							
GOAL: 10 - 15 Reps							
Week 1	Week 2	Week 3	Week 4	Week 5	Week 6	Week 7	Week 8
50 x 15	55 x 12	55 x 14	55 x 15	60 x 11	60 x 14	60 x 15	65 x 12

A safe, progressive and organized lifting program is recommended for the middle school (adolescent)-age individual. Introductory weight training should be enjoyable and is an opportunity to learn a new skill with constant improvement. The goal should always be to teach strength training basics and engrain great technique while increasing one's relative strength. Doing so can develop a strong work ethic and increase confidence. To avoid burnout, the SCP should stick with 2-3 sessions a week at about 30 minutes per session, and remember that supervision and constant coaching is vital to this group.

Conclusion

Strength training is an important part of physical preparation for athletics, and it has become more popular than ever. This is a great thing, but with this growing demand comes the need for excellent coaching. This is an exceptional opportunity for quality SCPs to make a tremendous impact on an entire generation of athletes.

Because strength training has become such a large part of every sport, responsibility is now placed in the hands of the SCP to administer safe and effective programs for young athletes. This responsibility does not stop with learning proper technique. The SCP must learn how to plan and implement a year-round strength training program that is appropriate for the sport and the population. This includes applying programming built around sound strength training principles and understanding training age and appropriate progression. Additionally, the SCP must teach the athletes to focus on the "process" rather than only the results. Selection of lifts and exercises should depend on identifying movements that are teachable, repeatable, and can be progressively overloaded along with determining the proper sequencing of lifts and exercises for any given training day is key.

For many professionals, determining the appropriate training plan to follow, given the number of training weeks allowed is an important first step, but determining how to use that time by prescribing appropriate intensity and volume necessary to meet the specific training goals is no less essential. As such, devising loading parameters that are safe and progressive for the duration of the training phase is a critical skill.

When creating programs, the SCP must keep in mind that strength training is not the actual sport for most athletes. In addition to strength training, allowing for time and energy to address other demands that are specific to the sport including conditioning, speed development, mobility, and most importantly, sport practice will help combat the natural tendency to over-prescribe exercise due to a myopic view of the athlete's total physical and mental demands.

The principles of strength training are time tested and will never change, but the SCP should constantly evolve and learn the newest ways to help the athletes we serve. This will allow us to make the greatest impact on these athletes and teach them lessons that extend well beyond the walls of the weight room. Such should be the goal of any coach.

References

1.   Rippetoe M, Baker A. *Practical Programming for Strength Training.* 3rd ed. Wichita Falls, TX: Aasgaard Company; 2013.

2.   Laputin P, Oleshko V. *Managing the Training of Weightlifters.* Kiev, Russia: Zdorov'ya Publishers; 1982.

3.   Niewiadomski W, Laskowska D, Gasiorowska A, Cybulski G, Strasz A, Langfort J. Determination and prediction of one repetition maximum (1RM): Safety considerations. *Journal of Human Kinetics.* 2008;19:109-120.

4.   American Council of Sports Medicine. *ACSMs Guidelines for Exercise Testing and Prescription.* Philadelphis: Lippincott, Williams & Wilkins; 2010.

5.   Aniceto R, Ritti-Dias R, Dos Prazeres T, Farah B, de Lima F, do Prado W. Rating of perceived exertion during circuit weight training: A concurrent validation study. *Journal of Strength and Conditioning Research.* 2015;29(12):3336-3342.

6.   Egan A, Winchester J, Foster C, McGuigan M. Using session RPE to monitor different methods of resistance exercise. *Journal of Sports Science & Medicine.* 2006;5(2):289-295.

7.   Helms E, Cronin J, Storey A, Zourdos M. Application of the repetitions in reserve-based rating of perceived exertion for resistance training. *Strength and Conditioning Journal.* 2016;38(4).

8.   Council on Sports Medicine and Fitness. Strength training by children and adolescents. *Pediatrics.* 2008;121(4).

9.   Dahab K, McCambridge T. Strength training in children and adolescents. *Sports Health.* 2009;1(3):223-226.

PRINCIPLES of
ATHLETIC
Strength &
Conditioning
The Foundations of Success in
Training and Developing
the Complete Athlete

CHAPTER 6

Explosive Training for Youth Athletes

Darl Bauer

Objectives

- Describe the stretch shortening cycle and discuss how it can be utilized to increase power production
- Be able to incorporate explosive training into an annual conditioning plan using appropriate volume and intensity prescriptions
- Be able to describe and coach low, moderate, and complex explosive exercises

Introduction

Developing strength and power is critical for many athletes as they progress into more competitive levels over time. As a result, effective explosive training for young athletes is essential as the athlete matures. This chapter first will cover foundational knowledge regarding explosive training while the second section will be more practical and will illustrate and explain the execution of different explosive training modes. Furthermore, the practical section will also guide the reader in understanding what types of exercises are appropriate for different training ages.

Foundational Knowledge

Explosiveness is one of the most sought-after attributes that an athlete can have. However, the term is ambiguous, subjective, and not consistently defined in either academic or practical settings. Some athletes are genetically gifted with the ability to be explosive, while others have to train for a long time. Other athletes have such low genetic potential they may never reach a great level of explosiveness. With proper programming, however, any athlete has the opportunity to maximize their genetic potential. Whether it is a basketball player driving up for a rebound, or a football lineman exploding out of his stance, being explosive can be the difference between winning and losing.

Being "explosive" is basically the combination of strength and speed expressed in a fluid, efficient manner. An explosive athlete can generate a tremendous amount of force in a very short period of time, and training to become explosive can be done many ways. The purpose of this chapter is to help the strength & conditioning professional (SCP) understand how to use various tools to make an athlete become more explosive, understand when it is appropriate to use each tool, and describe the proper execution of each movement.

What Does It Mean to be Explosive?

Explosiveness itself cannot be measured, it can only be observed. Power, force, and rate of force development (RFD) are qualities that contribute to explosiveness, and they can all be measured. Power, measured in Watts, is equal to work divided by time (P=W/T), indicating a reciprocal relationship between power and time. In other words, for a given amount of work, the faster an athlete can perform the movement or skill, the more power he or she produces.

While an athlete's overall capacity for explosiveness is largely determined by genetic factors, there are many trainable factors that can come into play.[1] Specifically, a number of trainable factors have been identified that can impact the expression of power by any athlete, including cross-sectional area, density of muscle unit per cross sectional area, intensity of recruitment, muscle synchronization, inhibition of fibers not contributing to movement, and cooperation of muscle fiber types.[2]

Greater cross-sectional area results in more cross-bridge attachments within the myofibrils, thereby increasing force production capacity. Overall muscle size is not the only contributing factor, but density within that space is important, as well. Increased density of muscle fibers in a small amount of space will lead to greater levels of force production. At the same time, neural factors play a role in performance, too. The motor unit can adapt just like anything else. If there is a stronger signal of intent sent to the motor end-plate, the intensity of the recruitment will increase. Muscle synchronization could be one of the most important trainable factors related to explosiveness, as getting muscles to fire with optimal timing and sequencing helps both muscle synergists and agonists work together to produce more efficient movement. Along those same lines, the body's ability to inhibit fibers not contributing to movement is essential in making motor skills more efficient. Lastly, muscle fiber type recruitment is critical for employing the appropriate motor units to meet the need at the moment, whether that be more fatigue-resistant but less powerful Type I fibers or more fatigable but high power-producing Type II fibers.[2]

When discussing the concept of explosive training, we must think in terms of rate of force development (RFD), maximal power output, and ground reaction force. RFD measures how quickly force can be produced, while maximum power output describes the peak level of power (measured in Watts) produced in a movement. Ground reaction force is the force exerted by the ground on a body in contact with it, most typically the athlete's feet.

An athlete can develop explosiveness in many different ways, including improved acceleration, change of direction skill, and jumping, punching, and rotating. First, acceleration involves going from zero velocity to max velocity and requires the combination of high RFD, running mechanics, and stride frequency. The athlete must have the explosive capabilities and the intent to gain velocity at a significant rate. Acceleration is defined by how fast the athlete can change velocity per unit of time. Next, being able to quickly change direction can separate a good athlete from a great athlete. Along with changing direction, it is important to note that the ability to decelerate takes great eccentric strength. This is another very important attribute that should be trained when attempting to increase explosiveness.

Jumping, punching, and rotating are also important skills. Jumping is probably the first thing that people think about when they picture an explosive athlete. In order to jump high, the athlete must have the ability to create a lot of force in a minimal amount of time. A popular cue for jumping is "load and explode." Upper body punching, either with both hands, or with one hand, is a vital motion for many sports. Just as the lower body can fire quickly to produce force, the upper body must be able to do the same. Lastly, sports like baseball, golf, and boxing rely heavily on rotational power. The ability for the core musculature to stabilize the spine while contracting peripheral muscles at a high level of force is critical. This is why core training—specifically rotational core training—should be an emphasis for many sports.

Training Elastic Strength (Tensile Strength)

It is important to understand the relationship between tendon and the muscle. Muscle tissue is contractile in nature composed of thousands of cells referred to as sarcomeres. When a motor unit (a single motor neuron and all the sarcomeres innervated by it) is recruited, the muscle attempts to contract. When the force generated by the muscle is greater than the resistance encountered, the muscle shortens and a concentric muscular action occurs. When the force is equal to the resistance, no movement occurs and the action is referred to as isometric in nature. When the force produced is less than the resistance encountered, the muscle resists lengthening and an eccentric muscular action occurs.

Connective tissue is composed of collagen fibrils that envelop the sarcomeres into bundles and also serve to connect the muscles to their proximal and distal attachment points. These fibers can be fascia that encase the muscle, tendons that connect the muscles to bones, or ligaments that connect bones together. Connective tissue is non-contractile in nature but can serve to absorb or dissipate force.

The musculo-tendon unit is comprised of a contractile component (muscle fibers) and an elastic component (tendon and fascia). Tendons are viscoelastic, meaning that a rapid stretch is followed by a return to the original length, while a prolonged stretch causes a more prolonged change in length.[2] This allows the tendon to stretch to accommodate high forces without rupturing. Additionally, tendons possess impressive tensile strength. When stretched quickly, tendon tissue can encounter tremendous forces as it resists lengthening. This action, coupled with a properly-timed muscular contraction, can serve to significantly magnify force production. Movements that require a quick eccentric deceleration followed by a rapid concentric contraction utilize elastic strength (i.e. barbell squat jump, clean, band box squat).

Stretch Shortening Cycle

The stretch shortening cycle (SSC) is a critical concept that a SCP must fully understand in order to effectively prescribe explosive movements to athletes. The SSC involves a preceding eccentric action, a brief coupling or amortization phase, and an explosive concentric action that leverages not only the elastic/structural capacity of the musculo-tendinous unit but also the enhanced muscular action through the muscle spindle fibers that facilitate stronger contraction. The SSC can result in force production that exceeds maximal isometric strength by as much as 50-100%.[3]

During the eccentric phase, the SCP should coach the athlete to quickly absorb force and land on the ground in a balanced position. The forces involved in the eccentric phase can be significant and injuries can frequently occur in this phase of movement, so the athlete should be coached to maintain proper knee alignment and to avoid valgus collapse.

Figure 6.1: Phases of plyometric activity. The goal is typically to minimize the amortization phase and maximize the concentric phase for maximum power output.

Next, during the amortization phase, the athlete transitions from eccentric to concentric action, and the athlete should be coached to minimize the time it takes in this transition in order to maximize force production. Lastly, during the concentric phase, the athlete releases stored energy and the explosive action occurs as quickly and forcefully as possible.

Intent

Of all the aspects associated with explosiveness, the concept of **intent** may be the most important. Intent is the determination to fulfill a purpose. When performing explosive movements, the athlete is not simply inducing fatigue. Rather, the reason for performing these exercises is to get the neuromuscular system to work faster and more efficiently. With this in mind, it is critical that maximal effort is given when performing explosive exercises. The best way to coach intent is to educate the athlete about the purpose of the training activity. An athlete who understands the process and perceives it to be beneficial will be more motivated to give an all-out effort.

Intent can be either voluntary or neuromuscular in nature. Voluntary intent involves a premeditated action with a specific goal in mind (box jump, kettlebell swing, etc.). On the other hand, neuromuscular intent involves reactivity to an unknown or incompletely known stimulus (i.e. depth jump, landing from a rebound, etc.) or using reflex mechanisms.

The SCP can measure intent through technology that measures power output or bar velocity. This technology can provide both the athlete and SCP with real-time data that quantifies these measurements and clearly illustrates how much power is being produced. This type of technology can increase the intent of the athlete and provide motivation to maximize explosive efforts while also measuring progress and introducing competition into the environment.

Safety

Prior to training an athlete to perform explosively, the SCP must be sure the athlete is adequately prepared. The forces involved in explosive training can be harmful to an athlete who is not properly prepared. Inexperienced or beginning lifters should not be required to include explosive training into their routine until they have established a foundation of basic strength. Although empirical evidence is currently lacking in this specific area, the addition of explosive training too early in development could conceivably lead to a variety of chronic injuries including tendinopathy, stress fracture, and low back pain or acute injuries such as tendon ruptures and muscle tears.

The best way to prevent injury in youth athletes who are engaged in explosive training is to be cautious and use a slow progression when introducing exercises. Basic strength training movements like push-ups, pull-ups, and lunges can provide large adaptations in young athletes. It can be easy for parents to get caught up in the desire for their young athlete to be successful, and many want to seek out the best training available. Parents and coaches should always contact an experienced and qualified SCP before allowing their child to participate in any sort of performance training, especially if it involves potentially dangerous movements or activities.

When a young athlete experiences a rapid growth spurt, he or she may be gaining height rapidly without the necessary strength to leverage this new height. This temporary mechanical disadvantage can create slow reaction times, weakness, and poor intermuscular coordination. When poor coordination is a factor for an athlete, it becomes extremely risky to introduce any type of explosive training where an external load is involved. This should be a time for improving movement quality, general strength and mobility in an effort to re-establish overall balance and coordination.

How Many Reps?

Due to the high forces experienced during explosive training, it is important that the athlete receives adequate rest time between efforts. The goal of explosive training is to maximize neuromuscular recruitment in the shortest amount of time. Explosive training performed in a repetitive fashion with no recovery limits recruitment due to the high fatigability of the type II motor units. As a result, it is recommended that an athlete have time for full recovery between repetitions (usually around a 1:20 work-to-rest ratio). The less intense the exercise the athlete is doing, the less rest is necessary to reload the musculature for another contraction. Conversely, the higher the intensity of the exercise, the fewer the reps should be performed.

When performing maximal power exercises, research has shown that peak power output drops quickly after about 5-6 reps.[4] Keeping this in mind, training for maximal power should generally be done with fewer than 6 reps. Less intense exercises that do not create maximal power (i.e. line hops, kettlebell swings, medicine ball throws, etc.) can utilize higher rep ranges

Practical Application

While a sound foundation is critical for understanding, implementation of explosive training is similarly important. The following section includes numerous examples of explosive training techniques and strategies to incorporate these approaches into programming. As detailed in the following, explosive exercises are best grouped by intensity (Grade I/low, Grade II/moderate, and Grade III/high) and age (6-9, 10-14, and 15+).

Table 6.1: Explosive exercise intensity continuum

AGE GROUPS		LOW (GRADE I)	MEDIUM (GRADE II)	HIGH (GRADE III)
PREPUBESCENT	AGE 6			
	AGE 7			
	AGE 8	SLED PUSH, KB SWING	DUMBBELL HI PULL, 1 ARM KB SWING	
	AGE 9		MB OV HEAD TOSS, MB EXPL FORW TOSS	
PUBESCENT	AGE 10	KB SNATCH	DOUBLE KB SWING, KB SWING HI PULL	
	AGE 11			
	AGE 12		EXP STEP UP, VERTIMAX, TIRE FLIP	
	AGE 13			
	AGE 14		DB SQ JUMP, DB JERK, BARBELL SQ JUMP	
	AGE 15			
YOUNG ADULT	AGE 16		SPEED & PAUSE SQUAT	DYN EFFORT BOX SQUAT, CLEAN & HANG CLEAN, SNATCH & JERK
	AGE 17			
	AGE 18			
	AGE 19			
	AGE 20			

Table 6.2: Exercise prescription suggestions for programming explosive movements

		AGEs 6-9	AGEs 10-15	AGEs 16+
GRADE I (LOW IMPACT)	KB SWING	VERY LIGHT WEIGHT	LIGHT - MODERATE	MODERATE -HEAVY
	SINGLE ARM KB SWING	VERY LIGHT WEIGHT	LIGHT - MODERATE	MODERATE -HEAVY
	DOUBLE KB SWING	VERY LIGHT WEIGHT	LIGHT - MODERATE	MODERATE -HEAVY
	DOUBLE KB SWING HI PULL	VERY LIGHT WEIGHT	LIGHT WEIGHT CHOICES	MODERATE WEIGHT
	KB SNATCH	VERY LIGHT WEIGHT	LIGHT WEIGHT CHOICES	MODERATE WEIGHT
	DB HIGH PULL	VERY LIGHT WEIGHT	LIGHT - MODERATE	MODERATE -HEAVY
GRADE II (HIGH IMPACT)	MED BALL OVERHEAD TOSS	VERY LIGHT MED BALL	LIGHT-MEDIUM MED BALL	MEDIUM WEIGHT MED
	MED BALL FORWARD TOSS	VERY LIGHT MED BALL	LIGHT-MEDIUM MED BALL	LIGHT-MEDIUM MED
	DB JERK	NOT RECOMMENDED	LIGHT WEIGHT CHOICES	LIGHT-MODERATE
	BARBELL SQUAT JUMP	NOT RECOMMENDED	BARBELL ONLY	NO MORE THAN 75 LBS
	DB SQUAT JUMP	NOT RECOMMENDED	LIGHT WEIGHT CHOICES	MODERATE WEIGHT
	EXPLOSIVE TIRE FLIP	NOT RECOMMENDED	USE SMALL TIRE	USE SMALL-MEDIUM
	EXPLOSIVE SLED PUSH	USE UNWEIGHTED SLED	LIGHTLY LOADED SLED	LIGHT-MEDIUM LOADED
	EXPLOSIVE STEP UP	NOT RECOMMENDED	BODYWEIGHT ONLY	USE LIGHT SANDBAG ON
	VERTIMAX	NOT RECOMMENDED	LOW BAND RESISTANCE	LOW-MODERATE BAND
GRADE III (HIGH IMPACT)	CLEAN/HANG CLEAN	NOT RECOMMENDED	NOT RECOMMENDED	USE ONLY UNDER QUALIFIED SUPERVISION. CAN BE DANGEROUS
	SNATCH	NOT RECOMMENDED	NOT RECOMMENDED	USE ONLY UNDER QUALIFIED SUPERVISION. CAN BE DANGEROUS
	JERK	NOT RECOMMENDED	NOT RECOMMENDED	USE ONLY UNDER QUALIFIED SUPERVISION. CAN BE DANGEROUS
	SPEED/PAUSE SQUAT	NOT RECOMMENDED	NOT RECOMMENDED	USE ONLY UNDER QUALIFIED SUPERVISION. CAN BE DANGEROUS
	DYNAMIC EFFORT BOX SQUAT	NOT RECOMMENDED	NOT RECOMMENDED	USE ONLY UNDER QUALIFIED SUPERVISION. CAN BE DANGEROUS

Grade I: Low Intensity

Grade I drills are low impact, voluntary-response movements usually used as movement preparation. Most athletes can participate in these movements with proper instruction/supervision regardless of underlying strength and neuromuscular coordination.

Kettlebell Swing

The kettlebell (KB) swing is an excellent low-impact explosive movement that is relatively easy to teach and execute. The athlete should begin by holding the KB firmly with both hands. Using a hip-hinge movement, the athlete should allow the KB to swing backward between the legs. As the KB slows down, the athlete should quickly push the hips forward, swinging the KB forward, away from the body in an arching motion. As the KB loses momentum, it will begin to descend. Keeping the arms straight, the athlete should return to the hip-hinge position to allow the KB to swing between the legs again. The action should

Figure 6.2: Kettlebell swing

take place at the hip joint, and the athlete's arms should not be used to move the KB. This exercise is typically done repeatedly.

Single Arm Kettlebell Swing

Similar to the traditional kettlebell swing, this alteration adds a rotational component to the exercise. Because only a single side is involved at a time, this can be an appropriate short-term alternative for an athlete with an upper extremity injury who is unable to perform with the involved side. The athlete should use the same guidelines as the KB swing described previously, except that the KB is only held with one hand. This exercise can be done repeatedly.

Figure 6.3: Single arm kettlebell swing

Double Kettlebell Swing

Using two kettlebells requires more power from the hips to accelerate and decelerate the weight. The athlete should use the same guidelines as the KB swing described previously, except the movement is performed while holding a KB in each hand. This is typically done with the KBs swinging between the legs, but another variation is to have the KBs swing outside the legs with a narrow stance. This exercise can be done repeatedly.

Double Kettlebell High Pull

Having to swing the kettlebell to a high-pull position requires even more hip extension and a rapid RFD. The athlete should allow the kettlebells to swing back between legs before extending the hips forward and upward, forcefully sending the KBs away from the body. As the KBs rise upward, the athlete should violently rip the resistance over the shoulders with the wrists locked and elbows high, then punch them back out on the same plane of motion. The athlete should allow control the KBs back to starting position, and repeat. This exercise can be done repeatedly.

Kettlebell Snatch

The kettlebell snatch is more complex than the KB swing because it is received overhead. The athlete should allow the KB to swing back between legs, then violently extend hips upward and forward. Once the hips are extended, the athlete should pull the kettlebell upward close to rib cage and attempt to "throw it back over shoulder." As the KB travels upward, it will pivot around the wrist as the athlete punches vertically in a locked-arm receiving position. By gripping the handle to control rotation, the KB should land gently on the posterior aspect of the forearm. To recover for the next rep, the athlete should bring the kettlebell down by supinating the wrist while bringing the KB to the front of the chest then thrusting it away from the body and returning back to starting position.

Figure 6.5: Kettlebell snatch

Dumbbell High Pull

The dumbbell high pull is a simple way to load the body safely while extending the hips through full range of motion. The athlete should begin with the dumbbells at the side. The athlete should then squat halfway down with the heels flat on the floor then explosively extend the hips and knees while "pushing the floor away" in a jumping movement without leaving the floor. Once the hips are extended, the athlete should rip the dumbbells up toward the armpits to reach full extension. The athlete should finally decelerate the dumbbells and return the heels to recover and reset between each rep.

Grade II: Moderate Intensity

Grade II exercises are high-impact explosive movements that are more complex than Grade I due to the increased eccentric loading and complexity of some activities. These movements should only be executed by athletes who have a sound strength and motor control foundation and a moderate to high training maturity.

Figure 6.6: Dumbbell high pull

Med Ball Explosive Overhead Toss

The athlete should begin with the med ball extended out in front of the face. The ball should then be forcefully brought down between the legs. Once the ball is back as far as possible, the athlete should then initiate a jumping motion. While keeping the elbows extended, the athlete should extend the hips and launch the ball back over the head. The goal is to throw the ball for both height and for distance.

Med Ball Explosive Forward Toss

The athlete should begin with med the ball on upper part of chest with palms underneath the ball and the thumbs up. Movement is then initiated by squatting down partially while rocking forward. Using a broad jump motion, the athlete should then forcefully extend the hips, putting as much force as possible into the ball while attempting to launch it out and up. The athlete should fully extend the hips and elbows in an attempt to gain as much height and distance as possible.

Dumbbell Split Jerk

Starting with the dumbbell at the shoulder in one hand in a clean catch position, the athlete begins by locking the wrist and making sure the forearm is perpendicular the floor with the dumbbell handle also parallel to the floor. The athlete should make sure the spine is neutral with the chest up. While keeping the heels on the floor, the athlete should then begin a quick and explosive dip portion by performing a quarter squat. The athlete should drive upward forcefully by extending the hips and pushing all force up into the dumbbell. Once the dumbbell has been accelerated away from the shoulder, the athlete should push the body down into a lunge/split stance in order to assume the receiving position. The opposite leg of the arm holding the dumbbell should plant one step forward, while the dumbbell-side leg should extend two steps back behind the athlete. The elbow should be extended and locked out and there must be stabilization in the receiving position before the recovery phase begins. Recovery from the jerk has three steps, as the lead foot is first stepped back under the hips, followed by the trail foot and then a controlled return of the dumbbell back to the clean catch position.

Barbell Squat Jump

The squat jump is one of the more overlooked explosive movements because it is easy to teach and execute. There must be great caution when executing the movement due to where the bar is located high on the spine. The athlete should begin with the bar high on the traps similar to a squat position then dip quickly into a half squat and explosively jump into the air. The athlete should then land softly on the front half of the feet (metatarsal heads) first to absorb impact, then heels down to fully load the feet. It should be the goal of the athlete to land as quietly as possible while maintaining a stabilized, neutral spine position.

Dumbbell Squat Jump

This is basically the same exercise as the barbell squat jump, but with the weight held at the sides to reduce spinal load. The athlete should begin with the dumbbells at sides, then dip quickly into a half squat and explosively jump into the air. The athlete should then land softly on the front half of the feet (metatarsal heads) first to absorb impact, then heels down to fully load the feet. It should be the goal of the athlete to land as quietly as possible while maintaining a stabilized, neutral spine position. This exercise can also be performed with a hex/trap bar.

Figure 6.6: Dumbbell squat jump

Explosive Tire Flip

This drill should be performed with a tire that is light enough to allow the athlete to move it with speed. This is a total-body movement that allows the athlete to transfer power from the lower body to the upper body. The athlete should begin at the bottom of a squat position with the feet close to the tire and hands under tire with elbows locked out. The athlete should apply tension to the grip and forcefully explode up and into the tire with the body acting as one unit. Once the hips are extended, the athlete should curl the arms into the tire and punch the tire forward.

Explosive Sled Push

The explosive sled push strengthens the muscles used in acceleration. With arms extended, the athlete should push the sled forward in a running motion, fully extending the drive leg hip with each stride.

Explosive Step Up

Using a box that is about knee-height, the athlete should begin by stepping on the box with the entire foot of the lead leg and driving the body upward. The athlete should be cued to then drive the knee of the trail leg upward and opposite arm backward, similar to sprint mechanics.

VertiMax

The VertiMax is an excellent training tool because it has a great takeoff and landing surface, resistance can be changed easily, resistance stays consistent, and a variety of movements can be performed. Specifically, the SCP may incorporate the VertiMax squat jump, pogo hop, or split squat jump.

Squat Jump

The athlete should use the same mechanics as a normal vertical jump while emphasize good form and quality landing mechanics. Movements can be done continuously or the athlete may reset between each rep.

Pogo Hop

This is a lower-leg explosive movement very similar to jumping rope but with more height. With knees fully extended and the body in an upright stance, the athlete should hop up and down on the front half of the feet using the calf muscles to forcefully plantarflex the ankles with minimal knee action. The athlete should dorsiflex the ankles while airborne and work to minimize ground contact time between hops. The athlete's elbows should be flexed to approximately 90 degrees and the arms should be used to forcefully assist each hop.

Split Squat Jump

Starting in the lunge or split stance position, the athlete should jump up as high as possible, alternate legs while in midair, and land with the legs split, controlling the deceleration of the body. This movement can be done continuously or reset between each rep.

Grade III: Complex Explosive Movements

The techniques involved in some of the Grade III movements are very complex and difficult. Therefore, the athlete must have a high training maturity, be relatively strong for their bodyweight, and the SCP must be capable of teaching these movements properly. These movements can be dangerous if not done properly and because of their inherent complexity, errors can occur very easily.

Olympic Weightlifting

Weightlifting movements are extremely popular because they demand and develop high power output, athletes can compare power between one another, and they include the forceful triple-extension (hips/knees/ankles) so important to many sports. They are, however, some of the most complex movements seen in all of sports. It is an Olympic sport in itself, but frequently used as a training tool for many other sports. If not done properly, the Olympic lifts can be dangerous.

Due to the high level of complexity in executing and the mastery necessary to teach the movements, it is not recommended for any athlete that is not considered a young adult to execute these movements with high loads. It is not recommended that these lifts be taught or prescribed by anyone who does not have the proper education and certification. That said, it is entirely appropriate to implement the teaching progressions for athletes as young as 9-14 years using a broomstick or PVC pipe, as such athletes are typically highly sensitive to motor learning and complex skills such as the Olympic lifts can be grooved easily for future loading when the musculoskeletal system is more developed.

It is also very difficult to adequately describe these in written form only, so consider this to only be an introductory description. The reader should watch videos, live repetitions, and be taught by a highly-qualified coach in order to perform these lifts properly. Olympic movements should only be performed with Olympic-style bars and specialized Olympic bumper plates. The lifts should be performed on an Olympic platform or designated area that has a clear workspace free of clutter and foot traffic.

Olympic movements should never be spotted. Athletes must be taught how to safely "miss" a lift and "bail" from a failed attempt (this is why the plates are rubber and platforms typically include a resilient floor suitable for missed loads). It is also suggested that the athlete drop the bar to blocks or to the floor. The reason for this is that it can be hard on the shoulder joints and lower back to allow the weight to drop and catch the weight in front of the body after each repetition.

Clean

The clean consists of a first pull, a scoop, a second pull, and a catch at shoulder height. The first pull should begin in a neutral position with the feet shoulder-width apart and the bar grasped slightly wider than shoulder width with an over-hand grip. The lumbar spine should be in neutral or slight lordosis and the hips hinged into flexion. The hips should be slightly higher than the knees. The athlete should keep the head in a neutral position, take a deep breath, and forcefully attempt to drive the heels through the floor. The athlete should make sure the shoulders drive up as the hips initiate the movement. The hips and shoulders should rise at the same time. The athlete should then extend the hips and knees, pulling the bar smoothly off the floor.

Next, the scoop phase consists of the bar transitioning between the completed first pull and second pull yet to come. Once the bar passes the knee, the knees will come forward quickly as the hips begin to

Figure 6.7: Clean start position

extend. For the second pull, with the bar now at mid-thigh, the athlete then explosively extends the hips, accelerating the bar into a power shrug position and driving force through the entire foot. Maximal force production occurs due to the intent of the athlete to push the ground. The goal is to extend the hips and knees as forcefully and explosively as possible. The athlete is not trying to leave the ground on purpose; this is simply a side effect of pushing the ground away aggressively.

Following the second pull, the bar is now in flight. The bar is used as a fixed object in space to accelerate the body under. Using high elbows and keeping the bar tight to the body, the athlete then quickly pulls the body under the bar, while simultaneously replacing feet to just past shoulder width (squat stance). As the bar comes back to the collar bone, the athlete should receive the bar in front squat position with the elbows punched up. The bar should be resting on the shoulders at this point. Many athletes need to release their grip on the bar so it rolls on to the tips of the fingers. The athlete should then stand up with the bar to finish the lift. When the lift is complete, the athlete simply drops the elbows and drops the bar to the floor.

Figure 6.8: Clean scoop

Figure 6.9: Clean second pull (start)

Figure 6.9: Clean second pull (finish)

Figure 6.10: Clean catch

Figure 6.10: Clean finish position

Snatch

The snatch is initially performed similarly to the clean with some key differences. First, instead of the shoulder width grip used in the clean, the snatch grip is much wider. To find the proper grip width for the snatch, the athlete should hold the bar at the waist with the elbows fully extended, then adjust the grip narrower or wider until the bar is level with the pubic bone. The other key difference is the catch position. Unlike the clean which is caught in a front squat/clean catch position at shoulder height, the snatch is caught overhead.

The snatch begins with the first pull. The athlete should begin in a neutral position with the feet in a shoulder width position and the bar grasped as previously described. The lumbar spine should be in neutral or slight lordosis and the hips hinged into flexion. The hips should be slightly higher than the knees and the head should be in a neutral position. The athlete should take a deep breath and forcefully

Figure 6.11: Snatch start position

attempt drive the heels through the floor, making sure the shoulders drive up as the hips initiate the movement. The hips and shoulders should rise at the same time. The athlete should then extend the hips and knees, pulling the bar smoothly off the floor.

Once the bar passes the knee, the scoop phase involves the transition between the completed first pull and the second pull yet to come. With the bar now at mid-thigh, the athlete should extend the hips fully and accelerate the bar into a power shrug position, driving the force through the entire foot. Maximal force application occurs due to the athlete attempting to forcefully push into the platform. The goal is to extend the hips and knees as explosively as possible. The athlete is not trying to leave the ground on purpose; this is simply a side effect of pushing into the ground aggressively.

From here the athlete is ready for the catch. As the hips fully extend, the bar will be propelled into flight. Once the bar is in flight, the athlete must pull the body under the bar while keeping the bar

Figure 6.12: Snatch scoop phase

Figure 6.13: Snatch second pull (start)

Figure 6.14: Snatch second pull (finish)

Figure 6.15: Snatch catch

Figure 6.16: Snatch finish position

close to the body. The athlete then quickly descends to the bottom of a squat position as the arms extend overhead. The wrists will turn over, providing a pocket in the palm where the bar should land. The bar should be caught directly over the shoulders and the head should be in front of the bar as though looking through an open window. The wrists, elbows, and shoulders should all be fully extended overhead with the elbows locked out. The athlete should stand up with the weight to complete the lift. To finish, he or she should take a small stop backward and drop the bar with control in front.

If the bar continues to go behind the athlete in the receiving position, the athlete must learn to properly "miss" the rep by pushing bar behind the body while simultaneously letting go and hopping forward. The athlete should never try to save a snatch that has been pulled too far back, as this can lead to serious injury.

Jerk

To begin, the athlete should start with the bar in the front of body across the shoulders in the clean catch/ front squat rack position. Grip should be just past shoul-

Figure 6.17: Jerk start position

der width, with all fingers wrapped around the bar. With the spine vertical, the athlete should then dip by sitting the hips back into a quarter-squat, pushing the knees forward and outward. This should be done quickly to take advantage of the stretch reflex.

exploding upward out of the quarter-squat and extending the hips and knees explosively. This will get the bar moving off the shoulders. Once the barbell is moving upward, the athlete then pushes the body down into the receiving position. The dominant leg will stride forward approximately one step while the trail leg will stride back two steps so the athlete will land in a lunge/split squat position with the bar overhead caught overhead. The elbows should be extended and locked out and the head will be forward. There must be stabilization in the receiving position before the recovery phase begins.

To recover from the receiving position, the lead foot should slide back quickly under the hips followed by the trail foot being brought forward under the hips. To finish the lift, the barbell should be brought down under control back to the collar bone. The athlete should drop the bar in front of the body on the platform if it is too heavy to control.

Figure 6.18: Jerk dip phase

Figure 6.19: Jerk receiving position

Figure 6.20: Jerk finish position

Hang Clean

The hang clean is a great movement to develop power, however it is frequently overused and under coached. It is identical in execution to the full clean, except for the setup. The hang clean begins by finding the same grip as the clean. With the lumbar spine in neutral or slight lordosis, the athlete deadlifts the bar and stands all the way up. The athlete then initiates the lowering phase by lowering the bar toward the knees, pushing the butt back and the chest pushing forward over the bar similar to the beginning of the Romanian dead lift or the hip hinge exercise. Once the bar reaches the lower thigh or top of the knees, the athlete will then decelerate the bar, reverse direction, and attempt to transition to the second pull via the scoop phase. With the bar at mid-thigh, the athlete initiates the second pull by extending the hips fully and accelerating the bar into a power shrug position while driving the force through the entire foot.

Figure 6.21: Hang clean start position

Following the second pull, the bar is now in flight. The bar is used as a fixed object in space to accelerate the body under. Using high elbows and keeping the bar tight to the body, the athlete then quickly pulls the body under the bar, while simultaneously replacing feet to just past shoulder width (squat stance). As the bar comes back to the collar bone, the athlete should receive the bar in front squat position with the elbows punched up. The bar should be resting on the shoulders at this point. Many athletes need to release their grip on the bar so it rolls on to tips of the fingers. The athlete should then stand up with the bar to finish the lift. When the lift is complete, the athlete simply drops the elbows and drops the bar to the floor.

Many athletes improperly catch the barbell in a "closed grip" position without the bar resting on the shoulder. This is often seen when performing multiple reps in a set. Catching improperly just to avoid re-gripping the bar and setting up properly is a common mistake that can lead to various injuries. The athlete should be coached to perform each rep separately and properly in order to avoid injury.

Performing the clean and hang clean without the catch is commonly referred to as a high pull or clean pull. This is an excellent variation that is usually easier to teach and perform because it does not include the catch. Likely because it is easier to perform, recent force plate evidence suggests that the mid-thigh clean pull has the capacity to create higher peak power outputs than the clean or hang

Figure 6.22: Speed squat start position

clean making it a viable option for the SCP.[5]

Speed Squat

The speed squat is a great explosive movement because it can be loaded easily and the coaching is very similar to a normal back squat. The load will be between 30-70% of 1RM so that the barbell can be moved fast enough to maximize power output.

Using the same technique for a traditional barbell back squat, the athlete begins by eccentrically lowering the bar in a controlled fashion. Once the top of the thigh is parallel to the floor, the athlete should accelerate out of the bottom forcefully, standing up as quickly as possible. It is crucial that the athlete's heels stay firmly planted following the concentric phase. This is not a jump-squat. Likewise, the barbell must be pulled down into the upper back of the athlete so that it never leaves the body, especially when the athlete finishes the concentric portion of the movement. Barbell velocity measurement technology is a great way to motivate athletes, create a competitive environment, and measure progress.

Pause Squat

The purpose of the pause squat is to eliminate the influence of the stretch reflex, thereby increasing the demand placed on the musculature during the concentric portion of the lift.

Set up just like a traditional squat with the barbell in a high-bar position on the traps, the athlete should take a deep breath and hold it prior to the eccentric phase of the movement. The movement begins by the athlete pushing the hips back and the knees slightly out. The athlete should squat the barbell down while attempting to keep the torso as vertical possible. At the bottom of the movement, the athlete will hold for no less than one full second, then aggressively accelerate the barbell upward into the concentric phase of the movement.

Figure 6.23: Pause squat isometric position

The weight must be much lighter than a traditional barbell back squat so that the barbell can be moved fast enough to generate maximal power. This is typically done with 30-70% of the athlete's 1RM. Again, barbell velocity measurement technology is a great way to motivate athletes, create a competitive environment, and measure progress.

Dynamic Effort Box Squat

Similar to the pause squat, the box squat is also used to eliminate the stretch reflex at the bottom of the squat and place more demand on the musculature of the athlete. Interrupting the stretch reflex can be beneficial in further developing the strength capabilities of the athlete.

The use of accommodating resistance from bands, chains, and other implements have been around for many years, but it has become popular with many powerlifting athletes. Accommodating resistance is typically done by adding bands or chains to a barbell. These external components decrease the resistance at the bottom of the movement and increase as the weight is lifted. This is an advanced progression that should be reserved only for highly trained athletes. Recommended loading is 30-50% of 1RM on the barbell, then estimate the external load in pounds that the athlete would be experiencing due to the bands or chains.

Bands may be attached to an anchor point even with the midfoot of the athlete when performing the box squat. The bands should be tight enough to eliminate slack when the athlete is at the bottom of the squat. The band is then wrapped around the bar just inside the inner collar on the outermost knurling. Chains should be anchored securely on the inside of the plates. There should be a smaller chain that loops around the bar and connects to a set of larger chains that are on the floor.

When performing the box squat with dynamic effort, the athlete should begin by un-racking the barbell under control. The feet should be just past shoulder width and the toes pointed out slightly. If bands or chains are being used, the SCP should make sure that they are anchored at the midfoot as described previously.

The box should be very sturdy and angled with one corner between the legs. The height of the box should be approximately two inches lower than the knees. The athlete should take a deep breath and begin the lowering phase by sitting back more than a normal squat. The hips should continue to travel backward as the athlete descends. The torso should be as vertical as possible during the lowering phase. The athlete will sit softly on the box in a strong position, and at no point during the seated phase does the athlete relax as the body remains tight and strong and the feet firmly planted. As soon as the tension is about to leave the feet, the athlete will reproduce the force and drive upward forcefully off the box as fast as possible. The athlete should not jump at the top but rather just stand up as quickly as possible.

Barbell velocity measurement technology is a great way to motivate athletes, create a competitive environment, and measure progress. This type of technology works great with any dynamic effort training methods.

Conclusion

Developing explosiveness can be done in many different ways, but it is up to the coach to understand the physiological demands of the training and appropriately prescribe training in a conservative fashion. Strength is always the prerequisite to explosive training. Once the athlete is strong enough to be able to handle some novice explosive movements, the SCP should start slowly and master techniques first before loading. Performance in most every sport is improved through the development of increased explosiveness, and it is a highly trainable trait. Increased rates of force development and power can be a competitive advantage over opponents in most cases.

References

1. Guth L, Roth S. Genetic influence on athletic performance. *Current opinion in Pediatrics.* 2013;25(6):653-658.

2. Verkhoshansky Y, Siff MC. *Supertraining.* Verkhoshansky; 2009.

3. Zatsiorsky V, Kraemer W. *Science and Practice of Strength Training.* 2nd ed. Champaign, IL: Human Kinetics; 2006.

4. Baker DG, Newton RU. Change in power output across a high-repetition set of bench throws and jump squats in highly trained athletes. *J Strength Cond Res.* 2007;21(4):1007-1011.

5. Comfort P, Allen M, Graham-Smith P. Kinetic comparisons during variations of the power clean. *J Strength Cond Res.* 2011;25(12):3269-3273.

CHAPTER 7

Plyometric Training

Adam Feit & Bobby Smith

Objectives

- Understand the importance of specific plyometric training for preparing the modern athlete

- Describe and be able to coach the athlete into each of the four foundational body positions

- Recognize the need for multi-directional jump training and be equipped to prescribe various exercises that train explosiveness in all planes

- Understand the zones of plyometric training, knowing when to prescribe exercise in each of the zones to best meet the needs of the developing athlete

- Know and understand how to design appropriate plyometric training programs that fit within a larger comprehensive strength & conditioning plan

Jump Training for Today's Athlete

The quest to jump higher, further, and move faster is a never-ending journey among athletes. Unfortunately, the use of plyometrics is often misunderstood and improperly programmed, particularly at the youth coaching level. Plyometric training refers to the use of jumping exercises where an eccentric lengthening of the muscle is rapidly succeeded by a powerful concentric contraction. The elastic energy produced through these powerful contractions allows an increase in force production, muscular power and running velocity/economy. The use of this muscle pattern, called the stretch shortening cycle (SSC), is the foundation of jumping and running for maximum height and speed.

Unfortunately, many strength & conditioning professionals (SCPs) rush this process and attempt to program advanced plyometric exercises before the athletes can control their bodyweight in space. This often sets up improper movement patterns which carryover to future injuries during competition. Jump training should serve as a foundational element of power training before any type of external loading is applied. Before SCPs ask their athletes to move fast with heavy loads, they should ensure proper form in bodyweight variations. This is the prerequisite of enhanced power development: take care of one aspect of training before moving onto the next.

Jump training is not only important for power development, but more importantly, for the reduction of future injury. Too many sports medicine professionals clear athletes for return to play without evaluating single-leg strength, stability, and power. Jump training can be performed in the warm-up, during movement, and throughout weight training sessions. After all, running, cutting, planting, pivoting, and jumping almost always occur with one leg at a time, so this should a priority.

Jump training for today's athlete is not about stacking bumper plates higher and higher or jumping off as fast as he or she jumped on. It is not jumping off rooftops and running into sprints, nor is it counting how many box jumps you can do in the workout of the day in a nearby parking lot. Instead, jump training for today's athlete is about elasticity, efficiency and energy transfers. It should involve teaching the athlete to absorb force and apply power, and it should reduce the risk of future injury and improve performance.

During competition, the athlete will have to cut, plant, pivot, turn, jump, rotate, twist, bound, and perform other feats of athleticism from one leg to the next. That is the nature of sports. By matching up joint angles, body positioning, and force-velocity dynamics, jump training has the potential to improve performance and decrease the risk of future injury. It is the goal of this chapter to explain the progressions and strategies to properly develop athletes through jump training for power development.

Foundational Four Body Positions

Proper jump training begins with proper positioning. Regardless of the level of athletic ability, SCPs can never underestimate the power of proper body position. If coaches are to take pride in taking athletes through squat and deadlift progressions, they must do the same when it comes to hinging and flexing. This is especially true when it comes to using kettlebells for teaching the swing, which is a natural and fundamental movement pattern used by almost every coach or trainer these days. Before a coach can ask athletes to hinge and snap through quickly, he or she must first make sure that each athlete can get into the hinge position slowly and under control.

Similarly, before actual jumping should commence, the SCP should spend time preparing the athlete how to get in the right position to jump and land. Special emphasis should be placed on the double-leg athletic/RDL position, the single-leg athletic/RDL position, the double-leg snapdown, and the single leg snapdown. For maximum effectiveness, the SCP should layer positions that will be repeated in future drills to improve the rate of retention. Notice the standard athletic position in Figure 7.1 from the lateral view.

In the athletic position, the feet are positioned under the hips with the toes straight ahead while the knees and hips are flexed. The head is set in a neutral/natural position while the shoulders are retracted with a slight forward torso lean. The athlete's weight is balanced on the middle portion of the feet and the arms are slightly flexed at the elbow and hands are at the hip.

The athletic position is the backbone to any movement skill taught on the field or weight room and also serves as the landing position of any type of jump. This is to remind athletes that starting/landing from a jump, performing an RDL, or setting up for a hang clean, are closely related movements. Having the ability to transfer body positions from one area to another is especially important when teaching new skills to athletes.

Figure 7.1: Establishing the standard athletic position

During the layering process of the athletic position, the SCP should emphasize proper chest, hip and knee angles upon takeoff and landing. ACL injuries often occur when posture and neuromotor control are not optimal, which may include internal rotation of the hip, valgus (inward) angle at the knee, and/or limited hip and knee flexion. There may be significant differences between athletes, so the SCP is encouraged to assess each athlete individually to ensure proper landing mechanics.

Once the athlete has mastered the basic athletic/landing position, the next progression is the single-leg version of this position, or the single-leg RDL. Jumping, running, and changing direction often occur on one leg at a time. Thus, it becomes paramount to master single-leg stability, balance, and control of the body during jumping exercises.

Once the athlete has mastered the RDL position, it is time to add the next factor in proper power development: speed. This is readily apparent when you look at any type of Olympic weightlifting exercise from the hang position. Oftentimes, the athlete will hinge too slowly to fully utilize the rapid stretch of the hamstrings to help transition the body into triple extension before the catch. What begins in somewhat of a slow-motion loss of energy turns into a "jumping jack, angry-starfish" catch on a clean or a giant "I'm a star" catch on a snatch.

Before any type of jumping, bounding, or hopping, the SCP can now implement the "snapdown" before the active jump. This is beneficial for four reasons. First, it helps the athlete shift and maintain static to dynamic body positions right before take-off, ensuring proper joint alignment BEFORE active jumping occurs, specifically at the hips, knees, and ankles. Next, it transfers the necessary speed for weight room movements like the Olympic lifts. It also allows the athlete to prepare mentally just before attempting a jump for maximal height or distance. Lastly, it provides another regression/progression in a SCP's layering system to benefit youth athletes throughout the training program.

A basic jump training preparatory program should follow a standard four-step progression:

- Double-leg athletic/RDL position

- Single-leg athletic/RDL position

- Double-leg snapdown

  - For a video demonstration of the double-leg snapdown, go to: https://vimeo.com/album/3578138/video/140224273 (password: jumpRYPT)

- Single-leg snapdown

  - For a video demonstration of the single-leg snapdown, go to: https://vimeo.com/album/3578138/video/140224322 (password: jumpRYPT)

Before the SCP requires the athlete to move quickly on one leg, the athlete must demonstrate the ability to control slower movement on one leg. Additionally, before moving on one leg, the athlete must master the speed and positioning of moving with two legs.

Classification of Jump Types

While it is common to borrow jumping variations from track and field, the exact drills and naming of these drills can create confusion among coaches and athletes. What may be read as a double-leg jump to one coach may be interpreted as a single-leg jump to another. More precisely, when working in any type of system, it is important to keep everyone on the same page when it comes to coaching terminology and technique. There should be very little wiggle room between a head coach and his or her assistants in regards to exercise naming and technique corrections.

For this discussion, the different types of jump training exercises can be broken down into four separate categories:

- **Jump:** A two-legged takeoff with a two-legged landing (e.g., vertical jump)

- **Hop:** A one-legged takeoff with a same one-legged landing (e.g., vertical hop)

- **Bound:** A one-legged takeoff with an alternate one-legged landing (e.g., lateral bound)

- **Hybrid:** A combination of any type of jump, hop, or bound with the possible addition of a medicine ball (MB) for upper body power development (e.g., lateral bound to double legged landing or a hurdle jump to MB punch)

The hybrid category may be the most important when working with youth athletes for three reasons:

1) It bridges the gap between double-leg and single-leg jumping exercises. With the use of the hybrid, SCPs can better prepare athletes for single-leg hops and bounds through the use of single-legged takeoffs with double-legged landings.

2) Rather than change exercises completely, coaches can simply add or remove one piece of the drill to change the stimulus to keep athletes progressing.

3) Coaches can analyze single-leg jumping and landing mechanics much earlier in the programming. Instead of wasting 4-6 weeks on primarily double-leg takeoffs and landings, coaches can work on the limiting issue (usually single-leg strength/stability/power) right away.

The Importance of Multi-Directional Jumping

In the weight room, coaches pride themselves on working through three-dimensional movements, using ground-based and multi-joint exercises. The same approach should be taken in regards to movement and jump training. Athletes simply do more than jump up and down or forward and back; they move in a manner that utilizes a combination of movements and directions.

Unfortunately, many programs base success on measureable standards, especially when it comes to jumping. Coaches will often hear about the highest vertical or longest long jump on the team to justify their ability to play the sport at the highest level. Coaches try to find correlations between their athletes' on-field explosiveness and the movements in the weight room (e.g., Olympic lifting) and assume that heavier weight equals better performance. That is true to a certain degree, but not as much as is often portrayed. In order to get better at jumping, one needs to jump. And in order to stay healthy through a high volume of acceleration, deceleration, planting, and pivoting, athletes need to be well-coached throughout jumping exercises in all planes of motion.

One look at the various invitational showcases, combines, and various testing protocols, two movements always seem to take center stage: the vertical jump and long jump. Why those two? They are easy to coach, easy to track, and essentially easy to perform. Like many other aspects of strength & conditioning, SCPs adapted these skills after football training programs that have traditionally tested vertical and long jumps.

Unfortunately, we are missing two key ingredients. First, neither assesses the athlete's ability to jump and land on one leg. Furthermore, neither skill assesses the athlete's ability to change direction. Vertical jumps are solely focused on jumping as highly as possible in the sagittal plane while long jumps are solely focused on jumping as far as possible in the sagittal plane. There is very little transfer from training to sport in regards to injury prevention on one leg since everything was being done on two legs. Since many lower body injuries occur during rotational movements, the SCP should make sure the athlete's ability to jump and land on one leg as well as change direction are both being adequately addressed.

The four directions in which jumps, hops, bounds, and hybrids may occur include vertically, linearly, laterally, and rotationally.

- **Vertical:** Jumping is done primarily in place, aiming to jump as high as possible. These would be your typical vertical jump, box jump, and squat jump progressions. The movement is done primarily in the sagittal plane.

- **Linear:** The goal is to jump as far as possible. These would be your typical long-jump and hurdle-jump progressions. The movement is done primarily in the sagittal plane.

- **Lateral:** The goal is to jump as high or far as possible from side to side. These would also include variations of jumps in the vertical and linear planes with an emphasis on frontal displacement. The movement is done primarily in the frontal plane.

- **Rotational:** The goal is to rotate the body during the jump and land accordingly. These variations are modifications of traditional hops, bounds, and jumps with a landing orientation different from the takeoff, usually by 90 or 180 degrees. The movement is done primarily in the transverse plane.

When coaches look at sports that require jumping on a frequent basis such as basketball, volleyball, and even football, it becomes clear that most landings are not perfect or stable. The question then becomes how frequently an athlete lands with both feet under the hips, striking the ground at the same exact time. Most injuries occur during the landing or deceleration portion of a movement, so athletes should be prepared for the loads, speeds, and movements they will be subjected to during competition. This is the true meaning of physical preparation, and coaches should use the appropriate means and methods to keep athletes healthy and productive.

Volume and Category Considerations for Jump Training

In this section, we will explore the common issues and concerns when programming jump training, such as:

- What makes a jump easy or hard
- How many reps should be performed
- How many sets should be performed
- How to know when athletes are prepared for jump training
- How to organize an exercise pool

The system of classifying jumping exercises is modified after the original 1970's research performed by Soviet Sport Scientist A.S. Prilepin. It is said that Prilepin analyzed the training logs and journals of more than 1,000 elite-level weightlifting champions and noticed a common theme: as the weight of the bar increased, the velocity of the bar decreased. This is now an accepted principle as displayed by the force-velocity curve.

Prilepin noticed which training percentages and set/rep schemes caused dramatic shifts in bar speed which mitigated the training effect of explosive strength. If a weightlifter did too many reps or sets at a certain training percentage, the lifter would reach a point of diminishing returns, and the efforts put forth would not yield optimal results. Based on this research, he crafted a very simple table outlining his findings, now commonly referred to simply as "Prilepin's Chart.

Table 7.1: Prilepin's Chart*

% of 1RM	Reps per Set	Total Reps	Optimal Reps
70%	3-6	12-24	18
80%	2-4	10-20	15
90%	1-2	4-10	7

*Originally presented in *Managing the Training of Weightlifters*[1]

When looking at the chart, the SCP assumes the following strategies in regards to load selection:

- When working with loads between 70-79% of an athlete's 1RM, reps should be kept between 3-6 per set and no more than 12-24 reps per session. The optimal amount is 18.

- When working with loads between 80-89% of an athlete's 1RM, reps should be kept between 2-4 per set and no more than 10-20 reps per session. The optimal amount is 15.

- When working with loads above 90% of an athlete's 1RM, reps should be kept between 1-2 and no more than 4-10 reps per session. The optimal amount is 7.

The term "optimal" is obviously very subjective, as It could be due to bar speed, reduction of training fatigue, or any combination of factors relevant to the coach and athlete. The main point to understand is that as load *increases*, volume *decreases*. Essentially, as the movements become more difficult to perform, the number of repetitions decreases, maintaining the integrity of each rep.

Over time, the chart has been modified by other SCPs. The Modified Prilepin Chart and its variations are frequently seen in the strength programs throughout the world. It includes a row of lower percentages (<70%) and additional volume recommendations for this training zone.

Table 7.2: Modified Prilepin Chart

% of 1RM	Reps per Set	Total Reps	Optimal Reps
<70%	3-6	18-30	24
70-79%	3-6	12-24	18
80-89%	2-4	10-20	15
90%	1-2	4-10	7

The Modified Prilepin chart has been used as a reference point for many SCPs when determining appropriate volume and intensity prescriptions. While the original chart was designed to accommodate the Olympic lifts, SCPs have extrapolated its recommendations to fit all strength development qualities under six reps per set. If jump training is utilized for power development, it seems logical to utilize a similar approach.

In other text books, plyometric training volumes are categorized by the number of jump contacts, based on the training age of the athlete. If coaches are to use jump training as a means to develop explosive power AND reduce the risk of future injury, it makes sense to utilize Prilepin's recommendations for Olympic lifting, not total foot contacts based off "plyometric experience."

Table 7.3: NSCA Plyometric foot contact guidelines*

Plyometric Experience	Beginning Volume (per session)
Beginner	80-100
Intermediate	100-120
Advanced	120-140

*Adapted from the *Essentials of Strength Training and Conditioning*[2]

Using the modified chart from Prilepin's research, jump training could now be based on the following considerations:

- Training age of the athlete

- Speed of drill (short response versus long response)

- Height of drill (hurdles and boxes)

- Number of foot contacts

- Planes of motion

- Takeoff and landing position

Keeping the emphasis on landing mechanics, injury prevention, and power development in mind, Prilepin's chart could be modified with the following changes:

- Instead of percentage of 1RM training zones, zones would reflect the intensity of the jump drill. Zone 1 would include lower-intensity jumps within each plane of motion and Zone 4 would include higher-intensity exercises.

- Each zone would be color-coded to help the SCP understand that as the intensity of the jumps increase, volume should be adjusted accordingly. The zones are divided as follows:

  o Zone 1 (green)

  o Zone 2 (yellow)

  o Zone 3 (orange)

  o Zone 4 (red)

- The total volume of each jump exercise, or sequence, would decrease as the intensity of the jump increased. Each repetition would be the actual repetition of the drill rather than how many foot contacts it used. For example:

  o A box jump would be classified as a Zone 1 jump, thus yielding sets no higher than 6 reps per set and a volume of no more than 30 reps per session. Coaches could program sets and reps such as 5x5, 4x6, etc.

  o A box jump to depth jump to repeat-3-hurdle-jump would be classified as a Zone 4 jump thus yielding sets no higher than 1-2 reps per set and a volume of no more than 10 reps total. Because this is hybrid among a variety of jumps in one sequence, its repetitions would be based on the drill, not foot contacts. Zone 3 and Zone 4 jumps should not include more than 6 foot contacts per sequence. The jump sequence noted above includes 6 total contacts:

    Box Jump (1) + Land from Depth Drop (1) + Land from Depth Jump (1) + 3 Hurdle Jumps (3) = 6 total contacts

With the zones and volume recommendations in place, the jump training chart is now shown in Table 4.

Table 7.4: Jump training chart

Level	Total Volume	Reps per Set
Zone 1	18 to 30	3 to 6
Zone 2	12 to 24	3 to 6
Zone 3	10 to 20	2 to 4
Zone 4	4 to 10	1 to 2

Zone 1

Before training force production through maximal jump training methods, the athlete should learn how to properly absorb forces in Zone 1. Similar to the catch on a power clean, the athlete must learn how to brace for impact and develop the eccentric strength to safely decelerate during a landing. Zone 1 jumps are primarily long-response double-leg drills that can utilize a "snap-down pause" before transitioning into the concentric jump action. This allows the athlete to re-set into a proper position before takeoff if needed. Each jump should be done as a "one-repetition masterpiece," allowing the athlete to stick each landing perfectly with enough time to reset before the next rep. A simple Zone 1 coaching cue is "jump and stick." Volume should be kept between 18-30 reps total, and each drill should fall between 3-6 reps per set.

Landing considerations include:

- Chest up, shoulders back with the front t-shirt "logo" readily viewable to the coach

- Knees behind toes and in line with the hip and ankle (not over and/or in)

- Impact should be minimal, and athletes should be encouraged to "land like a helicopter, not a space shuttle"

- Landing position should mimic starting position with no drop of the hips upon impact

Table 7.5: Sample exercise pool of Zone 1 jumps

Vertical	Linear	Lateral	Rotational
Snapdown	Snapdown	Snapdown	Snapdown
Box Jump	Long Jump	Box Jump	Box Jump
Vertical Jump	Hurdle Jump	Hurdle Jump	Hurdle Jump
Tuck Jump			Squat Jump

Zone 2

Once athletes have mastered basic landing mechanics and body positioning, a more specific power development model can be employed utilizing the stretch reflex from a powerful arm swing and short ground contact time. Zone 2 jumps are referred to as "medium response" where the athlete will jump more than once in a sequence. An example would be a repeat-2-long or hurdle jump where the athlete would perform two consecutive long jumps or hurdle jumps without a re-set between the jumps. This allows the athlete to take advantage of the recoil between successive jumps for a larger height or distance. A simple Zone 2 coaching cue is "jump, jump, and stick."

Zone 2 jumps include a multi-planar approach of up to two different planes of motion within a drill, thus challenging the athlete's proprioception and reactive ability to change direction. Examples include a long jump into a vertical jump, or lateral hurdle jump into a long-jump. Lastly, Zone 2 jumps include hybrid variations that introduce single-legged takeoffs into double-legged landings or double-legged takeoffs into single-legged landings. Depending on the intensity of the drill, some drills may not be appropriate until adequate single-leg strength is achieved. Thus, most double-legged takeoffs into single-legged landings are reserved for Zone 3. Volume should be kept between 12-24 reps total and each jump should fall between 3-6 reps per set.

Table 7.6: Sample exercise pool of Zone 2 jumps (DL=double-legged)

Vertical	Linear	Lateral	Rotational
Box Hop to DL Landing	Hurdle Hop to DL Landing	Bound to DL Landing	Box Hop to DL Landing
Split Jump	Hurdle Jump to Box Jump	Box Hop to DL Landing	Depth Jump to 90 Degree Landing
Vertical Hop to DL Landing	Repeat-2 Hurdle Jump	4-way Hurdle Jump	Bound to DL Landing

Zone 3

Moving along the zone continuum, it should be noted that Zones 3 and 4 should be reserved for advanced athletes only. The variability between planes of motion, use of external resistance, and elastic response to jumping is geared for athletes with a high training age.

Zone 3 jumps focus on the athlete's ability to sustain maximal levels of power and elasticity between repetitions. Jumps that generate high levels of power are performed in succession in Zone 3. These jumps follow a "quick, quick, and stick" coaching cue, emphasizing extremely little time on the ground between repetitions. These are reflected in repeated jumps such as hurdle jumps and hops as well as the introduction of alternate leg landings with bounding and split landings. Zone 3 jumps also utilize external resistance added to the jumps, forcing the athletes to accelerate their bodies faster through triple-extension and challenging their base of support on the landing. Lastly, these jumps begin to utilize hybrids between double-legged takeoffs with single-legged landings. Volume should be kept between 10-20 reps total and each jump should fall between 2-4 reps per set.

Table 7.7: Sample exercise pool of Zone 3 jumps

Vertical	Linear	Lateral	Rotational
Weighted Box Jump	Repeat Hurdle Hop	Box Jump to SL Landing	Hurdle Hop
Box Jump Medley	Weighted Long Jump	Lateral/Medial Hurdle Hop	Box Hop
Bound	Bound	Bound	Bound

Zone 4

The last zone of jump training includes multiple response jumps in multiple planes of motion. The addition of visual or audible commands further challenge the athlete's reactive abilities. Zone 4 jumps are also where the successful implementation of contrast or complex jumps are utilized throughout a weight training session. Joe Kenn is credited with the terminology of two types of complexes that can be used effectively during a period of peaking before competition:

- Strength/Speed Complex: Performed with a strength training primer (i.e. back squat) followed by a maximal jump with a 20-40 second break between exercises.

- Speed/Strength Complex: Performed with a jump primer (i.e. repeat vertical jump) followed by a strength exercise such as a hang clean or squat with a 20-40 second break between exercises.

Contrast jumps refer to a heavy/light approach where an athlete will perform a weighted jump (or series of jumps) before unloading to perform another un-weighted jump or series of jumps.

Volume should be kept between 4-10 reps total and each jump should fall between 1-2 reps per set. Remember that a repetition encompasses the entire sequence, rather than individual foot contacts.

Table 7.8: Sample exercise pool of Zone 4 jumps

Vertical	Linear	Lateral	Rotational
Band Resisted Jump	Reactive Long Jump	Band Resisted Jump	Repeat Hurdle Jump to Jump
Vertical Jump to SL Landing	Hurdle Jump to MB Punch	4-Way Hurdle Hop	Lat/Med Hop to Box Hop to DL Landing
Box Jump to Depth Jump Series	Long Jump to SL Landing	Hurdle Hop to Sprint	Lat/Med Hop to Box Hop

Programming Jump Training

The following steps should be considered when developing a jump training program:

1) Determine the number of weeks for the training season

2) Determine how many weeks will comprise each phase of training

3) Working backwards, select the specific jump training progression for the training season from hardest (or most specific) to easiest (or most general)

4) Start at the lowest number of repetitions per set in each zone

5) Gradually increase the number of repetitions per set each week

6) Finish with the highest volume possible within the zone parameters and allotted time or add a de-load week by decreasing total volume

7) Repeat for future phases within the training season

Organizing a training block is a relatively straightforward four-step process. First, the SCP should determine how many weeks comprise the training season. For example, let's say the coach has determined she has a total of 12 weeks. Next, the SCP should determine how many weeks will comprise each phase of training. In our example, it might be likely that the coach would designate four phases of three weeks each. Next, working backward, the SCP should select the specific jump training progression for the training season from hardest (or most specific) to easiest (or most general). For example:

a. Zone 4: Repeat-2 Hurdle Jump to Long Jump to Vertical Jump

b. Zone 3: Repeat-2 Hurdle Jump to Long Jump

c. Zone 2: Repeat-2 Hurdle Jump

d. Zone 1: Hurdle Jump

Lastly, the SCP should start at the lowest amount of repetitions per set for each required zone and gradually increase the volume each week. Again returning to the working example:

a. Phase 4 (3 weeks): Zone 4: 4x1, 4x2, 5x2

b. Phase 3 (3 weeks): Zone 3: 5x2, 6x2, 6x3

c. Phase 2 (3 weeks): Zone 2: 4x3, 4x4, 4x5

d. Phase 1 (3 weeks): Zone 1: 5x4, 5x5, 5x6

A basic 12-week jump training program could look like this:

Table 7.9: 12-week progression for hurdle jumps

Weeks	Phase 1	Phase 2	Phase 3	Phase 4
Exercise	Hurdle Jump	Repeat-2 Hurdle Jump	Repeat-2 Hurdle Jump to Long Jump	Repeat-2 Hurdle Jump to Long Jump to Vertical Jump
1	5x4	4x3	5x2	4x1
2	5x5	4x4	6x2	4x2
3	5x6	4x5	6x3	5x2

Table 7.9 illustrates a number of salient points. First, each week adds volume, either through an increase in repetitions or sets. Every 3 weeks, the exercise itself progresses and the starting volume for the next phase is reset to the minimum volume in that zone. Additionally, the exercise difficulty progresses from phase to phase, allowing enough time for the athlete to learn and master the movement pattern.

The number one deciding factor on programming of volume is TIME. If the SCP does not allocate the proper time for a specific jump training block, it simply will not be possible for the athlete to complete all of the reps and sets. Emphasis should be on quality, not quantity. There should be various times throughout the training season that the SCP allocates more or less time for this type of training, depending on the time of year. However, nothing is set in stone and some athletes will not progress at the rate of the training sheet. Rather than telling youth athletes to "work harder" and "be an athlete," the SCP should tailor the jump exercise to meet the athletes where they are in terms of physical ability, not where the SCP has decided that the athlete should be. This concept of layering will save coaches programming headaches, athlete injuries, and most of all, the stress and worry associated with an elegant and elaborately designed program that does not deliver intended results.

The layering process is very simple. Instead of establishing a baseline of where everyone should be starting in Phase 1, the SCP should implement a phase or two BELOW the baseline as well as small progressions with each phase to accommodate the athlete's athletic ability. This ensures that while everyone will be doing a jumping exercise, they might be in different stages of the progression. This is much easier than trying to over-coach a movement in an attempt for an athlete to "get it" or removing an athlete from a drill because he/she is slowing everyone else down.

Using our 12-week progression of hurdle jumps listed above, we can add two regressions to the exercise OR build in a smaller step within each phase and progress when the athlete is ready. Now, our progression looks like the following:

- Phase 4: Repeat-2 Hurdle Jump to Long Jump to Vertical Jump

  o *Regression: Phase 3 or add reset after Long Jump before Vertical Jump*

- Phase 3: Repeat-2 Hurdle Jump to Long Jump

  o *Regression: Phase 2 or add reset after Hurdle Jump before Long Jump*

- Phase 2: Repeat-2 Hurdle Jump

  o *Regression: Phase 1*

- Phase 1: Hurdle Jump

  o *Regression: Phase 0*

- Phase 0: Snap-down to Hurdle Jump

  o *Regression: (Base) Double Leg Snap-down with Band*

In the event an athlete was not ready for Phase 1, the SCP could start him/her at even lower regression at Phase 0. If Phase 0 caused issues, the SCP could then regress to the most basic jump preparatory movement for that exercise; in this case, a standard double-leg snap-down with band. It would be up to the coach's discretion on when to progress or regress the drill for each specific athlete. Sometimes an athlete only needs 1-2 sets of reintroduction before progressing back to the base level. Other times, an athlete may train at the regressed level for a few weeks to ensure proper movement patterns before progressing at the rate of the other athletes.

An important concept to remember is that the layering process should be used throughout the entire coaching process, not just at the beginning. Coaches must have the confidence to tell an athlete that he or she is not yet ready for the prescribed drill and do what is best for their long-term athletic development. A faster, more explosive athlete who continues to demonstrate a lack of body control is only destined for a faster, more explosive injury down the road.

Organizing Jump Training Into a Seasonal, Weekly, and Daily Plan

Utilizing the updated Prilepin chart and an exercise pool of jumps, the SCP can now set forth a plan for a jump training program that is systematic and progressive in nature based on a seasonal, weekly, or daily plan.

Seasonal Plan

Seasonal plans are catered to the traditional sport season and can last anywhere from 8-16 weeks. Once the SCP knows the length of the season, it can be split into three phases, each lasting approximately four weeks. For example:

- Fall: Two phases of four weeks, one phase of three weeks (11 weeks)

- Winter: Three phases of four weeks (12 weeks)

- Spring: Three phases of four weeks (12 weeks)

- Summer: One phase of four weeks, One phase of three weeks (7 weeks)

To start, the SCP should consider utilizing one jump training exercise per day and progressing accordingly throughout each phase. The amount of training days per week will dictate which planes of motion will predominate. An example of a weekly split might look like this:

- Four days per week

    o Day 1: Vertical or linear plane

    o Day 2: Rotational plane

    o Day 3: Lateral plane

    o Day 4: Linear or vertical plane

- Three days per week

    o Day 1: Vertical or linear plane

    o Day 2: Lateral plane

    o Day 3: Rotational plane

- Two days per week

  - Day 1: Vertical plane

  - Day 2: Lateral plane

For novice youth athletes, the SCP should consider sticking with one exercise per phase, culminating with a three-exercise progression within a 12-week season. An example would be:

- Phase 1: Day 1: (4 weeks): Box jump with depth drop

- Phase 2: Day 1: (4 weeks): Box jump with depth jump

- Phase 3: Day 1: (4 weeks): Box jump with depth jump to long jump

For advanced athletes, the SCP can consider splitting the four-week phase into two 2-week phases, thus effectively doubling the amount of jump training exercises. This provides a quicker coaching progression and allows the coach to cater to the athletes who need a quicker change to drive consistent improvements in performance. An example is shown below:

- Phase 1a: Day 1: (2 weeks): Box jump with depth drop

- Phase 1b: Day 1: (2 weeks): Vertical jump to box jump with depth drop

- Phase 2a: Day 1: (2 weeks): Box jump to depth jump

- Phase 2b: Day 1: (2 weeks): Box jump to depth jump to vertical jump

- Phase 3a: Day 1: (2 weeks): Box jump to depth jump to long jump

- Phase 3b: Day 1: (2 weeks): Box jump to depth jump to repeat hurdle jump to long jump

As you can see, the advanced jump training progression is simply additional exercises between each phase of jumping. By adding one different type of jump or direction, the SCP can provide the necessary overload to keep the athletes engaged and results moving forward. We have found that some of the most successful ways to progress between phases is to move to the next zone of jumping intensity, add an element of short response to the jump, or simply change the final orientation of the landing. This allows the coach to "vary within simplicity" by making the jumps be performed in a repeated sequence or having the athlete land facing a different direction. Once the SCP knows the exercises to be programmed, each phase can be split into their respective weeks. The coach can then plan their appropriate volumes based on the approach used previously.

Weekly Plan

Now that you have the exercises for the entire season organized by phase, we can program the appropriate volume for each week, within each phase. Going back to the step-by-step approach listed in the "Setting up a jump training program" section, the SCP can list out the respective volumes for each jumping exercise, making sure it stays within the respective zone recommendations. If an exercise stays within the same zone between phases, the coach has the option to repeat the previous volume, as the different exercise may be enough change without affecting total volume. As a reminder, each zone should incorporate the following:

- Zone 1: 18-30 reps total, 3-6 reps per set

- Zone 2: 12-24 reps total, 3-6 reps per set

- Zone 3: 10-20 reps total, 2-4 reps per set

- Zone 4: 4-10 reps total, 1-2 reps per set

Weeks	Phase 1	Phase 2	Phase 3

Table 7.10: Novice seasonal and weekly training plan

Exercise	Box Jump with Depth Drop	Box Jump with Depth Jump	Box Jump with Depth Jump to Vertical Jump
1	5x4	4x3	5x2
2	5x5	5x4	6x2
3	5x6	6x3	6x3
4	3x6	4x3	5x2

Notes:

- For the most part, each week adds one rep or one set until week 4

- Week 4 of every phase serves as a reload in training, so the volume is cut down

- As the intensity of the jump increases, the reps per set decrease

Weeks	Phase 1a	Phase 1b	Phase 2a	Phase 2b	Phase 3a	Phase 3b

Table 7.11: Advanced seasonal and weekly training plan

Exercise	Box Jump with Depth Drop	Vertical Jump to Box Jump with Depth Drop	Box Jump to Depth Jump	Box Jump to Depth Jump to Vertical Jump	Box Jump to Depth Jump to Long Jump	Box Jump to Depth Jump to Repeat Hurdle Jump to Long Jump
1	5x4	4x3	5x2	5x2	5x2	4x1
2	5x5	5x4	6x2	6x2	5x3	4x2

Notes:

- Like the novice plan, each week adds one rep or one set until the next phase

- As the intensity of the jump increases, the reps per set decrease

It is also important to remember that while the advanced program progresses faster than the novice program, the use of layering must be implemented with greater detail. It may take athletes more than two weeks of training to master the jump sequence fully, thus the coach may have to either a) decrease the amount of change and extend the phases from two to three weeks or b) effectively regress as needed throughout the season.

Daily Plan

The first step in this process is determining when the jump training will take place. Knowing which part of the session the jump training will occur will allow the SCP to shape the session to maximize time, efficiency, and overall performance of the athletes. The coach should consider if the jump training will occur during the warm-up, after warm-up before movement, after movement but before training, or during training.

We have found that the most appropriate time for jump training is either right after the warm-up or directly before the weight training session. These two times are when the body is at its peak condition to produce explosive efforts without the residual effects of training fatigue. At no point would we want to teach advanced jump training exercises at the end of a weight training session or after conditioning.

While it can serve a purpose to train explosively during times of fatigue, when working with youth athletes, we want to perform these drills when the body is fresh and maximally attentive. Once athletes have mastered the performance of these drills in a fresh state, the SCP can then experiment with changing the order of these drills within each session, specifically between weight training exercises during the utilization of complex and contrast training methods. In a 90-minute total sports performance program, jump training could take place right after a movement session to act as a primer for the Olympic lifting about to occur in the weight room.

Additional Considerations

To maximize the nervous system and its application toward sports performance, the SCP can combine all jump training exercises with an upper body explosive exercise, primarily through the use of medicine ball throws. This will allow the coach to split the group in half and provide better coaching as well as adhere to a more manageable work-to-rest ratio of 1:5 to 1:10 to ensure proper recovery between repetitions and exercises. During this time, the focus should be on maximum acceleration of the body or medicine ball as well as proper deceleration upon its impact.

The SCP can also implement a "jump prep" sequence into each of the warm-ups to incorporate some extra low-level, single-leg landing mechanics with bare feet. This will allow the coach to stimulate the intrinsic muscles of the feet as well as prepare the athlete for more advanced jump training drills to follow. By including some preparatory exercises into the warm-up, we are able to better program upcoming exercises that the athletes will perform. For example, by practicing the single-leg snapdown in the warm-up, the coach is preparing for the single-leg vertical hop in the jump training block.

Lastly, it is important to note that each day should have a specified plane of motion for jump training exercises (hybrids are an exception). Depending on how many days per week the athletes train will dictate which planes of motion will be programmed on each day. Using a four-day per week training model, the coach can insert where each plane would be programmed on each day. From there, the coach can validate which plane of motion takes priority based on the amount of sessions per week and where the athlete is in the competition cycle.

Table 7.12: Four-day per week model

Day of the Week	Movement	Weight Training	Planes of Motion
1	Linear speed	Upper body	Vertical or Linear
2	Multi-directional speed	Lower body	Rotational
3	Combination	Upper body	Lateral
4	Lateral speed	Lower body	Linear or Vertical

Table 7.13: Three-day per week model

Day of the Week	Movement	Weight Training	Planes of Motion
1	Linear speed	Lower body	Vertical or Linear
2	Lateral speed	Upper body	Lateral
3	Multi-directional speed	Lower body	Rotational

Table 7.14: Two-day per week model

Day of the Week	Movement	Weight Training	Planes of Motion
1	Linear speed	Lower body	Vertical or Linear
2	Lateral speed	Upper body	Lateral

References

1. Laputin N, Oleshko V. *Managing the Training of Weightlifters.* Livonia, MI: Sportivny Press; 1982.

2. Haff G, Triplett N. *Essentials of Strength Training and Conditioning.* 4th ed. Champaign, IL: Human Kinetics; 2016.

PRINCIPLES of ATHLETIC Strength & Conditioning

The Foundations of Success in
Training and Developing
the Complete Athlete

CHAPTER 8

In-Season Training Considerations

Blair M. Wagner

Objectives

- Describe and discuss the factors unique to training the in-season athlete

- Identify strategies necessary to prevent overtraining while maintaining factors of athleticism in the in-season athlete

- Be able to apply contemporary concepts to specific sport seasons to most benefit the in-season athlete

Introduction

The last month of any season is where programs are defined, and this critical period of the annual training plan should keep athletes in peak condition through the season. Athletes are either progressing, remaining healthy, and playing their best or they are barely hanging on, weak, tired, and uninterested in the remainder of the season. The strength and conditioning professional (SCP) should work collaboratively with the sport coaches to develop an in-season plan that allows the team to be at their best during the season.

In-season training should share a lot of similarities between other periods of the training year, but the SCP must understand that the demands of training cannot interfere with sport practices and competitions during the season. The key to a great in-season program is figuring out how to maintain (or even build) strength/power without inducing fatigue that will have a negative impact on practices and competitions. Manipulating volumes and intensities, adjusting the program when necessary and scheduling appropriately will help the SCP put athletes in a position to achieve success.

Regardless of the time of year, coaches should expect athletes to show up on time, ready to train, with a focused mindset. In order to maintain consistency throughout the training year, a list of standards and principles should be developed in order to produce a positive training environment and consistency throughout the season.

Standards of Training

In-season training standards should be no different than what is expected throughout the rest of the training year. The SCP should have clearly defined standards such as:

- Safety First: "Make training count, not cost."

    o The coach's training prescription should meet the demands of the sport and the stress for the given period of the year. These dosages will dictate whether athletes are improving from week to week, falling short of their abilities, or potentially at risk for injury.

- Quality vs. Quantity: "It's now how much you do, it's how you do it."

    o No one gets more than 24 hours in a day. Know what is needed, what is wanted, and how both can be accomplished in the most effective and efficient way.

- Execution > Innovation: "Put the *base*, back in basics."

    o Some of the best athletes in the world repeat the same drills every day for years. Mastery comes through repetition, not by gimmicky training methods and equipment. The in-season training phase is not the time to try out new ideas and intensive modes of exercise prescription.

- Adaptable: "Plan on changing your plan."

    o Know when to change course of direction in order to meet the final goal.

    o Sometimes what is planned won't hold up during unexpected events. Practices are bound to go long, sport coaches will cancel lifts, and teams might have a case of nagging injuries.

- o Be able to modify and adjust on the fly. This could be due to a shortened training session, an athlete who is orthopedically limited to what they can do, class schedule conflicts or weather conditions.

Training Principles

When the SCP begins to put together the in-season training program, it is imperative to have goals and a road map to meet them. This will help put athletes in the best situation possible during competition. The following is a list of items to think about when drawing the training road map.

Athletic-Based

Perform exercises that utilize multiple joints, multiple muscles, and multiple planes of movement.

Balanced

Use movements that balance the ratio of pulling to pushing, incorporate both uni-lateral and bi-lateral movements, and take advantage of appropriate intensities and velocities.

Competitive

Having small competitions that live inside the training environment can help keep the weight room fun, especially for developmental groups who are not competing during the season.

Consistent

Regardless of what is going on during the season, winning or losing, the SCP should maintain a consistent approach. For example, a high-energy coach should remain high-energy during every training session.

Detailed

Time is critical during the in-season training period. The coach should have a detailed outline of how long the training session should take to complete. Have structured times for movement preparation, prep sets, time between sets, etc. so that time is spent efficiently.

Educated

The coach should make the decision to the best of his or her ability for what constitutes a quality training session.

Efficient

The coach should look to get the most bang for their buck with the time they are allotted. This comes down to preparation. Try to make sure the flow of the training session is set up for success. For example, if cleans are programmed for that day, use that same implement for a barbell hip bridge or RDL later in the session because the barbells are already set up.

Effective

Does the training session elicit the physiological stimulus you are seeking? Because in-season training takes a back seat to the sport season, try to use the smallest amount of time and energy to elicit results without creating unnecessary fatigue.

Evolving

The coach should take notes from season to season and know what worked and what did not. Evolving means always seeking the next best thing that prepares athletes for the demand of the sport.

Injury Resistant

The SCP should always look to implement the most orthopedically-sound exercise selection for each athlete to build resilient bodies that can withstand the demands of their sport.

Motivating

There are several motivating tactics that a coach can use in order to produce a positive outcome. It is the SCP's job to build relationships with each athlete in order to know which buttons to push during the training session.

Periodized

The coach should have a plan of what they want to accomplish on a daily, weekly, monthly basis. This plan will be the framework on which to act. It may change, but it is a guiding light in which to progress throughout the season.

Positive

The coach should be positive when engaging with athletes during training sessions. The coach has the ability to see a different side of an athlete and often builds a relationship that fosters an outlet to discuss and address in-season frustrations.

Progressive

The coach should aim to provide realistic and achievable training sessions while in-season. The appropriate progressions for exercise selection, intensity, and volume (overload) will help athletes improve their performance over the course of the season.

Purposeful

The coach should be specific on the purposes and intentions of the training session. If the purpose of the lift is to move the bar as fast as possible, the coach should clearly instruct athletes to perform the movement in such a manner.

Scientifically-based

The coach should always use scientifically backed research and methods in developing the in-season program. Having a basic understanding of exercise physiology will help in determining proper loads during specific periods of the year.

Sport Specific

The coach should adapt and modify the in-season program with exercises and energy system development that is specific to that sport. If the coach is programming for a sport that already involves high velocity sprinting, multiple change of direction, and jumping in practice, the amount of these activities should be limited. The coach should aim to give the athlete a training session that that can help balance the demands of the sport during this period of the year.

In-Season Planning

The major objective in training is to induce specific adaptations in order to improve sport performance. Coaches can also refer to this as the SAID (specific adaptations to imposed demands) principle. What athletes repeatedly do should yield positive (or negative) results in the manner in which they are doing them. If the coach has their athletes completing Olympic lifts three days per week with proper execution, technique, and load, those athletes are probably going to become proficient at performing the Olympic lifts. Similarly, if the coach has athletes constantly working on the bench press while neglecting the lower body and upper body strength development, those athletes will most likely end up with an awesome bench press along with musculoskeletal imbalances and nagging injuries.

Designing an in-season training program can look very different depending on the sport in which the SCP is planning. The needs of a court or field based team will be different than a swim team or cross country team. Regardless of the demands of the sport, many concepts for in-season training will hold true. The sport becomes the primary focus while training becomes a means to ensure athletes are prepared to perform at an optimal level. In-season volume, intensities, frequencies, and durations will—for the most part—typically decrease. A strong emphasis should be placed on restorative methods and movements that will help to keep the athlete healthy during the in-season period. The SCP should develop the in-season training schedule based around the competition schedule from the first game to the final post-season competition.

Consistency is very important for in-season training. Athletes often get sore and tight when a new training stimulus is introduced, but this quickly stops happening when exposure to the same stimulus occurs consistently. For these reasons, it is advisable to begin a strength program well before a season begins. The off- or pre-season strength program should get the athlete accustomed to this stimulus so that soreness can be minimized during the season.

When strength training is stopped for a couple weeks, soreness often re-occurs after the next lifting session. This is why coaches should not eliminate lifting for extended periods of time. Many coaches stop lifting for multiple weeks during tryouts and early-season practices, then re-introduce lifting again. In this case, most athletes will experience at least some muscular soreness following conditioning, which can lead to injury during subsequent practices. It would be much better to continue lifting just once a week during this period in order to maintain strength levels and reduce soreness when lifting is reintroduced.

The SCP must also understand that in-season training means plenty of program adjustments. Practice times change, injuries occur, and general fatigue builds. Factors like these need to be taken into consideration, and the SCP needs to adapt the program accordingly. For example, the plan may call for three sets of squats at 80%, but if a particular athlete's knee is hurting from an injury sustained the night before, the SCP will need to find an alternative that does not cause pain or exacerbate injury while still being able to train the athlete's lower body. Several exercises may be attempted before it becomes clear that a single-leg glute bridge is the answer for that day.

Another example may be a practice that runs very late. The SCP may have had a 60-minute lifting session planned, but practice ran over by 30 minutes. In this case, the program is going to change and the SCP must quickly decide what is most important. Should volume be reduced or should exercises be removed completely? Should warm-up or cooldown time be eliminated or should something else change? Being able to make decisions quickly based on unforeseen circumstances is vital in these situations.

In-Season Training Frequency

The number of training sessions per week depends on a number of factors. The number of competitions will dictate how frequently and consistently athletes train. For the SCP working with football, the schedule will consist of one competition per week. The SCP should know exactly how many days there are between competitions well in advance, so training can be very consistent.

Other sports have very different competition schedules, so the frequency of training may not remain constant throughout the season. There will be periods of the season when one training session per week is adequate, and other weeks that allow for multiple workouts (e.g. bye-week). The

SCP should work collaboratively with the sport coach to determine the frequency of training sessions throughout the season. This will help the SCP prepare an appropriate program.

There is a simple formula to help the SCP determine the number of training sessions that should take place each week. First, determine the number competitions and days off for the week. Subtract these days from the number 7 and divide by 2. The final answer is an estimated amount of time (in hours) that the team should be dedicating to strength & conditioning that week. Below is an example if the sport were to only consist of one competition during the week along with one off-day.

$$7 - (1+1) / 2 = 2.5$$

Days in the week - (# of Days of Competition + # Days Off) / 2 = Number of hours to devote to training for the week

The SCP can use the amount of time over the course of 1-3 days depending on the schedule. If 2.5 hours will be devoted toward strength and conditioning, the SCP could schedule 2 to 3 training sessions during the week. If the SCP chooses to utilize two days, the sessions would be a maximum of 75 minutes each. If the SCP chooses to utilize three days of training, two of those training sessions could be 60-minute strength training sessions and the third training session could be 30 minutes of recovery methods and body restoration. How the time is used may change throughout the season and should be discussed with the sport coaches. This will ensure that the needs of the athletes/team are being addressed appropriately.

Table 8.1: In-season scheduling possibilities for various sports

Sport	Days of Competition	# of Days Off	# of Hours for Training	# of Days to Utilize Time	Training Session Duration (min)
Baseball	3	1	1.5	2	45
Football	1	1	2.5	3	2x60, 1x30
Track & Field	2	1	2	2	45
Swimming	1-2	1	2-2.5	3	45-60
Golf	2-3	1	1.5-2	2	45-60
Soccer	2	1	2	3	1x60, 2x30

A training session should be viewed as any time that is devoted to the development, recovery, or improvement of athletic performance outside of competition or practice. The location, equipment, and methods can all change from day to day and week to week. If athletes are involved in a sport which demands sprinting, jumping, reactive agility, and change of direction, an emphasis of this type of training may not be appropriate for in-season training sessions. However, if athletes are lacking proficiency in a particular area, in-season training time may be focused on these deficiencies in order to be better prepared for competition.

Let's use a high school football team as an example, with a game on Friday night. Saturday could be used as recovery day that may include activities such as medical treatments, flexibility/mobility, and a low-intensity run and strength training session. If a pool is available, this may be a good time to do a low-intensity pool workout instead of the run. Sunday would be an off-day, and the team would begin their week of practice on Monday. A more intense strength training session could be scheduled on Monday, with additional conditioning done after practice on Tuesday. Normal practices and game preparation would occur on Wednesday along with a low volume, upper body emphasis lift to conclude the third training session for the week. It should be noted that strength training could be done on Thursday or Friday for any return-to-play athletes or athletes that will not be playing on Friday night.

On the other hand, the schedule for a basketball team with games on Tuesday and Friday would look very different. A strength training session could be done on Saturday or Sunday along with flexibility/mobility work and medical treatments. The team would have a standard practice on Monday, game on Tuesday, and a second strength training session after practice on Wednesday. Thursday would be a standard practice before the second game of the week on Friday. This schedule allows the team to complete two strength sessions per week without interfering with games.

In-Season Training Intensity & Volume

It is very important to balance training intensity and volume during the season. As stated earlier, the SCP must understand that in-season training takes a back-seat to actual sport practice and competition. The purpose of in-season training is to allow athletes to practice harder, longer and without negative impacts to training. If training intensity and volume are too high, athletes will be too fatigued to meet these demands. This can also lead to overtraining issues if adjustments are not made. The goal should be to use the lowest volume and intensity possible (which produces the least fatigue) and still elicit results.

Training intensity and volume will usually be measured in four different ways: percentage of an athlete's 1RM, number of repetitions per set, the number of sets during a training session, and the total amount of work that is performed during the training week (training density or frequency). All of these factors need to be managed in an effort to create a training effect without inducing unnecessary fatigue.

When prescribing resistance training loads based on an athletes 1RM, off-season testing numbers should be adjusted to account for the demands of the season. It is very difficult for athletes to train at high intensities during the season, so it is recommended to reduce an athlete's 1RM by 5-7% when prescribing loads for strength and power based movements. For example, an athlete with a 200 lbs. max bench press at the end of the pre-season would use a max of 185 – 190 lbs. to determine in-season loads. All prescriptions of volume and intensity should be based off the individual athlete when possible. Certain individuals will be able to handle higher intensities and volumes more than others.

Volume must also be controlled during the season in an effort to reduce systemic fatigue. When intensities are high (i.e. high percentage of 1RM), volume must be lowered. Keeping intensity high and volume low helps maintain (or even improve) in-season strength levels. Here is an example of an in-season strength progression for core lifts. Notice that the intensity (as a percentage of 1RM) stays high, while volume remains low.

Table 8.2: In-season core exercise progression chart

Week 1	3 X 3 @ 75%
Week 2	4 X 3 @ 75%
Week 3	3 X 4 @ 75%
Week 4	4 X 4 @ 70%
Week 5	3 X 3 @ 77%
Week 6	4 X 3 @ 77%
Week 7	3 X 4 @ 77%
Week 8	4 X 4 @ 72%
Week 9	3 X 3 @ 80%
Week 10	3-4 X 3 @ 80%
Week 11+	2-3 X 3 @ 80%

In this example, athletes will still be able to perform 2-4 sets of 3 reps at 80% of the 1RM at the end of the season. Of course, the sets, reps and percentages can all be adjusted as this is just a sample program.

In-Season Training Duration

The time devoted to the in-season training program will be reduced compared to the off-season training period. With the demands of the student-athlete schedule, efficiency and effectiveness will benefit both the coach and athletes. Proper planning and logistics of the training session should be well thought out prior to finalizing any training program. Equipment set-up should flow from one exercise to another without causing traffic congestions with large groups of athletes. The set-up and function of the training session will depend entirely on the facility size, equipment, number of athletes training, number of coaches, and duration of the training session.

The SCP should prepare the facility for the upcoming training session prior to athletes arriving to maximize time spent for strength training. If the SCP has multiple teams coming through the weight room during the day, the set-up and break down should be well thought out to minimize transition time between teams. Proper time should be allotted for a warm-up, strength/power/speed/conditioning, and a cooldown or flexibility work. Duration of the training session should remain between 30-60 minutes.

The training session should include the needs of the athlete and, if time allows, any accessory work that will aid in the development of performance and injury protection. In order to reduce overall training volume and fatigue, more time should be spent on multi-joint lifts so that more musculature can be stimulated with fewer exercises. These exercises should focus on the principles of the SCP and be specific in nature to the demands of the sport. If possible, strength training sessions should be done several hours before (i.e. in the morning) or directly before practice for optimal results and to avoid excess fatigue that may result in uncontrolled practice conditions. By keeping intensity moderate to high and volume low, the duration of a training session and muscle soreness can be significantly reduced.

Sample Schedules & Programs

Collegiate Football

Event	Sunday	Monday	Tuesday	Wednesday	Thursday	Friday	Saturday
Off Day		x					
Competition							x
Travel / Walk-Thru / Light Practice	x					x	
Practice			x	x	x		
Recovery Methods / Lift	x						
Resistance Training	x		x		x		
Plyometric Training			TBD		TBD		
Agility Training			TBD		TBD		
Conditioning	x		x				

High School Football

Event	Sunday	Monday	Tuesday	Wednesday	Thursday	Friday	Saturday
Off Day	x						
Competition						x	
Travel / Walk-Thru / Light Practice					x		
Practice		x	x	x			
Recovery Methods / Lift							x
Resistance Training		x		x			
Plyometric Training			TBD				
Agility Training			TBD				
Conditioning		x					

Collegiate Volleyball (Conference Schedule)

Event	Sunday	Monday	Tuesday	Wednesday	Thursday	Friday	Saturday
Off Day		x					
Competition	x					x	
Travel / Walk-Thru / Light Practice					x		x
Practice			x	x			
Recovery Methods / Lift							x
Resistance Training			x	x			
Plyometric Training			TBD				
Agility Training				TBD			
Conditioning			TBD				

High School Wrestling

Event	Sunday	Monday	Tuesday	Wednesday	Thursday	Friday	Saturday
Off Day		x					
Competition				x		x	x
Travel / Walk-Thru / Light Practice					x		x
Practice			x				
Recovery Methods / Lift							x
Resistance Training	x		x				
Plyometric Training			TBD				
Agility Training				TBD			
Conditioning		x					

High School Basketball (Non-Conference Schedule)

Event	Sunday	Monday	Tuesday	Wednesday	Thursday	Friday	Saturday
Off Day	x						
Game			x			x	x
Travel / Walk-Thru / Light Practice					x		
Practice		x		x			
Recovery Methods / Lift		x			x		
Resistance Training		x		x			
Plyometric Training		TBD					
Agility Training				TBD			
Conditioning		TBD					

Football

Day 1: Weight Room

Athlete Protection Plan (shoulder protection, warm-up, activation, technical prep): 15 minutes

- Manual neck flexion 2x10 (2.2.2.2)
- Complete upon entry with coach
- Single-arm dumbbell shrug 2x10 each

- A1: Block clean pull (below knee)
  - Prep sets 1x3, 1x3, 1x3
  - Work sets 3x3 @ 80%
- A2: Landmine split jerk
  - 3x3 each
- B1: Back squat
  - Prep sets 1x5, 1x3, 1x3
  - Work sets 3x3 @ 80%
- B2: Active hip mobility 3x:60s
- B3: Thoracic passes: Foam roller 3x:60s
- C1: Dumbbell bench press
  - 1x6, 1x8, 1x8-12
- C2: Barbell bent-over row (Deadstop) or seated cable row
  - 3x10
- C3: Stability ball rollouts
  - 2x15
- C4: Contralateral kettlebell RDL
  - 2x6 each

Day 2: Weight Room

Athlete Protection Plan (shoulder protection, warm-up, activation, technical prep): 15 minutes

- Manual neck extension 2x10 (2.2.2.2)
- Complete upon entry with coach
- Barbell shrug 2x12

- A1: Neutral grip bar bench press or bench press
  - Prep sets 1x3, 1x3, 1x3
  - Work sets 3x3 @ 80%
- A2: Single-arm dumbbell row (hand/knee supported) or single-arm Meadows row
  - 3x8 each
- B1: Hang snatch pull or kettlebell swing
  - Work sets 4x3 @ 70% or 3x8
- C1: Neutral-grip chin-up or lat pull-down
  - 1x8, 1x8, 1x8-12
- C2: Lateral shoulder raise
  - 3x8-10
- C3: Landmine rotations or cable press to rotation
  - 3x6ea

Day 3: Pool & or Field Session (Active recovery)

Volleyball

Day 1: Weight Room

Athlete Protection Plan (shoulder protection, warm-up, activation, technical prep): 15 minutes

- Just Jump monitoring 1x3 non-countermovement, 1x3 countermovement
- Complete Upon Entry with Coach

- A1: Hang clean pull
  - Prep sets 1x3, 1x3, 1x3
  - Work sets 3x3 @ 80%
- A2: Half-kneeling kettlebell bottoms-up press
  - 3x5 each
- B1: Rear foot elevated single leg squat

- o Prep sets 1x3, 1x3
- o Work sets 3x3 @ 75%
- B2: Active hip mobility
  - o 3x:60s
- B3: Forward facing wall slides
  - o 3x6 each
- C1: Split stance single arm cable press
  - o 3x8 each
- C2: TRX inverted row
  - o 3x10
- C3: ½ kneeling band chop
  - o 2x10 each
- C4: Glute/ham raise
  - o 2x6

Day 2: Weight Room

Athlete Protection Plan (shoulder protection, warm-up, activation, technical prep): 15 minutes

- Ankle Mobility / Knee Stability Series
- 2x10ea

- A1: Single arm dumbbell incline press
  - o 3x6 each
- A2: Band pull-apart
  - o 3x12
- B1: Snatch grip single leg RDL
  - o 3x4 each
- C1: Single arm cable pull-down
  - o 2x8 each
- C2: Dumbbell front raise
  - o 2x10
- C3: Body saw
  - o 2x12

Wrestling

Day 1: Weight Room

Athlete Protection Plan (shoulder protection, warm-up, activation, technical prep): 15 minutes

Weigh-in prior to lift. If athletes are cutting weight, may need to monitor working sets and percentages. Heavy weights should stick to the training percentages.

- A1: Hang power clean
    - Prep sets 1x3, 1x3, 1x3
    - Work sets 3x2 @ 70%
- A2: Rear foot elevated hop
    - 3x4 (during prep sets)
- B1: Trap bar deadlift
    - Prep sets 1x3, 1x3
    - Work sets 3x3 @ 70, 75, 80%
- B2: Neck harness extension
    - 2x8 (during prep sets)
- C1: Barbell floor press
    - 1x10, 1x8, 1x6
- C2: Meadows Row
    - 3x8 each
- C3: Weighted front plank
    - 3x:30s

Day 2: Weight Room

Athlete Protection Plan (shoulder protection, warm-up, activation, technical prep): 15 minutes

Weigh-in prior to lift. If athletes are cutting weight, may need to monitor working sets and percentages. Heavy weights should stick to the training percentages.

- A1: Single arm dumbbell snatch
    - 4x3 each
- A2: TRX-assisted squat jump
    - 4x5 (continuous)
- B1: Pull-up (weighted if possible)
    - 3x6-8

- B2: Kettlebell front rack reverse lunge
  - 3x4 each
- C1: Band rip downs
  - 2x10
- C2: Single arm dumbbell farmer carry
  - 2x60 ft (1 arm down, 1 arm back)
- C3: Medicine ball rotational slam
  - 2x5 each

Monitoring on a Budget

Isaiah Gonzales, University of California Berkeley

Sport science is often thought to revolve around technology and fancy gadgets; however, the term "sport science" simply means the science of sport. While many of these products are very expensive, it is not necessary to spend a lot of money to collect data. Those with a limited budget can choose to find inexpensive ways to monitor athletes such as questionnaires, sleep monitoring apps, or measuring vertical jump height and bodyweight.

Before even considering more expensive options, a great place to start is by tracking body weight. It is simple, effective, and reliable. The amount of information or questions that can be derived from monitoring body weight are extensive. Body weight provides insight into the fluctuations of athletes' hydration levels, weekend behavior trends, travel trends, health and other stressors. It allows the SCP to communicate with athletes about other stressors they may be experiencing that are not on the surface. Weight changes can lead to in-depth questions regarding academic stress, relationship issues, family problems, etc. and can alert athletes to potential problems that would otherwise go unnoticed.

Vertical jump testing is another highly efficient, inexpensive, and repeatable way to monitor central nervous fatigue.[1] Studies suggest that as little as a 6% decrease of vertical jump effort compared to mean vertical jump efforts can indicate central nervous system fatigue.[2]

The SCP can create a live excel file that automatically updates the athlete's vertical jump average and tracks personal records. It can also be set up to alert the user when a jump is outside of the normal range. For most athletes, a 6% decrease is less than 1.6 inches. 1.6 inches is such a small difference that it is difficult to determine if the athlete is truly fatigued or just did not have a great jump. A 10% decrease, on the other hand, usually has a range of 2-3 inches, and gives a more accurate depiction of fatigue. Even with a technical error or poor effort, most athletes are not going to jump 3 inches less than their average unless there is significant fatigue present. Once the season has begun, the SCP can utilize the information derived from the vertical jump monitoring to aid in daily training selection and emphasis.

As previously stated, it is probably unnecessary to modify a workout based on a small (i.e. 6%) drop in vertical jump performance unless other variables such as travel, practice schedules, etc. have changed. Modification would be reserved for larger drops in performance and would be accompanied by additional investigation and a discussion with the athlete. When an athlete has any significant increase in vertical jump height, it is usually a good indication that the intensity of the workout can be increased that day.

It is highly recommended to track body weight and vertical jump on the same spreadsheet so that power-output numbers can be automatically calculated using Sayers formula: PAPw (peak anaerobic power output) (Watts) = 60.7 · jump height(cm) + 45.3 · body mass(kg) – 2055.[3] The same concept can be applied utilizing Reactive Strength Index (RSI) which would provide the SCP further insight to athlete fatigue by analyzing Ground Contact Time (GCT) and Jump Height. This is an important piece of information because it allows the SCP to track athletes over time. For example, we may see an athlete who remains constant on the vertical jump but gains body mass will exhibit higher power even though the vertical jump has not increased. We may also see an athlete that continues to have a jump height consistent with his/her average, however the GCT is significantly longer. This could indicate CNS fatigue with a mechanical compensation. This helps the SCP to track progress over time and determine whether the training program has been effective and where it can improve.

In short, daily monitoring can be done on a very limited budget as long as some effort and attention to detail are applied. The data derived through this can help guide programming and will often lead to teaching opportunities for the strength and conditioning professional.

References

1. Gathercole R, Sporer B, Stellingwerff T, Sleivert G. Comparison of the capacity of different jump and sprint field tests to detect neuromuscular fatigue. *J Strength Cond Res.* 2015;29(9):2522-2531.

2. Ronglan L, Raastad T, Borgesen A. Nuromucular fatigue and recovery in elite female handball players. *Scand J Med Sci Sports.* 2006;16(4):267-272.

3. Sayers S, Harackiewicz D, Harman E, Frykman P, Rosenstein M. Cross-validation of three power equations. *Med Sci Sports Exerc.* 1999;31(4):572-577.

PRINCIPLES of ATHLETIC Strength & Conditioning

The Foundations of Success in
Training and Developing
the Complete Athlete

CHAPTER 9

Training the Mulit-Sport Athlete

Fred Eaves

Objectives

- Identify the issues associated with early adolescent athletes, including biological vs. chronological age

- Describe and discuss challenges associated with training the multi-sport high school athlete

- Describe the factors to be monitored and adjusted when training the multi-sport athlete to ensure optimal results without overtraining

Introduction

One of the most difficult questions in strength and conditioning is how to train the multi-sport athlete. This has been a controversial and frustrating topic for many high school and middle school coaches across the country for quite some time. The following chapter is designed to help outline some strategies that have proven effective in optimally developing athletes who participate in multiple sports.

The strength & conditioning professional (SCP) must understand that his/her program is a small part of a larger puzzle. The program should be designed to keep athletes healthy and elicit results without inducing unnecessary fatigue. It is a balancing act that needs to be taken seriously if long-term success is expected.

Training young athletes (i.e. middle school and high school levels) should focus on foundational elements of physical preparation and should be very general in nature, particularly for those just entering formal training. The reduction in physical education at both the elementary and middle school level has had profound effects on the mobility, stability, relative body strength, and athleticism of adolescents entering their high school years. Young athletes are also exposed to more specialized sport training than ever before. This is a generation that has been over-specialized and under-generalized in its development due to the intense focus on developing sport-specific skill. Early specialization can be very counter-productive to producing a healthy, mobile, and strong athlete.

It is especially important for the SCP to focus on foundational principles when dealing with multi-sport athletes. This philosophy of general development is congruent with the physical development that high school students are experiencing during these formative years. Unfortunately, this philosophy of foundational development is counter-cultural to what parents are usually pursuing with travel teams, year-round game play, and highly specialized training. The athlete's strength training program is one of the last places the athlete can receive appropriate instruction for his or her physiological age.

In-Season Success

The multi-sport athlete will spend at least two out of three school seasons in competition. There are two important issues the SCP must address in order to help the multi-sport athlete experience progress physically. First, understanding how to progress athletes who are constantly in-season can thwart efforts to address deficiencies and help athletes fully develop. Secondly, knowing how to progress athletes without compromising health and performance during periods of competition and high stress is critical for physical and psychological well-being and injury prevention.

It is important to apply simple solutions in order to solve these very complex problems. It must be understood that the athlete's sport is the most important priority during the in-season period. This is a very difficult prospect for the SCP who is pressured by the football coach to attain big numbers for his players while these athletes may also be involved in basketball, baseball, or any number of sports at the interscholastic level. This can be a difficult balancing act for the SCP in this situation. It is important to establish realistic expectations for development on the front end with both coaches and administrators in order to avoid future issues. If an athlete is in-season for a majority of the year, it is important to determine what constitutes success for the in-season in each situation. For example, in most situations, maintaining somewhere between 88-90% strength levels in terms of pre-season numbers can be viewed as a success and an appropriate progression.

At the high school level, what determines whether a program is successful or not can also be very specific to the situation. There are several factors that influence the ability to train at a particular intensity during the in-season, including strength of schedule, incidence of injury, workouts completed, and a number of other related factors. There is anecdotal evidence that it is feasible to make gains during the sport season at the high school level. The takeaway is that the SCP should strive to keep his or her athletes within 10% of their pre-season numbers throughout the season, assuming the athlete has not been subjected to significant injury or ill health during that time period

Program Design Factors

Biological Age vs. Chronological Age

Early adolescence is a period of tremendous physical growth, with males growing as much as 20 inches and females as much as 9.5 inches between the ages of 13-18 years old.[1] These young athletes are going through puberty and experiencing significant physiological changes while also beginning what may be their first organized training program. It is important that the SCP factor these changes into the program design model for their athletes. Developing a program in this manner also promotes a safe training environment by progressing the athletes according to what they are truly ready for from a physical standpoint. Recognizing biological age is of great importance to determining appropriate exercise selection and load that will enable the athlete to achieve long-term success in the training program. It is important to begin with the end in mind when developing the training curriculum. Backward design is a very effective way to accomplish this goal and also achieve the goal of long-term athletic development.

Challenges of the High School Strength & Conditioning Program

There can be multiple challenges at the high school level that can be quite different from other environments, including group size, varied training ages, limited access, stress, facilities, staffing, and outside factors. In order to best address each of these issues, it is important to examine each individually.

Group Size

Most high school strength and conditioning settings are filled with large groups with usually only one coach to facilitate the training session. This is problematic for several different reasons, but namely from a safety and quality of instruction standpoint.

Multiple Training Ages

The high school weight room can also be very dynamic with different physiological ages, emotional maturity levels, opposite genders, and ability levels. This is one of the most challenging aspects of program design at the high school level. It is important to account for the safety and quality of training for each of these constituents.

Limited Access

Many high school schedules only allow for somewhere between 1.5 to 7.5 hours of contact time per week in a training environment. There are many different types of schedules implemented at high schools across the country. A public-school block schedule allows for the most with 90-minute class periods five days per week. The drawback to this type of schedule is that students can be enrolled for one semester and then gone the next because they have received their credit.

Many private schools have implemented rotating block schedules that allow instructors to have students 3-4 times per week for 50-minute classes. There are variations of these two, but these are two very common models. The drawback to the 50-minute class is that 20 minutes of class time is often used simply for transition between classes. A 30-minute class dictates the need for the training session to be thoroughly planned and very efficient in nature.

Many athletes do not have any access to training during the school day, so everything must be accomplished before or after school. This introduces additional issues such as transportation, conflicts with practices and other after-school activities, academic demands and simply overwhelming a person with after-school activities. In some cases, however, the weight room may be the safest and most productive place an athlete can be, so it is important to know as much as possible about each athlete.

The yearly school schedule itself is filled with vacation days, holidays, teacher planning and in-service days, etc. that interrupt a regular training schedule. Some other areas that take contact time away are unplanned assemblies, crisis management drills, and inclement weather days. Class interruption can be very frequent at the high school level, which makes planning, efficiency, and execution extremely important to ensure success.

Stress

Stress is a very real concern when planning for the multi-sport athlete. The demands on the high school athlete are very unique. It is crucial to understand that athletes at the high school level may also be participating in multiple sports or on multiple teams simultaneously. An example of this would be a high school football player attending a baseball showcase during the football season. The bylaws of each state's athletic association vary, but there has recently been a movement toward less regulation on this type of activity. Additionally, when academic, social, and civic responsibilities and activities are factored in, the athlete may very well be over-scheduled and unable to fully benefit from even the most elegant and well-designed training plan.

Facilities

The size and availability of the facility and the quantity and quality of the equipment available for use should play a large role in the design of the program. Designing a program without taking these factors into account can lead to inefficiency, safety issues, and frustration for all parties involved in the strength and conditioning program. If there is a lack of resources in any of these areas, it can be a significant determinant on how the coach must program for the facility. Each situation at the high school level is unique, and there are always multiple solutions available. It is important that the SCP be extremely adaptable in order to deal with such challenges.

Staffing

Appropriate staffing is a major concern in most school settings. Quite often, the high school coach works under a very large coach-to-athlete ratio, sometimes as high as 20 or 30:1. It is important for the coach to plan for this by being realistic in his/her programming. Implementing a full Olympic lifting program in a room where one coach is responsible for 30 or more athletes can be very difficult and also dangerous due to the highly technical nature of those lifts. A more practical approach may look to use derivatives in order to elicit the benefits of the Olympic lifts while removing complicated components of the lift in order to simplify and add safety. This type of thought process should be the standard at the middle school and high school levels. The question that should be asked is, "How do I get the greatest benefit for the smallest cost?" If a school has multiple coaches working in the room, it allows the coach to expand the program and differentiate at a much higher level. Multiple staff members is ideal, but not realistic in many environments.

Outside Factors

There are also outside stresses that athletes deal with including academic stress, personal stress, and training outside of the school program. The stress of the training is the easiest to manage because the SCP has direct control. Constant communication with everyone involved is highly valuable in determining the appropriate amount of stress to apply. There are multiple solutions for how to deal with these issues, but it is imperative that the SCP communicates well and works to create an environment that best serves the athlete.

Program Design

Because multi-sport athletes rarely engage in extended periods of intense training, it is important to keep program design simple and efficient. Breaking exercises into basic categories will allow the SCP to easily adapt workouts for multi-sport athletes. The three most common categories are total body, lower body, or upper body focus. These categories allow for easy adjustments due to academic and competition schedules. Joe Kenn is often credited with creating these categories in his Tier System. Kenn defines the Tier System as "the daily rotation of exercises from three basic movement categories."[2]

Keeping these categories broad allows for significant latitude in program design. This enables the coach to adapt the exercises to the needs of his or her athletes according to stress, developmental level, and technical proficiency. The highest tier is the main emphasis for the day and also has the highest volume and intensity for the workout. Volume and intensity decrease in the lower tiers. The ability to categorize movements this way allows a lot of flexibility in programming for the multi-sport athlete.

Table 9.1: Tier system example (3x3)

	Monday	Wednesday	Friday
Tier 1 (Priority)	Total body	Lower body	Upper body
Tier 2 (Major)	Lower body	Upper body	Total body
Tier 3 (minor)	Upper body	Total body	Lower body

Technique, Velocity, and Load

Competitive powerlifter, established author, and NCAA Division I strength & conditioning coach Bryan Mann advises a basic concept in strength training for young athletes: focus on technique, velocity, and load. In order to get this point across simply, this concept has also simplified to "how good, how fast, and how much." It is very important to follow this model with all athletes, but it becomes especially important when dealing with young athletes. High school athletes are at a formative age physically, mentally, and emotionally, and this philosophy sets such athletes up for long-term success.

Technical Proficiency

It is very important to ingrain proper movement patterns with developmental athletes. The movement patterns that are developed at a young age will set the foundation for each athlete's training and athletic career moving forward.

From a safety standpoint, it is also very important that proper technique is taught and enforced at all times in a weight room environment. Teaching proper technique will pay dividends down the road when the speed of the bar and load are both increased. It is important to spend the appropriate amount of time equipping athletes with tools to be successful and safe.

Velocity

Once the athlete is proficient in basic movements, it is acceptable to begin to perform the movement with more speed and greater intent. The specific adaptation to imposed demands (SAID) principle is applied in order to elicit a positive response from athletes in the training program. Young athletes will quickly show improvement through enhanced neural function by using proper technique and increasing the speed of the movement. It is important to master technique and velocity in order to feel confident enough to increase the load of the exercise.

Progressive Overload

Progressive overload is a simple method that is characterized by the gradual increase of stress in training to produce strength gains. A simple example of this is as follows: An athlete trains his squat with 135 pounds for five sets of five on week one. The athlete completes the prescribed reps and weight for all sets and adds five pounds to increase the weight to 140 for five sets of five the next week. The athlete would continue to add weight each week as tolerated with good form. This is an oversimplified example, but it should illustrate the simplicity of this method. Developing athletes respond very well to this training and multi-sport athletes can take advantage of simple versions of progression.

APRE/RPE Method

It can be difficult to train on a purely percentage-based program due to the variable readiness of the multi-sport athlete. It is important that the SCP considers all outside influences in order to adjust programming to meet the needs of each athlete. The autoregulatory progressive resistance exercise (APRE) protocol is an extremely adaptable method that can help the coach achieve all of these goals. Traditional APRE protocol will have the athlete work to failure on the last two sets of an exercise. An example would be this:

APRE 8

Set 1- 10 reps @ 50% of 8RM

Set 2- 8 reps @ 75% of 8RM

Set 3- 2 reps @ 85% of 8RM (neurological adaptation)

Set 4- 2 reps @ 95% of 8RM (neurological adaptation)

Set 5- Reps to failure @ 8RM

Set 6- Adjusted reps to failure

This is a tremendous method to build strength quickly, but can be very taxing due to the nature of training to failure on the final two sets. Because this type of program will induce fatigue, the SCP must take the competition schedule into consideration.

Combining the APRE protocol with the rate of perceived exertion (RPE) concept is another highly effective method to increase strength and help protect an athlete who is under significant stress for a large portion of the year. The RPE protocol allows the athlete to become an active participant in his or her training in order to rate how the last two sets felt. Many variations can be used, but a simple example is a 10, 9, 8, 7 scale for the last set of an exercise. This RPE scale is as follows:

10= 0 reps left

9= 1 rep left

8 = 2 reps left

7= multiple reps left

The weight on the final set can then be based on how the athlete rates the 5th set in order to regulate intensity. This can help avoid excessive fatigue before a competition. If the workout calls for sets of 8 reps, the athlete will not train over 8 reps and an RPE of 8 would call for the athlete to end the set when he/she feels like two more reps could be completed. A 6-set example of this would look like the following:

Set 1- 10 reps @ 50% of 8RM

Set 2- 8 reps @ 75% of 8RM

Set 3- 2 reps @ 85% of 8RM (neurological adaptation)

Set 4- 2 reps @ 95% of 8RM (neurological adaptation)

Set 5- RPE @ 8RM

Set 6- Adjusted reps to 8RM

Developmental Levels

Accounting for individual differences and training ages can be done by creating different developmental levels. A logical way to organize this is to develop multiple groups or levels that differentiate the exercises, volume, and intensity the athlete is exposed to in training. Here are some examples of different developmental levels.

Level 1: Developmental (Middle-school, Freshman and Junior Varsity athletes)

There are few modifications from the off-season training program. There is a high emphasis on technique and proper patterns in this level in lieu of load. This is a time to create familiarity with the program and improve relative body strength in order to create a strong foundation for more intense training down the road in the program. These athletes typically train on a 3-day off-season program during this stage.

Table 9.2: Sample Level 1 routine

Session T	DAY 1 WILDCAT BLOCK 0	Week 1 Volume	
T	KB Sumo Deadlift + Wall Taps + Scap Retractions	6x5/ 3x10/ 3x15	
L	Eccentric BW OH Box Squat + DB Farmer Walk + T Raise	3x10/ 2x30 yds/ 3x10	Slow 6 sec down
U	Modified Push-up + Batwing Hold + Eccentric Russian Lean	3x10/ 3x10- 5 sec hold/ 3x6	
T	PVC RDL + PUPP + Manual Iso Neck	3x5/ 3x10 sec/ 3x10- 5 sec hold	
L	BW Eccentric Reverse Lunge + DB Curls	3x6/ 3x10	Slow 6 sec down
Session T	DAY 1 WHITE BLOCK 1		Tempo/Velocity
T	4 Block Hex Bar Deadlift+ Wall Taps+ Scap Retractions	APRE 5/ 3x10 / 3x12	
L	Eccentric PVC OH Squat+ DB Farmer Walk + T Raise	3x10/ 2x30 yds/ 3x10	Slow 6 sec down
U	Elevated Pushups + Batwing Hold + Eccentric Russian Lean	3x10 / 3x10- 5 sec hold/ 3x6	
T	Hang Jump Shrug + PUPP+ Manual Iso Neck	3x5/ 3x10 sec/ 3x10- 5 sec hold	
L	Eccentric Reverse Lunge + DB Curls	3x6/ 3x10	Slow 6 sec down
Session T	DAY 1 GRAY BLOCK 2		
T	3 Block Hex Bar Deadlift+ Wall Taps+ Scap Retractions	APRE 5/ 3x10 / 3x15	
L	BB OH Squat+ DB Farmer Walk + T Raise	3x8/ 2x30 yds/ 3x10	
U	DB Half Kneeling Military Press + Batwing Hold + Eccentric Russian Lean	3x10/ 3x10- 5 sec hold/ 3x6	
T	Hang Jump Shrug + PUPP+ Manual Iso Neck	3x5/ 3x10 sec/ 3x10- 5 sec hold	
L	DB Eccentric Reverse Lunge + DB Curls	3x6/ 3x10	Slow 6 sec down
Session T	DAY 1 GOLD BLOCK 3		
T	2 Block Hex Bar Deadlift+ Wall Taps+ Scap Retractions	APRE 5/ 3x10 / 3x15	
L	Front Squat+ DB Farmer Walk + T Raise	3x8/ 2x30 yds/ 3x10	0.8-1.0 AV
U	DB Half Kneeling Military Press + Batwing Hold + Eccentric Russian Lean	3x10/ 4x10- 5 sec hold/ 3x6	
T	Hang Jump Shrug+ PUPP+ Manual Iso Neck	3x5/ 3x10 sec/ 3x10- 5 sec hold	
L	DB Eccentric Reverse Lunge + DB Curls	3x6/ 3x10	Slow 6 sec down
Session T	DAY 1 BLUE BLOCK 4		
T	1 Block Hex Bar Deadlift+ Wall Taps+ Scap Retractions	APRE 5/ 3x10 / 3x15	
L	Back Squat+ DB Farmer Walk + T Raise	3x8/ 2x30 yds/ 3x10	0.8-1.0 AV
U	DB Half Kneeling Military Press + Batwing Hold + Eccentric Russian Lean	3x10/ 4x10- 5 sec hold/ 3x6	
T	Hang Jump Shrug+ PUPP+ Manual Iso Neck	3x5/ 3x10 sec/ 3x10- 5 sec hold	
L	DB Eccentric Reverse Lunge + DB Curls	3x6/ 3x10	Slow 6 sec down

Level 2: Advanced Developmental (Role/practice athletes)

This is the in-between stage with high school athletes. This is an athlete who has a significant role at practice, but plays limited varsity snaps. From a programming standpoint, it is important to recognize that the work being put in during the practice week may be low even though technically the athlete is competing. Modifications are made at this stage to account for the added stress of practice, and these athletes will train on a three-day modified program.

Table 9.3: Sample Level 2 routine

Session U	DAY 2 BLOCK 0	Week 1 Volume	
U	Barbell Overhead Press-Hold + TGU Practice + Band Pull Aparts	4x10- 5 sec hold/2x2/ 3x15	
T	PVC RDL & Jump Shrug + BW Box Squat + Y Raise	3x5/ 3x10/ 3x10	
L	Eccentric Split Squat + Banded Duck Walk + Hip Thrust	3x6/ 3x10 yds/ 3x10	Slow 6 sec down
U	Chin-up Hold + MB Rotate & Throw + PUPP	3x10 sec/ 3x10/ 3x10 sec	
T	Slow Crawl + SA Tricep Pushdowns+ DB Hammer Curls	4x30 yds /3x10/ 3x10	

Session U	DAY 2 WHITE BLOCK 1		
U	Log Bar Overhead Press+ TGU+ Band Pull Aparts	APRE 8/ 3x3/ 3x12	
T	4 Block Hex Bar Clean Pull + KB Goblet Squat + Y Raise	3x5/ 3x3/ 3x10	
L	DB Bulgarian Split Squat + Banded Duck Walk + Hip Thrust	3x10/ 2x10yd/ 3x10	
U	BA Chinup + Jammer Rotation + PUPP	3x10/ 3x10/ 3x10 sec	
T	Slow Crawl + SA Tricep Pushdowns+ DB Hammer Curls	4x30 yds /3x10/ 3x10	

Session U	DAY 2 GRAY BLOCK 2		
U	Log Bar Bench Press+ TGU+ Band Pull Aparts	APRE 8/ 3x3/ 3x15	
T	3 Block Hex Bar Clean Pull + KB Goblet Squat + Y Raise	3x5/ 3x3/ 3x10	
L	DB Front Bulgarian Split Squat + Banded Duck Walk + Sand Bag Hip Thrust	3x10/ 3x10yd/ 3x10	
U	BA Chin Up + Jammer Rotation + PUPP	3x10/ 3x10/ 3x10 sec	
T	Slow Crawl + SA Tricep Pushdowns+ DB Hammer Curls	4x30 yds /3x10/ 3x10	

Session U	DAY 2 GOLD BLOCK 3		
U	Swiss Bar Bench Press+ TGU+ Band Pull Aparts	APRE 8/ 3x3/ 3x15	
T	2 Block Clean Pull + KB Goblet Squat + Y Raise	3x5/ 3x3/ 3x10	
L	BB Bulgarian Split Squat +Banded Duck Walk +RDL	3x10/ 2x10yd/ 3x10	
U	Chin Up + Jammer Rotation + PUPP	3x10/ 3x10/ 3x10 sec	
T	Slow Crawl + Tricep Rope Pulldowns+ DB Hammer Curls	4x30 yds /3x10/ 3x10	

Session U	DAY 2 BLUE BLOCK 4		
U	Swiss Bar Bench Press+ TGU+ Band Pull Aparts	APRE 8/ 3x3/ 3x15	
T	1 Block Clean Pull + KB Goblet Squat + Y Raise	3x5/ 3x3/ 3x10	
L	BB Bulgarian Split Squat + Banded Duck Walk +RDL	3x10/ 2x10yd/3x10	
U	Chin Up + Jammer Rotation + PUPP	3x10/ 3x10/ 3x10 sec	
T	Slow Crawl + Tricep Rope Pulldowns+ DB Hammer Curls	4x30 yds /3x10/ 3x10	

Level 3: Varsity (Starters/key athletes)

Level 3 athletes are under significant stress during the sport season. This group will likely battle injuries and fatigue as the season progresses. This group requires constant attention and monitoring due to the stress of the season. It is important to monitor and limit load when necessary and seek opportunities to increase intensities when appropriate. These athletes have two regular training days per week that are modified with volume and intensity reductions. There is also a third day that would be more geared toward technique and activation.

Table 9.3: Sample Level 2 routine

Session L	DAY 3 BLOCK 0	Week 1 Volume	
L	Eccentric MB Box Squat + Banded Side Walk + Face Pulls	5x10 /2x10 yd/ 3x10	Slow 6 sec down
U	Barbell Push-up + Seated Rope Sled Pull + Deadbug	3x10/ 3x20 yds/ 3x10	
T	PVC Hang Jump Shrug + Hurdle Over/Unders + JGXT Inverted Row	3x5/ 3 rounds/ 3x10	
L	BW Box Step Up + Hurdle 1&2 in each hole + Curl Up	3x10/ 3 rounds/ 3x10 - 10 sec hold	
U	DB Half Kneeling Military Press + Manual Iso Neck+ DB Shrugs	3x10/3x10- 5 sec hold/ 3x10	
Session L	DAY 3 BLOCK 1 WHITE		
L	Eccentric KB Goblet Squat+ Banded Side Walk+ Face Pulls	4x6 /2x10 yd/ 3x10	Slow 6 sec down
U	DB Bench Press+ SA Row + Dead Bug	3x10/ 3x12/ 3x10	
T	4 Block Clean Pull+ Hurdle Over/Unders + Inverted Row	3x5/ 3 rounds / 3x10	
L	BW Box Step Up + Hurdle 1&2 in each hole + Curl Up	3x10/ 3 rounds/ 3x10 - 10 sec hold	
U	DB Half Kneeling Military Press + Manual Iso Neck+ BB Shrugs	3x10/3x10- 5 sec hold/ 3x10	
Session L	DAY 3 BLOCK 2 GRAY		
L	Front Squat+ Banded Side Walk+ Face Pulls	APRE 8 /2x10 yd/ 3x10	
U	DB Bench Press+ SA Row + Dead Bug	3x10/ 3x12/ 3x10	
T	3 Block Clean Pull+ Hurdle Over/Unders + Inverted Row	3x5/ 3 rounds/ 3x10	
L	DB Front Box Step Up + Hurdle 1&2 in each hole+ Curl Up	3x10/ 3 rounds/ 3x10 - 10 sec hold	
U	Landmine Press+ Manual Iso Neck+ BB Shrugs	3x10/3x10- 5 sec hold/ 3x10	
Session L	DAY 3 BLOCK 3 GOLD		
L	Front Squat+Banded Side Walk+ Face Pulls	APRE 8/2x10 yd/ 3x10	
U	DB Bench Press+ SA Row + Dead Bug	3x10/ 3x12/ 3x10	
T	2 Block Snatch Pull+ Hurdle Over/Unders + Weighted Inverted Row	3x5/ 3 rounds/ 3x10	
L	BB Box Step Up + Hurdle 1&2 in each hole + Curl Up	3x10/ 3 rounds/ 3x10 - 10 sec hold	
U	Landmine Press+Manual Iso Neck+ BB Shrugs	3x10/3x10- 5 sec hold/ 3x10	
Session L	DAY 3 BLOCK 4 BLUE		
L	Back Squat+Banded Side Walk+ Face Pulls	APRE 8/2x10 yd/ 3x10	
U	DB Bench Press+ SA Row + Dead Bug	3x10/ 3x12/ 3x10	
T	1 Block Snatch Pull+ Hurdle Over/Unders + Weighted Inverted Row	3x5/ 3 rounds/ 3x10	
L	BB Box Step Up + Hurdle 1&2 in each hole+ Curl Up	3x10/ 3 rounds/ 3x10 - 10 sec hold	
U	Landmine Press + Manual Iso Neck+ BB Shrugs	3x10/3x10 - 5 sec hold/ 3x10	

Stress Management

Reduction of Exercises

One very simple method to reduce volume is to eliminate tiers. This allows the coach to differentiate between off-season and in-season students in the same class or group. Eliminating tiers automatically reduces the volume significantly by reducing the number of exercises to be completed. Reducing exercises during a sport season is a sound strategy to account for the stress that athletes experience at that time. There should be an emphasis on major core movements in the first three tiers.

Reduction of Sets

Another method of reducing physical stress is reducing the volume of workout or individual tier. For example, an off-season program may call for 5 sets of 5, whereas an in-season program may be reduced to 3 sets of 5. Completing 3 sets of 5 reduces 10 reps from the exercise. This simple method can be a very effective way to reduce stress and accommodate multiple sport participation.

Intensity Reduction

Intensity can be measured in many different ways, but the most tangible would be reducing the percentage of the athlete's 1RM. Reducing the intensity of the exercise and working in lighter ranges allows the athlete to maintain strength without inducing unnecessary fatigue. There must be stress in order to elicit an adaptation and this can still be accomplished in-season, but it is important to not stress the athlete beyond capacity. This is extremely important with school-aged athletes who have a tendency to eat, sleep, and hydrate very poorly during their teenage years.

Exercise Modification

Exercise modification is another valuable tool in which stress can be reduced for the multi-sport athlete. Although a number of strategies may be used, the SCP can apply modifications such as eliminating the catch from Olympic movements, restricting range of motion on upper body movements, or restricting range of motion on lower body movements.

Movement Training & Conditioning

Multi-sport athletes often spend a lot of time sprinting at full speed and conditioning during sport practice and competitions. The SCP must take this into consideration when implementing a speed, agility, or conditioning program with a multi-sport athlete. It is very easy to over-train a multi-sport athlete with high levels of conditioning, so it is important to communicate regularly with the sport coach about this.

The movement training emphasis for an in-season athlete should be on technical proficiency. Rather than performing long-duration conditioning drills that create large amounts of fatigue, short bouts of high-quality sprinting or acceleration work are more appropriate here. The SCP should keep in mind that it is not necessary to have everyone in a group or class perform the same exact workout. It is totally acceptable (and even encouraged) to have a group of off-season athletes doing one workout while a separate group of in-season athletes do a different workout. These athletes are at different points in their training cycles, so they should be performing different workouts. Some coaches feel as though they are being too "soft" on the in-season athletes, but that is not the case. Creating workouts that are appropriate for each athlete and situation is what is most important and needs to be understood by everyone involved.

It wouldn't make sense to do an intense conditioning workout with a football player on game day because it could have a negative impact on his ability to compete. Likewise, it isn't appropriate to have an in-season middle distance track runner perform conditioning drills in class during the school day. When training a multi-sport athlete, it is important to understand how training fits into the overall schedule.

Conclusion

Training the multi-sport athlete can be a very complex endeavor, but it can pay long-term dividends when done correctly. It is important to have an easily adaptable plan, and an open line of communication with everyone involved. The SCP must understand that his or her program is one small piece of the overall puzzle, and it must fit into a plan that moves each athlete forward. When all factors are taken into consideration, the multi-sport athlete can make progress without over-taxing the system. This will lead to long-term success and a healthy athlete who is far more likely to actually look forward to training.

References

1. McArdle W, Katch F, Katch V. *Exercise Physiology: Nutrition, Energy, and Human Performance.* Baltimore, MD: Lippincott Williams & Wilkins; 2010.

2. Kenn J. The TIER System: A Systematic Program Design Model. Paper presented at: Hammer Strength Clinic; May 19-20, 2002, 2002; Cincinnati, Ohio.

CHAPTER 10

Neck Strengthening

Greg Pyszczynski

Objectives

- Understand the importance of specific neck strengthening to help prevent injury

- Be able to incorporate various forms of neck strengthening into any program, including isometric, manual resistance, resistance band, machine resistance, and weight plate/medicine ball resistance

- Incorporate trapezius strengthening to further augment other forms of neck training

Introduction

The strength and conditioning professional (SCP) has the responsibility to prepare athletes for the rigors and demands of sport play. The development of the head, neck, and trapezius muscles is critical when dealing with contact or collision-sport athletes. Strengthening these areas is important for all athletes regardless of the sport and has become increasingly important with the relatively recent increase in scrutiny surrounding prevention of concussion. The benefits of training the neck complex include protecting the athlete from injury, enhancing the ability to move the head quickly, and improving respiratory system function through improved head and airway positioning.

Strengthening the Neck Complex

The neck complex can be trained in a variety of ways using different equipment and machines to provide resistance. It should be noted that a high-quality neck machine can be considered the "gold standard" for strengthening this area because it allows the SCP to quantify and individualize each rep/set and provide a systematic progressive overload of the musculature. Unfortunately, many SCPs do not have access to even one high-quality neck machine, let alone enough units to efficiently train an entire team. Because of this limitation, this chapter will outline several alternative training methods than can be used to safely and effectively train the neck. This includes training the neck in flexion, extension, and lateral flexion as well as the muscles responsible for head protrusion/retraction, scapular elevation/depression, and scapular retraction. Although rotation is another motion of the cervical spine, because it can be so difficult and dangerous to overload, it is not typically trained.

There are seven modes of safely and effectively training the neck that will be discussed in this chapter. While there are certainly other modes, bracing, braced movements, isometric bracing, neck machines, manual resistance, bands, and free weights are used most frequently. This order also provides a basic structure for the progression/regression of exercises. In general, the SCP should begin a neck training program teaching the concept of non-resisted bracing. Once bracing is understood, non-resisted braced movements should be performed. When the athlete is proficient at performing non-resisted braced movements, resistance can be applied isometrically to the braced positions. After that, the SCP will decide which method is most appropriate for the situation. This will depend on the available equipment, maturity of the athlete, and personal preferences of the SCP.

The rest of this chapter will be organized into seven sections discussing the main training modes described above, with each section describing how to train each movement – flexion, extension, lateral flexion and protraction/retraction. After that, shrugging and scapular movements will be discussed and the chapter will conclude with sample training routines. Keep in mind that the SCP does not have to choose the same mode for all movements. For example, flexion and extension could be trained using manual resistance while lateral flexion is trained with isometric bracing and protraction/retraction trained with bands.

Bracing

Bracing consists of creating tension throughout the neck complex as if preparing to absorb the shock of a collision. The athlete essentially needs to learn how to flex the neck musculature and maintain this tension for a period of time. This is the first step in a quality neck strengthening program and should be taken seriously. For maximum development and effectiveness, it is important for the athlete to learn how to activate and utilize the neck musculature.

Figure 10.1: Neck bracing

Figure 10.1 shows a braced neck complex. Notice how different the structure appears when it is fully engaged. The platysma, which is a thin, broad sheet of muscle fibers extending from the collarbone to the jaw, is activated in bracing and much more visible than in a relaxed state. Although not required, a mirror allows an athlete to see the bracing take place in a neutral position. The mirror allows the athlete to actually see the platysma contract, which is an excellent visual cue to reinforce the proper braced position. Once bracing can be maintained for at least ten seconds, the athlete is ready to move on to braced movements.

Braced Movements

Braced movement is nothing more than slowly moving the head/neck through different ranges of motion while holding the braced state. Because no partner or outside resistance is required for braced movements, many SCP call this type of training "self-serve." The four self-serve movements that can be performed with bracing include neck flexion, neck extension, neck lateral flexion, and head protraction/retraction.

It is again recommended to teach the athlete braced movements while watching in a mirror, as the visual feedback can help ensure that tension is maintained and that the movements are being done is a slow, deliberate manner. Each movement should take about 2-3 seconds to move in one direction. There should be a one second pause in the fully contracted position before taking another 2-3 seconds to return to the original position. This pace will feel slow and deliberate, and it becomes difficult to maintain the tension of the fully braced position.

Braced movements are typically done for time (i.e. 20 seconds), but can also be done for a specific number of reps. Initially, it may be difficult to maintain the braced position for very long, so the athlete should begin with one set of each movement for just 10 seconds. Over time, the athlete should slowly progress to longer durations (up to 60 seconds) and use additional sets.

Braced Flexion & Extension

Starting from a neutral, braced position, the athlete should lead the chin downward until contact is made with the upper chest as seen in Figure 10.2. A common coaching cue is to "drive the chin to the chest." At this point, the athlete should continue to drive the chin through the upper chest for one second. This will force the athlete to pause in the fully contracted position for one second before returning to the neutral position and finally into full neck extension as seen in Figure 10.3. Coaching cues for extension are "look above your eyebrows" or "chin up and away."

Figure 10.2: Braced flexion

Figure 10.3: Braced extension

Points of emphasis for braced flexion & extension include establishing and maintaining a braced position, maintaining neutral body position, maintaining constant tension through the neck & platysma, and using a full ROM without forcing the head into a painful position.

Braced Lateral Flexion

When engaging in braced lateral flexion, the athlete will begin in neutral head position then bring the starting side ear toward the same shoulder as shown in Figure 10.4. Again, the athlete will pause for one second at the furthest range of motion specific to the individual. Most athletes will be able to complete 20-45 degrees of motion from the neutral position. Each athlete

Figure 10.4: Braced lateral flexion

will have a unique ROM dictated by anatomical structures. Never force an athlete into an uncomfortable position.

The athlete should move the head slowly through this side-to-side motion, pausing at each end of the ROM. Additionally, the athlete should attempt to limit rotation so that the chin always points forward. Coaching cues include "squeeze the ear toward the shoulder" and "keep the face parallel to the mirror or wall." Points of emphasis include establishing and maintaining the braced position, maintaining a neutral body position, avoiding head rotation, and maintaining tension through the neck & platysma.

Braced Protraction/Retraction

The athlete will begin this movement by pulling the head straight back into retraction, forming a "double chin" before pushing the chin forward as seen in Figure 10.5. The athlete should pause at each end of the motion while maintaining constant tension. One coaching cue is to tell the athlete to act as though a table is under the chin, and he/she is trying to push a box across the table with the chin. Another cue is to tell the athlete to act as though he/she is reaching over a pie trying to get a sniff.

Figure 10.5: Braced protraction

Figure 10.6: Braced retraction

Coaching cues for this movement include "reach the chin, then form a double-chin," "slide the chin across the table then bring it back," or "sniff the pie." Points of emphasis include establishing and maintaining the braced position, maintaining a neutral body position, sliding the chin forward and back without dropping the head into flexion, and maintaining tension through the neck & platysma.

Braced Isometric (Static) Holds

Once the athlete is able to perform these braced movements, isometric, or static, holds should be incorporated, and resistance can quickly be added to these holds. Because the athlete will already be familiar with bracing and braced movements, progressing to isometric holds should be very easy to coach.

To perform any braced isometric hold, the athlete should start in the neutral position, move into the fully contracted position of a braced movement (i.e. flexion, extension, lateral flexion or protraction/retraction), and hold that position for a specified amount of time (progress from 10-60 seconds in each position). Because the athlete has slowly progressed to this point by learning bracing and braced movements, he or she should quickly become proficient at holding these positions with tension. At this point, the athlete is ready to add resistance to the hold.

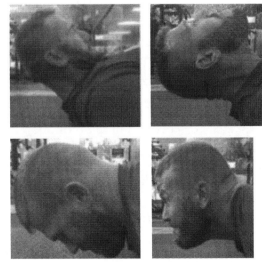

Figure 10.7: Braced isometric holds

The athlete should begin with the head in neutral while a partner places a hand on the head to create tension in the neck. The athlete should push his or her head into the partner's hand, but the head should not move. The partner should basically be an "immovable object" that the athlete is pushing against. Some SCPs prefer to add resistance at different points in the ROM. The position at which the resistance is applied is up to the SCP, but the neutral position is the most common because this is the position an athlete is usually trying to maintain during competition.

The amount of pressure will vary greatly at each position, but the athlete should attempt to push the head into the partner's hand as hard as possible to create the greatest training effect. Partners should provide constant feedback to the trainee to encourage effort throughout the hold. This is a pre-cursor to the next progression of neck strengthening, so it is important for an athlete to learn how slowly and deliberately apply pressure through the neck musculature.

Once isometric holds can be performed for 60 seconds at each position, the SCP can decide which mode to utilize to further progress the training process. To stimulate further development, additional resistance through a range of motion will be necessary, so the SCP will need to incorporate a more advanced training progression, which may include manual resistance, neck machine resistance, resistance bands, or free weights. Regardless of which modes are available, it is up to the SCP to decide which mode is most appropriate for his or her situation.

Manual Resistance

Manual resistance (MR) is one of the options for progressing into resisted movements. One of the main benefits of MR is that it can be done anywhere, anytime, without any equipment. It is absolutely critical, however, that the person providing the resistance **must** be fully knowledgeable of the rules of manual resistance and how to safely apply resistance to a partner.

In order to maximize safety, efficiency and effectiveness, it is critical for both the partner and the athlete to understand the MR guidelines. In a perfect setting, the qualified SCP would provide resistance to every athlete, however this is not always realistic, and athletes will often need to learn how to work with each other. Therefore, it is recommended that the SCP perform MR with each trainee 2-4 times before that person is allowed to spot a fellow trainee. This will help provide a thorough understanding of the MR guidelines and a better understanding of how MR feels in order to better train his or her teammates. If manual resistance is going to be an important part of the SCP's overall program, the MR guidelines should be posted visibly throughout the facility in order to be constantly read and discussed. This will help maintain a high level of success and accountability.

Manual Resistance Guidelines

Dan Riley is often credited with introducing the concept of manual resistance to neck strengthening to SCPs in the United States. Riley referred to the partner who provides resistance as the spotter, while the athlete performing the exercise is referred to as the lifter. Both the spotter and the lifter must understand the manual resistance training guidelines before starting a manual resistance exercise. The first repetition is not an all-out effort, but effort must increase for every subsequent repetition. Maximum effort should be given on every rep after the first 2-3 reps. The spotter should provide an appropriate amount of resistance to induce momentary muscular fatigue by 6-12 reps.

The spotter should allow the lifter to perform each repetition at the same pace throughout the set. This will require different amounts of pressure by the spotter during the rep (due to changes in lever arm length). The lifter will feel as though the resistance is similar at all joint angles (the resistance will feel smooth). It will also require the spotter to gradually reduce the resistance as fatigue sets in during the set.

A good repetition should require 2-3 seconds to move the body part concentrically. Next, there will be a 1-2 second pause with tension at the "top" of the movement. Lastly, the eccentric portion should take 4-5 seconds with control and constant tension. The spotter must make sure that the lifter generates more force during the eccentric phase of each repetition. The lifter should continually contract target musculature during the concentric and eccentric phase of every repetition. The lifter should feel like he or she is constantly trying to raise the involved body part.

The spotter must give feedback to the lifter to ensure there is always a constant contraction on every repetition performed. The spotter should identify any relaxation or loss of force by the lifter during the movement. The lifter should tell the spotter if more or less tension is needed. Additionally, the lifter should pause with pressure against the spotter's resistance at the top of every movement. Pausing with pressure and no relaxation is difficult, but an important part of the process.

The spotter should ensure the lifter is applying force at the top of the movement before slowly easing into the lowering phase of the exercise. Slowly easing into the lowering phase of the movement increases the safety of the movement. The set is completed when the athlete reaches momentary muscular failure, or cannot perform another repetition.

The SCP should emphasize a number of points for all manual resistance trained movements. First, the athlete should maintain tension on the structure throughout the repetition. Next, the spotter must adjust application of force as fatigue occurs and momentary musculature failure is achieved. Both the lifter and the spotter must continually communicate both verbally and non-verbally in order for resistance to be optimal throughout the entire range of motion being performed. The spotter should maintain pressure at the pausing points (top and bottom positions of the movement).

Specifically, a number of movements can effectively strengthen the musculature of the neck using manual resistance. This includes manual resistance neck flexion, manual resistance neck extension, and manual resistance neck lateral flexion. These movements will not only help develop concentric strength, but also significantly reduce the likelihood of injury from eccentric load as often encountered in athletic participation.

Manual Resistance Neck Flexion

Manual resistance neck flexion can be performed from a supine/supported position or progressed to a seated/non-supported position. The supported position protects the athlete from accidently being forced into hyper-extension if the athlete completely relaxes or if the spotter does not sense the lifter is at the point of fatigue. Conversely, the unsupported position allows for greater ROM and requires better neuromuscular control and endurance, so some SCPs may feel that it is beneficial.

In addition to positional progressions, resistance application can be modified, as well. The spotter can utilize a two-hand "cupped" hand placement to stabilize both the head and the chin or a single hand placement on the forehead alone. Athletes who are inexperienced or otherwise uncomfortable with manual resistance training typically prefer the supported position with the cupped chin hand placement, as it typically accommodates easier control for the athlete.

The cupped hand placement also seems to work better for less experienced spotters because pressure can be felt in both hands. The forehead position is not necessarily an advanced position, however athletes who have had more experience with manual resistance tend to do a better job with this position as they are aware of the pattern being trained.

Figure 10.8: Manual resistance neck flexion (single hand placement)

Supported positions are favorable when first starting manual resistance training as they help to protect the athlete from over-extension. When first initiating manual resistance, the athlete's ability to fully brace and maintain throughout the set is usually very challenging. It may take time for the spotter to learn how to "feel" when the athlete is on the verge of reaching momentary muscular failure. Learning to apply manual resistance appropriately is an acquired skill that takes time to develop.

Manual Resistance Neck Extension

Neck extension can either be performed in a supported quadruped position ("all-fours") or prone on a bench. Both are performed in the same manner, so it is a matter of personal preference and equipment availability. Likewise, spotter position can be selected from two options, as well. First, the spotter can position him or herself at the lifter's side with one hand cupping the back of the skull and the opposite hand maintaining light pressure on the middle of the back. Alternatively, the superior or front position involves positioning near the crown of the lifter's head with both palms on the lifter's upper posterior skull.

Figure 10.9: Manual resistance neck extension

Both positions are acceptable as long as the spotter applies pressure evenly in an arching path and allows the athlete to achieve maximum extension at the top of each rep. The back of the head should go slightly past the neutral position at the bottom of each rep but should not be forced into extreme flexion as this can increase the risk of injury.

The lifter should lift the head upward as high as possible as if looking at the sky. There should be a distinct pause at the top of the movement with an isometric hold for 1-2 seconds. The spotter should then apply more pressure as the lifter resists until the head reaches the bottom/starting position (slightly past parallel) of the movement. The lifter should never relax in the bottom position. Instead, he or she should constantly attempt to raise the head throughout the set.

Manual Resistance Lateral Flexion

It is strongly urged that those committing to train manual resistance lateral flexion have considerable knowledge and understanding of the ranges of motion and the unique aspects of lateral neck flexion. Lateral flexion ROM ranges from 20-45 degrees, however range of motion is highly individualized. Because of this, an understanding of the individual is critical, as not all athletes will have the same range of motion.

Manual resistance lateral neck flexion can be performed with the lifter either in sidelying or seated upright. In sidelying, the lifter lays on one side while the spotter places his or her hand or hands on the lateral aspect of the lifter's head just above the temple. The lifter should begin from the neutral position and forcefully press into the spotter's hand(s). This helps the spotter feel the lifter's ROM. After a momentary pause at the fully contracted position, the spotter should gently push the lifter's head back to the neutral position. It is recommended to stop this movement at the neutral position. After the lifter completes all reps, the exercise should be repeated on the other site.

From the seated position, the lifter should sit tall on a bench with the spotter positioned behind. The spotter should place one hand on the lateral aspect of the lifter's head just above the temple. The spotter should position his or her opposite foot on the bench with the leg placed firmly against the lifter's shoulder/arm. This leg will help provide support for the lifter as he or she applies pressure. Beginning from the neutral position, the athlete should then press the head against the spotter's hand. After a momentary isometric pause at the fully contracted position, the spotter should gently push the lifter's head back to the neutral position. As in the prone version, it is recommended to stop this movement at the neutral position to avoid any dangerous positions.

Figure 10.10: Manual resistance lateral flexion

The lifter should complete all reps then repeat the exercise on the other side.

Manual resistance is an excellent way to strengthen the neck, but there are certainly limitations. For example, the spotter must be able to apply pressure safely and effectively. Additionally, there is no real way to accurately measure how much pressure is applied, just as there is no accurate way to track strength development over time or a way to guarantee progressive overload. However, the addition of manual resistance neck exercise is beneficial despite these shortcomings.

Neck Machine Movements

As stated earlier, a high-quality neck machine is considered the gold standard for strengthening the neck because it allows the SCP to individualize and track the load used on each rep and set. This allows for a slow and systematic overload of the muscles and motions. Because each machine is slightly different, proper set-up for each exercise is crucial. This should be a priority for any SCP with access to neck resistance training machines. The SCP is advised to consult the specific equipment manufacturer and/or other SCPs about how to properly use each piece of equipment prior to implementing these exercises into any routine or program.

The following section shows the main movements performed on a high-quality neck machine, including machine neck flexion, machine neck extension, and machine neck lateral flexion.

Machine Neck Flexion

The athlete should begin the machine neck flexion movement with a slightly raised chin and the head slightly behind the neutral position. The torso should be vertical, tall, and stabilized and the head pad should be "loaded at neutral." The athlete should drive the chin into the chest in a controlled manner before holding the fully contracted position isometrically for one second. The athlete should then slowly return to the start position before performing the next repetition. Maintaining slow, controlled movement with a slow transition at the beginning and end of each repetition is key to proper performance.

Figure 10.11: Machine neck flexion

Machine Neck Extension

The athlete should begin with the chin slightly forward from the neutral position with the torso vertical, tall, and stabilized. The athlete should then tilt the head backward as though looking at the ceiling. Once the end range of motion is reached, the athlete should isometrically hold the top of the movement for one second before slowly returning to the starting position slightly past neutral. Again, maintaining slow, controlled movement with a slow transition at the beginning and end of each repetition is key to proper performance.

Figure 10.11: Machine neck extension

Resistance Bands

Resistance bands are a great alternative if no equipment is available and set up is very simple. On a squat rack, the SCP should begin by setting the safety pins at a height that allows the band to just barely sit on the bench. The athlete should then lay on the bench and place the bands across the forehead. Depending on the strength of the athlete, either both or one side of the band can be utilized. The movement patterns are the same as described above in the manual resistance section. It is recommended that a supported position be utilized prior to an unsupported position. As a side note, whenever utilizing bands with neck training, band maintenance and daily safety checks prior to training are necessary to ensure there are no rips or tears in bands.

Flexion with Band

Figure 10.12: Neck flexion with band resistance

Extension with Band

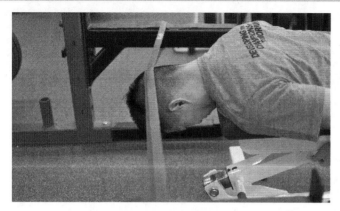

Figure 10.13: Neck extension with band resistance

Free Weights/Medicine Balls

Using free weights or medicine balls to provide resistance is not the preferred way to strengthen the neck, but it is an alternative that can be used when other equipment is unavailable. This section will show a few examples of how to use plates/balls to resist neck movements. The motions should be performed in the same manner as each movement in the manual resistance section. All movements should be slow and controlled, with a distinct pause in the fully-contracted position.

Neck Flexion with a Plate/Ball

Figure 10.14: Neck flexion with plate resistance

Neck Extension with a Plate/Ball

Figure 10.15: Neck extension with plate resistance

Protraction/Retraction with a Plate/Ball

Figure 10.16: Neck extension with med ball resistance

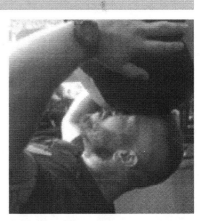

Trapezius Development

The trapezius is a large muscle that is important to develop as a part of a complete neck complex strengthening program. All shrugging variants are important; however, a number of movements have been identified as preferred due to their effectiveness and ease of implementation.

Basic Shrug with Barbell or Dumbbells

All shrugs should be completed with an up-and-down motion as the athlete attempts to raise the shoulder girdle as high as possible on each rep. There should be a distinct isometric pause at the top of every rep.

Single-Arm Shrug

The upper trapezius needs resistance on the occiput and back of skull for optimal development. This is achieved through the head protracted single arm shrug. The head protracted single arm shrug should be performed while sitting on a box or a bench and the athlete should fix the non-involved side by grasping the bench in order to keep the torso vertical and the chest up. With the opposite hand, the athlete should grasp the dumbbell, shrugging for maximum height. As with other exercises, the athlete should incorporate a brief 1-2 second isometric hold at the top of the movement.

Figure 10.17: Single-arm shrug

Scapular Retraction

One movement particularly well suited to develop the lower trapezius is scapular retraction, sometimes called the Kelso shrug. An underhand grip on either a band, barbell, or 3-way row machine should be utilized. The athlete should take the grip and retract the scapulae fully before completing a full rowing motion. The scapular retraction and row are separated into distinct movements using a four count: 1) retract scapulae, 2) row (concentric), 3) return (eccentric), 4) relax scapulae. The athlete should again pause in the fully retracted position for an isometric hold before slowly returning to the start position.

Figure 10.18: Row with scapular retraction

Head Nod & Tilt

The final movements to be considered are the head nod and tilt. These movements are very small and require great concentration on the part of the athlete. There is no actual neck movement in either of these motions; they are simply movements that rotate the skull around the spine. The tilt consists of pushing the jaw slightly forward and upward without letting the neck to extend backwards. It is basically a chin lift. Meanwhile, the nod is essentially the opposite of the tilt. It is a slight chin tuck without allowing the neck to flex forward. Both of these movements activate the small positional muscles responsible for subtle skull and cervical spine movements and stabilization. These movements can be performed with no resistance at all or can be resisted using all of the modes described previously.

Sample Programming

Day 1	Day 2	Day 3
Neck – Flexion	Neck – Extension	Neck – Lateral Flexion
Head – Nod	Neck – Protraction	Head – Tilt
Trap – SA Shrug, Low Row	Trap – OH Shrug variant	Trap – SA OH Shrug Variant, Low row

Day 1	Day 2	Day 3	Day 4
Neck – Flexion	Neck – Extension	Head – Nod & Tilt	Neck – Lateral Flexion
Trap – SA Shrug	Neck – Protraction	Trap – SA OH Shrug	Trap – DA Shrug
Trap – DA OH Shrug	Trap – Low Row	Trap – Shrug to Lat. Raise	Trap – Low Row

Day 1	Day 2
Neck – Flexion & Extension	Neck – Lateral Flexion
Neck – Protraction (gives full Ext. ROM)	Head – Tilt & Nod
Trap – SA Shrug, OH Shrug variant, Low Row	Trap – SA OH variant, DA Shrug, Low Row

PRINCIPLES of ATHLETIC
Strength & Conditioning

The Foundations of Success in
Training and Developing
the Complete Athlete

CHAPTER 11

Injury Prevention

Selena Budge

Objectives

- Be able to discern common myths from facts regarding athletic injury risk

- Understand the primary differences between traditional strength training programs and contemporary injury risk-reduction programming

- Be able to effectively develop a comprehensive injury risk-reduction program to help protect athletes from common sources of athletic injury

- Be able to progress training in an injury risk-reduction program to ensure optimal athlete adaptations and improvements

Introduction

Athletic injury is the wildcard that can undermine months of sport preparation and training in an instant. Subtraction of a single athlete due to injury can cost a team irreplaceable skilled performance and leadership while also upsetting the delicate blend of team chemistry. In a fraction of a second, one missed step, improper positioning, or unfortunate break can change a season's trajectory. The cost of injury goes far beyond physical. It can take an emotional, psychological, and financial toll on the athlete. Additionally, every injury has lasting implications for long-term joint health and sustainability.

There is still a persistent, pervasive, and inaccurate belief that injury is usually the result of "bad luck" that seems difficult to overcome for the strength and conditioning professional (SCP). By extension, under this commonly-held notion, athletes who are often injured are labelled as victims who are the helpless recipients of the undesirable effects of being born "injury-prone." However, decreasing any athlete's risk of injury is more controllable than many SCP's may recognize. However, staying healthy is a skill and should be developed like any other sport skill that athlete's train for. Successful injury prevention programming requires the same effort, evaluation, analysis and implementation as other aspects of sports performance and preparation.

Injury Myths

There are a number of myths surrounding injury that continue to impede progressive understanding of injury prevention. Clarification of these myths will help set the foundation for creation of successful injury prevention programs.

Myth #1: Injury Risk Cannot be Assessed

Truth: Injury Risk CAN be Assessed

More specifically, non-contact injury risk can be assessed. A non-contact injury is an injury that is sustained in the absence of contact with an external force (object or another athlete). An ACL injury that occurs directly after cutting, pivoting, or landing (without additional player contact) is an example of a non-contact injury. Many non-contact injuries are the result of inadequate mobility/flexibility, strength, and neuromuscular control. The result of these inadequacies is faulty biomechanics that result in high risk positioning, often leaving the athlete out of position and unable to stabilize appropriately.

In the case of non-contact injuries there are often what are referred to a "biomechanical sleeper issues." This is a movement pattern displayed by an athlete that lends to a high-risk injury environment but has not yet manifested as an actual injury. Sleeper issues can also manifest as multiple minor injuries prior to catastrophic injury. If these issues can be accurately identified early, they can provide valuable information regarding an athlete's likelihood for injury, as well as the type of injury that might pose the biggest risk to the athlete.

Myth #2: Injury Risk Cannot be Reduced

Truth: Injury Risk CAN be Reduced

Again, specifically in the case of non-contact injuries, several factors contribute to risk for injury, many of which are modifiable.

Injury Risk Factors

Figure 11.1: Modifiable vs. non-modifiable risk factors

Modifiable	Non-Modifiable
Biomechanics	Hormones
Neuromuscular control	Maturation
Strength	Joint laxity
Flexibility/mobility	Anatomic variants
	Genetic risk factors
	Gender

In many cases, modifiable factors may have a much larger contribution to injury occurrence than non-modifiable factors. What is more, modifiable risk factors are all under the control of the athlete and the SCP, meaning that training can serve to improve these factors and thereby reduce the likelihood of injury. This is also ideal because it suggests that the identification and resolution of modifiable risk factors can alter an athlete's injury trajectory. For example, anterior cruciate ligament (ACL) rupture is one of the most common and physically devastating injuries for the competitive athlete. However, athletes at risk for ACL injury can be identified and their risk significantly reduced through an appropriate injury risk reduction (IRR) program.

Myth #3: If an Athlete Gets Injured, He or She Will be Injured Again

Truth: This is a More Complicated Myth with Several Caveats

While it is true that one injury can increase the likelihood for another injury, this blanket statement can be a misleading. Research suggests that almost 30% of athletes suffer a second ACL tear within the first two years of returning to sports.[1] It is obviously advantageous to avoid catastrophic injury altogether, however, when injury does occur, there are a number of actions athletes can take to mitigate their risk for future injury. The athlete must work intentionally in order to stay healthy throughout the remainder of their career. Consistent compliance to the appropriate IRR program can result in a long, relatively healthy career. In fact, some athletes demonstrate improved biomechanics (compared to some uninjured athletes) after returning from injury because time spent in rehabilitation can help improve inadequate or inappropriate movement patterns. While it is ideal to implement an IRR program as a preventative measure, it is imperative the athlete with a history of injury to participate in preventative and maintenance exercise to combat any increased risk of injury.

Myth #4: A Good Strength Program Will Prevent Injury

Truth: This is Often the Most Controversial of Myths

An improperly designed strength program will definitely contribute to injury; however, a well-designed strength program is no guarantee to prevent all injuries. To be clear, a solid strength foundation is absolutely necessary to combat injury. Strength alone is not enough. Even athletes who participate in excellent strength programs are still at risk for injury. Acute dynamic injuries (e.g. ACL injury) continue to occur despite superior strength, explosiveness, and athleticism. If strength alone were adequate in preventing acute non-contact dynamic injuries, one would assume that strong athletes would not get injured. However, there are numerous examples of strong, elite-level, highly-trained and highly-explosive athletes who still suffer non-contact ACL injuries. Strong athletes do not continue to experience ACL injuries because absolute muscular strength is lacking, but most often because the neurologic control necessary to recruit muscles appropriately is inadequately developed. In the presence of adequate strength, ACL and other such acute dynamic injuries are often the result of a timing issue (the speed at which the injury occurs vs. the speed at which the muscle is recruited to react). A supplemental IRR program is required in addition to strength programming in order to address this timing gap and prevent acute dynamic injury.

Specifically, ACL rupture occurs rapidly following the initial aggravating non-contact incident. The ACL is torn within 100 milliseconds (ms) (most occurring between 50-100 ms) following the cut/pivot/landing event. Exercises that focus on enhancing strength, power and explosiveness (squats, hang cleans, etc.) are motor cortex driven. It takes at least 120 ms for the motor cortex to send a signal to a muscle to activate following an injurious stimulus. This 120 ms (at best) reaction time lends to an unfortunate timing gap between when the ACL is rupturing and how quickly the muscle(s) can be activated to stabilize the joint.

The timing of this sequence demonstrates the reason why strong athletes still get injured. Once this sequence is set in motion, the strength of the muscle becomes inconsequential because the window of opportunity to prevent the ACL rupture through dynamic stabilization via the hamstrings is closed before the muscles can react. This timing mismatch is the reason additional IRR exercises are required to supplement traditional strength training exercises. Exercises maximizing strength and power will not necessarily prevent injury, and exercises intended to prevent injury will not necessarily lead to significant strength and power gains, thus, the two must be done in collaboration for best results.

Injury risk-reduction exercises should be primarily cerebellar-driven and employed to address the previously discussed timing mismatch. Cerebellar-driven exercises, also referred to Stability Enhancement Systems (SES) train faster muscle activation pathways as compared to motor cortex-driven exercises. SES exercises are stability-based exercises that utilize cerebellar muscle activation pathways with latencies between 50-80 ms. This faster reaction time enables the muscle to be activated and to stabilize the joint during a timeframe where the ligament is exposed to potentially injurious load but not yet injured. Appropriate dynamic stabilization via muscular action during this window of risk is paramount in preventing a potential injury from progressing and mitigating damages.

Strength training programs are an essential component of injury prevention in that they can assist athletes in avoiding compromising positions, but strength alone is not the answer. It is vital for athletes to develop adequate stability (through SES training programs) to supplement strength and address the injury timing gap. The combination of a well-executed strength and IRR program can significantly improve an athlete's chances of staying relatively healthy and promote maximum sport performance.

Myth #5: Athletes Who Are More Athletic Are Less Likely to be Injured

Truth: Unfortunately, This Is Not True

In some respects, stronger, faster, more explosive athletes are likely at *higher* risk of injury if landing mechanics, stability, and/or neuromuscular control are compromised. More explosive (athletic) athletes create greater torque, and increased torque can compromise a joint if the dynamic stabilizers and/or neuromuscular control is lacking.

Strength Programs vs. Injury Risk Reduction (IRR) Programs

There are major goal, construction, theory, and progression differences between strength training programs and IRR programs. Fundamental program theory divergences emphasize the necessity for these programs to run in parallel. Neither should be used to replace the other.

Strength vs. Stability

Understanding the difference between strength and stability is paramount in developing effective IRR programs. As it relates to sport performance, strength is the ability to produce force while stability is the ability to control force. Injury risk reduction programs should focus primarily on correcting movement through enhanced joint stability. Improved joint stability is achieved through systematically and progressively training cerebellar pathways through SES exercises. While the goal of a strength program is to develop maximum strength, the goal of an SES program is to prevent injury through enhanced stability and enhanced muscle reaction time.

Figure 11.2: Strength training vs. stability enhancement systems/injury risk reduction training

STRENGTH TRAINING vs. SES/IRR TRAINING

	STRENGTH PROGRAM	SES/IRR PROGRAM
Program Goal	Sport performance	Injury reduction
Program Target	Strength, speed & explosiveness	Stability, biomechanics & neuromuscular control
Primary Muscle Activation Center Used	Motor Cortex	Cerebellum/Brainstem
Motor Response Method	Voluntary motor response	Subconscious motor response (Long loop reflexes)
Program Achievement Measure	Force Production	Balance/Stability
Program Methodology	Volume—reps/sets/weight	Proprioceptive enrichment
Susceptible to Deconditioning	Yes	Yes

Motor Cortex vs. Cerebellum

Strength programs train the athlete primarily from the motor cortex and the movements performed are a result of voluntary motor response. Use of the motor cortex and voluntary motor response utilize higher-order processing (e.g. athlete thinks about squatting and then proceeds to execute the squat). Voluntary motor response has longer latencies (120+ ms) because of this higher order processing.

SES programs, on the other hand, are controlled primarily from the cerebellum and movements are chiefly the result of sub-cortical motor response. These movements are more automatic and reactive in nature and are not processed higher (e.g. athletes balancing reactively correct to maintain balance rather than actively thinking about movements they are producing). This type of muscle activation is not processed in the motor cortex and thus has a shorter latency (50-80 ms).

Program Achievement and Methodology

There is a misconception that strength is the achievement measurement for both sport performance programs and IRR programs. Perpetuation of this myth results in ineffective IRR programs with significant inadequacies. Enhanced force production is the goal of strength training. Force production and power is achieved through progressive overload and the manipulation of repetitions/sets/weights.

Balance and stability are the goals of IRR training. It is trained through progressive proprioceptive enrichment and the manipulation of surface stability. Unstable surfaces are not typically used in strength training programs because they substantially reduce the amount of load that can be lifted and may therefore limit strength gains. The use of unstable surfaces is incongruent with the goal of strength programs (to maximize strength), which is why supplemental IRR programs are crucial. IRR programs are primarily meant to improve muscle reaction time (as it relates to injury timeframes) not strength, which is achieved though unstable surface SES training.

Injury Risk Evaluation Techniques

There are multiple injury-risk evaluation techniques available. The most challenging element of evaluation is not in conducting the test, but in interpreting the results and determining the implications. There are a few important elements to consider when choosing assessment methods. It is wise to utilize a battery of evaluation methods because no single test provides every piece of data you desire. However, for the purposes of practical implementation (as opposed to academic and research-driven projects), it is important to choose evaluation techniques that are succinct, efficient, relevant and specific/sensitive/reliable. There is a delicate balance between choosing evaluations that are comprehensive while simultaneously producing data that can be easily filtered through. For example, 3-D motion-capture is the gold standard for movement analysis—however, filtering and interpreting the data produced is cumbersome, time-intensive, and complex. As a result, it is usually far more practical to choose less detailed assessments that adequately provide relevant information, instead of being overwhelmed by a mountain of exhaustive data that may never be analyzed.

Succinctness

Time is a diminishing resource and utilizing succinct assessment methods is logistically important. Assessments that can be administered concisely provide a streamlined experience for the athlete (who may not always demonstrate the most robust attention span) and the evaluation administrator. Uncompromising time constraints and scheduling barriers can cause coaches to be protective of relinquishing time with athletes. A succinct, streamlined evaluation is significantly more palatable for time-strapped coaches. Assessment proctors also benefit from utilizing concise processes because the easier testing goes, the more likely it is to be incorporated into programming long-term.

When deciding which battery of tests to utilize, the SCP is best served by eliminating extraneous information that likely will not be used. It is best to collect only the information that is absolutely necessary during initial evaluation. Once preliminary data has been analyzed and interpreted, individual-specific assessments can be conducted as needed to follow-up on initial testing results requiring further exploration.

Efficiency

Efficient testing has two determinants—time and information. The SCP should consider if testing was efficient from an execution standpoint and if testing was efficient from an information-gathering standpoint. Like anything, efficiency of injury risk (IR) assessment execution improves with experience and frequency. There are a few key factors that will improve execution efficiency tremendously.

- Have all paperwork organized prior to testing—fill out everything that can be filled out beforehand.

- Be well-versed on the evaluation you are administering and how to explain it. Practice phrasing instructions—be simple, complete, direct and objective. Consistency in instruction-delivery will be helpful in streamlining the evaluation process. It may be beneficial for some administrators to write out instructions and directly read them to athletes.

- If available, an assistant is key—an additional person who can manipulate testing equipment (many tests require multiple equipment configurations) and take notes is a tremendous asset and exponentially improves efficiency. It is not necessary for the assistant to possess a complete understand of testing; however, it is imperative that he or she understand the overall testing protocol. It is beneficial to run through a few practice evaluation sessions so that the assistant can become familiar with the testing process/flow and evaluator nuances. An ill-prepared testing assistant is worse than no assistant. Evaluators must be diligent in sufficiently preparing any assistant.

- The SCP should test teams in groups rather than individually. Testing in groups of approximately 8-20 (depending on the SCP's comfort/familiarity with the testing process) is ideal from an efficiency perspective. In general, there is a point of diminishing returns with larger groups. The combination of increased distractions and athlete wait-time can often lead to systematic breakdown and overall inefficiency. For example, if the evaluation being administered has five different movement components, the proctor should explain/demonstrate the first movement, then each athlete should perform that movement. This process should then be duplicated for all subsequent movement components. This system minimizes repetition of directions and minimizes confusion/questions (athletes who were not paying attention during instruction can watch teammates ahead of them perform the movement). This approach also minimizes equipment configuration manipulation.

- If testing requires equipment (it typically does) and the budget allows, purchasing multiple sets of testing equipment (2-4 sets, maximum group of 20-25 athletes) will greatly decrease exchange time between athletes and benefit overall efficiency enormously.

- Athletes often have questions and want explanations during the evaluation (e.g. "What do those numbers mean? What are you looking for?"). Questions pertinent to correct testing execution should be addressed immediately, while non-essential athlete inquiries should be deferred until testing is complete.

Efficient information-gathering is crucial in selecting the battery of tests used in an IR evaluation. The SCP should choose the minimum combination of assessments (approximately 2-4 depending on the sport) that return the maximum breadth of relevant information and supplement the shortcomings of one another. While some information redundancy amongst assessments is helpful in reducing error, test combination arrangements should support unique value added by each assessment. The comprehensive synthesis of unique, complimentary data provided by each assessment will facilitate the most useful injury-risk profiles for each athlete. In general, the specific combination of injury-risk assessments should collectively provide objective measures regarding functional flexibility/mobility, functional strength imbalances, functional neuromuscular control/stability, and sport/speed-specific biomechanics. All of these elements help inform one another and ultimately explain the movement patterns an athlete has adopted.

Relevance

Specific injury-risk evaluation combinations should be relevant to the movement patterns and injury trends of the given sport. It is crucial to have at least one assessment that captures the athlete in sport-specific conditions (e.g. basketball athlete jumping, soccer athlete cutting, etc.). Creating an assessment that mimics sport-like conditions (speed and movement specific) is essential in deciphering an athlete's default movement patterns. Assessments that solely examine movement in a controlled, intentional, non-specific, and low-intensity environment are not sufficient in determining injury risk. These types of assessments provide useful information, but must be used as a supplement to sport/speed specific assessments in order to obtain the most-informed IR profile.

Sport/speed specific assessment of biomechanics provide the most relevant insight into an athlete's default movement patterns. Analysis of the athlete's default movement patterns offers meaningful information regarding sport injury-risk. Many athletes are able to mask high-risk biomechanics during low-intensity assessments; however, under sport-specific conditions, these sub-optimal movement patterns are revealed. Thus, it is crucial to accurate injury-risk analysis and programming to examine athletes under parameters that mimic sport demands.

Specificity, Sensitivity, and Reliability

Assessment techniques should be specific, sensitive, and reliable. Evaluation techniques that are supported in sports medicine research are ideal. There are assessment techniques with unconvincing levels of support in the literature. These may still be useful to an overall injury-risk profile when paired with other well-supported objective assessments, but sports medicine research can provide significant insight and sample methodologies for implementing injury risk evaluations. It is important to choose assessments that accurately measure what is being examined and possess strong test-retest reliability to quantify progress.

Creating an Injury Risk Reduction Program

Athlete injury-risk can be reduced through SES programs centered on resolving existing high-risk movement patterns. Faulty biomechanics are systematically corrected through specific and progressive interventions that target the development of inherent stability, which ultimately facilitates safer movement. SES programming shares certain construct principles with strength training. Similar to strength training, SES programs are specific, progressive, and gains are susceptible to regression with poor adherence. Athletes are often given the same five "injury prevention" exercises to perform over and over. No other sport skill is acquired with this static approach, and injury prevention is no different. This stagnant method will not usually trigger meaningful results. IRR programs need to be layered and cumulative in order to be effective.

Figure 11.3: Stability enhancement systems training characteristics and considerations

	SES PROGRAM CONSIDERATIONS
Program Advancement	Approximately every 2-3 weeks
Program Frequency	At least 3x/week
Program Theory	Multiple deficiencies tackled simultaneously and collaboratively
Program Progression	(1) Surface changes (2) introduction of a secondary task (3) multi-planar movement (4) increased demand dynamically (5) increase task complexity (6) Double-leg vs. single-leg
Program Time Requirement	Approximately 10-15 minutes
Program Placement	Ideally, prior to lifting or practice
Program Equipment	*BOSU, Stability Ball, Side-Stepping Band, Foam Roller*, Airex, Dyna Disc, TRX, Medicine Balls, (only italicized equipment is essential)

Mobility/Flexibility

Joint mobility and tissue flexibility impairments should be addressed initially to ensure athletes have access to the appropriate range of motion (ROM) requirements. Impaired ROM will contribute to poor movement patterns and adopted compensations. Sufficient ROM is the first building block in effective injury-risk reduction.

Strength

Any observed strength deficit or imbalances should be addressed once range of motion is normalized. SES programs should support strength achievement through adequately strengthening residual deficits in stabilizing muscle groups. Sufficient stabilizing muscle strength is an import precursor to future programming and stability development.

Stability

Stability development is the crux of SES programming and the critical element in training the faster cerebellar-driven muscle activation pathways discussed previously. It is not enough for an athlete to jump in front of a mirror 20 times trying to "keep their knees out." Athletes are not focused on keeping the knees apart when landing in a game, thus they typically default to high-risk biomechanics in competition. This lack of skill transfer highlights the need to correct poor biomechanics at a subconscious (cerebellar) level. Training this type of foundational stability is required to promote safe biomechanics and facilitate inherent adoption of safer default movement patterns.

Program Frequency and Advancement

While hypertrophy and strength gains begin to be seen several weeks after initiating a strength-training program, neuromuscular-driven changes can be seen after just two weeks of initiating a stability program. This rapid rate of acquisition for stability tasks allows athletes to demonstrate significant improvements in a relatively short amount of time. This quick development of added stability with adequate practice allows SES programming to be advanced every 2-3 weeks (as long as the athlete has consistently practiced their exercises). SES exercise frequency should be at least 3x/week in order to sufficiently master a series of exercises in a 2-3 week period of time. However, stability-based exercises should be practiced daily if possible. Mastery and benefit are directly related to amount of practice.

Program Theory

The human body is a complex machine with multiple dynamic systems interacting with and influencing one another. The approach to injury risk reduction must adequately address the complexity of human movement. An issue at any given joint is likely not an isolated issue, but most often the symptom of many compromised biomechanical components interacting. While specific progressions within SES programs are linear in nature, the overall program is layered and spatial, tackling multiple deficiencies simultaneously.

When correcting human movement, it is important to recognize that an isolated deficiency may be the limiting factor for the primary issue, thus the program must address the entire kinetic chain. For example, an athlete may not master a complex lower-extremity stability task because an unresolved core deficiency is negatively impacting the successful execution of the task. The core issue should be addressed beforehand, or concurrently, to support achievement of the lower-extremity exercise. If this collaborative foundation setting is overlooked, the athlete may practice the activity sufficiently in controlled environments but will not actually adopt the change in unpredictable circumstances. The goal of an SES program is not to fix an issue at one joint but to create safe default movement patterns that protect joints.

Program Principles and Application

Specificity should be applied to programming once athletes have been evaluated for injury risk. Programming can be completely individualized (each athlete receives their own program) or tiered (athletes are sent down 1 of 3 tracks based on their deficiency grouping) based on the characteristics of the athletic program. SES programs manipulate several variables to systematically progress programs. While advancement in strength programs is primarily a function of manipulating weight and power demands, SES programs use minimal weight (usually <15 lbs.). The main variables include bilateral/unilateral limb support, surface changes, addition of a secondary task, eyes open/closed, single plane/multi-plane, linear/rotational, static/dynamic, and degree of reactivity required.

These variables should be manipulated within specific progressions to support the overall theme of program progression, which is increasing stability demands under sport-like conditions. Athletes should advance to various sport-specific stability tasks once prerequisite levels of strength and stability have been achieved. Figure 11.4 shows progression principles for a lower-extremity, non-jumping SES exercise progression.

Weightlifting exercises often require high levels of skilled feedback regarding task execution (e.g. squat or clean form). This level of feedback is necessary because it is possible for the athlete to successfully complete a lift with improper technique. On the contrary, SES exercises are generally constructed to require minimal external feedback on execution success because the goal is to execute

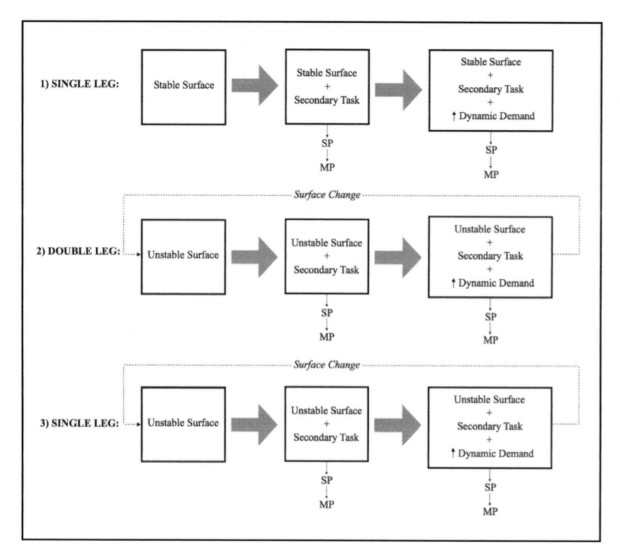

Figure 11.4: Stability enhancement systems progressions. SP=single plane. MP=multi-planar. Tier 1 represents single-leg progressions done on a stable surface. Military press (0-5#) is an example of a single-plane secondary task while a chop is an example of a multi-planar secondary task (tier 1, column 2). A ball toss is an example of a secondary task with increased dynamic demand (column 3). Once Tier 1 is mastered, the athlete should progress toTier 2: double leg on unstable surfaces. Difficulty level is progressed similarly to Tier 1, however, an athlete can repeat Tier 2 with a more challenging stability surface. Once Tier 2 is mastered, the athlete should progress to Tier 3: single leg on unstable surfaces, which progresses similarly to Tier 3. This figure represents general SES progression structure. Highly skilled athletes may skip some progression steps if they are not challenged at the current level.

the movement correctly without conscious thought (external feedback is appropriate if the athlete is unsafe or unable to independently correct despite best efforts). This is achieved by creating tasks that result in obvious failure/incompletion if the task is not executed correctly.

When an SES task is failed (i.e. the athlete loses his or her balance, etc.), the athlete should begin to inherently problem-solve and implement new strategies in order to complete the task (a process that occurs at a subconscious level). Once the athlete's neuromuscular system has identified a successful stability strategy, it is re-enforced into habit. This stability strategy acquisition is refined through practice and progressive training. The culmination of this strategy acquisition is a fine-tuned muscle stabilization response that deploys automatically when the body senses joint instability. This automatic deployment allows the muscle to activate faster in order to prevent injury.

The appropriate order for stability surface progressions follows a general trend, but may vary based on athlete-specific deficiencies. For example, a single-leg RDL stability surface progression (floor→Airex→Dyna Disc→BOSU) could be employed in conjunction with collaborative stability exercises to help an athlete master the single-leg RDL stability series over a 6-8-week period of time.

Figure 11.5: Stability training through SES RDL progression utilizing increasingly difficult stability surfaces. Utilizing unstable surfaces is paramount to a successful ACL injury risk-reduction program.

SES programs are meant to be a time-efficient (10-15 min) method of incorporating injury-risk reduction into an existing program structure. Athletes are assigned 3-4 exercises for 2-3 weeks that are performed at least 3 times per week. Every 2-3 weeks exercises are progressed and 3-4 new, more challenging exercises are assigned. This process continues to repeat in order to systematically train the athlete's inherent stability. Low-level SES programs often focus on resolving flexibility/mobility, stabilizing musculature and foundational stability deficiencies. As the program progresses the exercises require higher stability demands and mimic sport-specific movements.

It is important to measure program efficacy through re-assessing athletes periodically. A full or partial re-evaluation is valuable in tracking progress and adjusting programs. Biomechanical improvement is the main marker of success. Athletes will have varying improvement rates based on a number of variables (baseline stability, motor skill acquisition, etc.). Although athletes may improve at different rates, ideally, an overall improvement trend should be seen for each athlete.

Conclusion

The goal of injury risk-reduction programs should be to create safe default movement mechanics in athletes through progressive step-wise stability training. Programs must collectively address mobility, strength, and stability deficits to be effective. The construction, philosophy and goal of an injury risk-reduction program is very different than that of a strength training program, thus, the two must supplement one another. Reducing likelihood for injury is paramount to the physical, psychological, emotional, and long-term well-being of athletes. Athletic programs must make an intentional effort to meaningfully combat sports injury epidemics in order to foster competitive, sustainable athlete and program success.

Reference

1.   Paterno M, Rauh M, Schmitt L, Ford K, Hewett T. Incidence of second ACL injuries 2 years after primary ACL reconstruction and return to sport. *Am J Sports Med.* 2014;42(7):1567-1573.

CHAPTER 12

Considerations for Female Athletes

Kristin Shuman

Objectives

- Identify the most common methods utilized to accurately determine various aspects of physique
- Recognize normative values of body composition based on age, gender, and sport participation
- Describe and discuss physiological differences in the female athlete
- Discuss and describe the uniqie nutritional needs associated with the competitive female athlete

Introduction

Female participation in athletics and sport became increasingly common when Title IX of the Education Amendments was passed in 1972.[1] Prior to Title IX, it was quite uncommon to see female athletes participating in sport, and even less who prepared for their sport by utilizing resistance training in a weight room or on a field/court.[1] The growth of opportunities for women in athletics since the passage of Title IX has strongly encouraged strength and conditioning participation by females, as training and improved performance is now a common thread amongst all athletes, oftentimes regardless of age, gender, and/or level. There are both similarities and differences between male and female athletes, and as strength and conditioning professionals (SCPs) in control of developing weight lifting and running skills, we should recognize the importance of these factors.

Physique

Fat Free Mass (FFM)

Fat deposition and distribution in males and females occurs quite differently. Hormone production plays an important role in when and how the body develops. Puberty increases hormone production in females (estrogen), which encourages development of fat and breast tissue, while males encounter high levels of testosterone during puberty, which encourages the formation of bones and increases protein synthesis. This results in more fat free mass (FFM) in males as opposed to females.[2]

There are myths and beliefs that if a female lifts weights similarly to a male, that she will get "too bulky" or "look like a man." These thoughts are simply false. There are many factors that prevent a woman from looking like a man due to weight training. First, females do not have the testosterone content within the body to develop muscle like males do. Next, the chemical-alteration on magazine covers give the wrong impression of traditional weight training and females tend to lean out muscle rather than bulk up, due to low testosterone levels. Additionally, muscle bulk involves very high volumes of work at lower intensities than most athletes tend to train. Lastly, bulking up does not happen overnight and is calorie-dependent.

Body Composition

Typical techniques of anthropometry (skinfold calipers, hydrostatic weighing tank, DEXA, Bod Pod, etc.) are often utilized to determine the percentage of body fat on an athlete. This measurement not only allows the athlete to determine how much FFM or lean muscle mass exists on the body (comparative to fat stores), but it also allows the strength and conditioning coach to measure sites that directly reflect the work assigned within a program. If site measurements are not changing throughout the course of a progressive program, the design of the program or the effort of the athlete can be addressed in order to receive the best result possible from body fat measurement.

Body fat percentage is divided into two categories: Storage fat and essential fat. Storage fat, the fat stored in adipose tissue, is quite similar in males and females; 8.4% and 8.5%, respectively. Essential fat, that which is required to perform normal bodily functions and provide protection to the major internal organs, differs between males and females. Females require almost four times more essential fat than their male counterparts (6.8% compared to 2.1%), which increases the overall body fat percentage and content of the female body.[2] Classification of body fat percentage is dependent upon age and gender. Figures 12.1, 12.2, and 12.3 represent normative data on body fat percentage for general population by age and gender (males and females), and athletes by sport, respectively.

20-29 yrs	30-39 yrs	40-49 yrs	50-59 yrs	60-69 yrs	70-79 yrs	Rating
4.2	7.3	9.5	11	11.9	13.6	Very Lean
6.4	10.3	12.9	14.8	16.2	15.5	
7.9	12.4	15	17	18.1	17.5	
9.1	13.7	16.4	18.3	19.2	19	Excellent
10.5	14.9	17.5	19.4	20.2	20.1	
11.5	15.9	18.5	20.2	21	21	
12.6	16.8	19.3	21	21.7	21.6	Good
13.8	17.7	20.1	21.7	22.4	22.3	
14.8	18.4	20.8	22.3	23	22.9	
15.8	19.2	21.4	23	23.6	23.7	
16.6	20	22.1	23.6	24.2	24.1	Fair
17.5	20.7	22.8	24.2	24.9	24.7	
18.6	21.6	23.5	24.9	25.6	25.3	
19.7	22.4	24.2	25.6	26.4	25.8	
20.7	23.2	24.9	26.3	27	26.5	Poor
22	24.1	25.7	27.1	27.9	27.1	
23.3	25.1	26.6	28.1	28.8	28.4	
24.9	26.4	27.8	29.2	29.8	29.4	
26.6	27.8	29.2	30.6	31.2	30.7	Very Poor
29.2	30.2	31.3	32.7	33.3	32.9	
33.4	34.4	35.2	36.4	36.8	37.2	

Figure 12.1: Body composition evaluation for males (general population) (% body fat)[3]

20-29 yrs	30-39 yrs	40-49 yrs	50-59 yrs	60-69 yrs	70-79 yrs	Rating
11.4	11.2	12.1	13.9	13.9	11.7	Very Lean
14	13.9	15.2	16.9	17.7	16.4	
15.1	15.5	16.8	19.1	20.2	18.3	
16.1	16.5	18.3	20.8	22	21.2	Excellent
16.8	17.5	19.5	22.3	23.3	22.5	
17.6	18.3	20.6	23.6	24.6	23.7	
18.4	19.2	21.7	24.8	25.7	24.8	Good
19	20.1	22.7	25.8	26.7	25.7	
19.8	21	23.7	26.7	27.5	26.6	
20.6	22	24.6	27.6	28.3	27.6	
21.5	22.8	25.5	28.4	29.2	28.2	Fair
22.2	23.7	26.4	29.3	30.1	28.9	
23.4	24.8	27.5	30.1	30.8	30.5	
24.2	25.8	28.4	30.8	31.5	31	
25.5	26.9	29.5	31.8	32.6	31.9	Poor
26.7	28.1	30.7	32.9	33.3	32.9	
28.2	29.6	31.9	33.9	34.4	34	
30.5	31.5	33.4	35	35.6	35.3	
33.5	33.6	35.1	36.1	36.6	36.4	Very Poor
36.6	36.2	37.1	37.6	38.2	38.1	
38.6	39	39.1	39.8	40.3	40.2	

Figure 12.2: Body composition evaluation for females (general population) (% body fat)[3]

Figure 12.3: Body composition evaluation for athletes (NCAA – all divisions included) (% body fat)[4]

Sport	Male	Female
Baseball	12-15%	12-18%
Basketball	6-12%	20-27%
Football (Backs)	9-12%	No data
Football (Linemen)	15-19%	No data
Gymnastics	5-12%	10-16%
High/Long Jumpers	7-12%	10-18%
Ice/Field Hockey	8-15%	12-18%
Distance Running	5-11%	10-15%
Rowing	6-14%	12-18%
Shot Putters	16-20%	20-28%
Sprinters	8-10%	12-20%
Soccer	10-18%	13-18%
Swimming	9-12%	14-24%
Tennis	12-16%	16-24%
Volleyball	11-14%	16-25%
Wrestlers	5-16%	No data

Strength and Power Output

When measuring resistance training loads, absolute and relative values are both used to make comparative analyses between and amongst genders. Absolute values show that females have approximately two-thirds the strength of men, however, when utilizing relative values, incorporating the body weight of the athlete into the equation, the difference between male and female strength and power output is significantly reduced.[5] The reason for this reduction in difference when relative values are incorporated is due to the cross-sectional area of the muscle compared to the overall size of the athlete; gender no longer remains a factor.[5] This same concept is responsible for the higher absolute strength value for men. The overall size of the male musculature is often larger than their female counterparts, allowing for more force production. When upper body absolute strength is concerned, females are often around 50% lower than males, while the lower body difference is closer together at approximately 30% less.[2]

Physiological Responses

Delayed Onset of Menstruation and Cancer Risk

Young active female athletes can encounter a delayed onset of menstruation (amenorrhea), which in turn can pose beneficial results.[2] With fewer ovulatory cycles and less estrogen production, the risk for cancers are reduced. Female athletes who begin training for sport before or during high school have a reduced risk of developing breast, reproductive, or non-reproductive cancers throughout their lifetime compared to their inactive counterparts.[2] Research concerning older active women who exercise regularly also shows a decrease in reproductive cancers compared to the less active population of the same age range.[2]

The hormonal differences between females and males are apparent in the research. The primary hormones involved in muscle growth and synthesis are: (a) testosterone; (b) growth hormone; and (c) insulin-like growth factors (IGFs).[2] Females have 15 to 20-fold lower concentrations of testosterone than males do, as it is the primary male sex hormone (estrogen is the primary female sex hormone, which does not play a positive role in muscle synthesis). Even with increased resistance training, females do not show a pattern of increased testosterone production within the body (this may vary by individual, as some females have a higher concentration of testosterone to begin with).[5]

The Female Triad

The Female Triad is a collection of conditions which can affect the female athlete. In 1992, the Female Triad was first defined as a disorder that includes three interrelated conditions: (1) eating disorder; (2) amenorrhea; and (3) osteoporosis.[1,6] In 2007, the American College of Sports Medicine (ACSM) updated the concept of the Triad to include a spectrum that involved three distinct areas of health status: (1) energy availability; (b) menstrual function; and (3) bone mineral density.[1,6] Diagnosis and management by a strength and conditioning coach can prove difficult with the Triad components. While the strength and conditioning coach oftentimes has the most contact with an athlete, there are varying degrees of each prong of the Triad, which allows medical professionals and physicians to make better diagnoses, order tests, and determine the necessary treatment going forward. Each factor moves individually along their respected spectrums at different rates, making this condition difficult to both diagnose and manage.[6] Recognition of abnormal fatigue or behavior of the athlete by the strength and conditioning coach could assist in exposing any prong of the Triad for further review by medical professionals.

Energy Availability

Energy availability is strongly correlated to caloric balance. The body is like a car; it needs fuel to run and keep it running. If we do not put enough fuel in our body to balance the amount of energy that we expend (negative caloric balance), our energy level will not be high enough to complete the tasks that are required of us as athletes. Over time, weight loss (lean muscle and/or fat store) is often the result. If we put too much fuel in our body and the balance at the end of the day is higher than what we have expelled physically (positive caloric balance), decreased performance and weight gain are often the results. Eating disorders are calorically related to energy availability in female (and male) athletes.

Menstrual Function

There are many different types of menstrual function from normal to abnormal and in between. According to the ACSM (2007), the spectrum of menstrual function includes: (a) eumenorrhea (normal menstrual function); (b) subclinical menstrual disorders; and (c) amenorrhea (the absence of menstrual function longer than 90 days).[6] Oligliomenorrhea (menstrual cycles occurring at intervals longer than 35 days) falls into the middle subclinical disorder category, which can also involve other irregularly patterned menstrual cycles (may involve the follicular and/or luteal phase of menstruation).[6] Amenorrhea, the delayed onset of (primary) and/or the absence of menstruation longer than 90 days after onset (secondary), is a rare condition, yet easily recognizable.[3] Research involving animals discovered that pre-pubertal energy deficiency suppresses growth and delays sexual development.[6,7]

The SCP should build quality relationships with the female athletes for whom they are responsible, and in turn be able to discuss any menstrual irregularities that may occur during training. By addressing an issue, the management of how training is prescribed and implemented can benefit the athlete, rather than breaking them down further due to bad timing or poor communication.

Bone Mineral Density

The strength of a bone is dependent upon the density and internal anatomy. The quality of minerals and proteins within the structure of the bone play a very strong role in which bones encounter fractures, and which do not.[4] Bone mineral density is measured along a spectrum that allows an individual to fluctuate dependent upon the BMD score provided for specific factors including age and sex.[6] Athletes who participate in resistance-loaded sport activities generally have a BMD 5-15% higher than their non-athletic counterparts.[6] Over time, low BMD can lead to osteopenia, which can increase the incidence of fracture and further increase the likelihood of long-term osteoporosis.[6] Amenorrhea is linked to demineralization of the skeleton over time and can move an individual toward the low end of the BMD spectrum. Due to the fluctuation on the spectrum, being aware of the current BMD and also knowing how it moves along the spectrum over time is quite important at this level.

By educating athletes on proper nutrition and what contributes to increased bone mineral density, the SCP can attempt to reduce the effects of this component of the Triad.

Injury Prevention in Female Athletes

The most predominant injury in young female athletes involves the anterior cruciate ligament (ACL). Researchers have been attempting to solve the puzzle of why female athletes see an increased occurrence of this injury (30% or higher) as opposed to their male counterparts.[8] Theories behind this increased incidence involve: (a) anatomical issues (valgus knees and Q angle); (b) lower neuromuscular control in female athletes associated with pubertal development; and (c) menstruation. While no theory has ever been completely proven and supported by the literature, all of these factors can be taken into consideration when training female athletes.

Valgus Knees and Q Angle

When the knee joint is angled toward the midline of the body while the individual is standing, this is referred to as a valgus knee position (Figure 12.4). The angle that is created from the pelvis to the knees is referred to as the Q angle (Figure 12.5). When an individual has a dramatic angle from the pelvis to the knee joint, the Q angle is increased. Some research states that increased Q angle is involved with an increased incidence of knee pain and ACL injury.[8] While other researchers dispute the idea that anatomical issues are related to all ACL injuries, and support the idea that each case is unique and must be confirmed individually.[9,10]

Some basic suggestions for the strength and conditioning professional in correcting or attempting to correct valgus knee position could be to position the athlete so that when the knee is flexed at any time, the patella (kneecap) stays in a direct line with and remains posterior to the foot of the athlete. Attempts like these help to produce muscle memory and build up the often-underdeveloped musculature surrounding the knee joint, which can help to improve the position toward the normal position (see Figure 12.5).

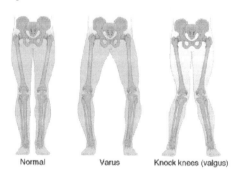

Figure 12.4: Knee alignments. The valgus position (right) is particularly high risk. http://unorllamsi.moxo.sk/category.php?n=265-valgus-of-knee

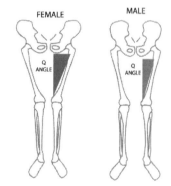

Figure 12.5: Q angle.
http://www.insidelacrosse.com/article/a-pound-of-prevention-minimizing-your-risk-for-acl-injuries-/13186

Program Design Considerations

Physiologically, the muscular structure of the human body is essentially the same in both genders (minus hormone content and concentration), so altering a progressive resistance program based on female or male anatomy is unnecessary. Rather than changing the training protocol for gender, incorporating training protocols based on the needs and goals of the athlete involved to benefit them in their specific sport can be much more beneficial.[5]

One consideration that the SCP should address when female athletes initially start a training program is their personal level of comfort in the weight room. This will also lend itself to how the confidence of that athlete grows over time. From personal experience, bringing female teams into the weight room by themselves or with very little outside influence of other athletes, can make them feel more comfortable. Teaching female athletes how to correctly lift weights along with safe progressions over time and positive coaching can also improve the confidence level of female athletes in the weight room.

Nutritional Concerns

Eating Disorders

Anorexia nervosa and bulimia nervosa are the two most common forms of eating disorders.[6] Anorexia involves restricted eating habits paired with negative self-view of weight, while bulimia involves binging and purging on a regular basis and may also include excessive exercise.[4] Certain criteria separate these disorders into subcategories dependent upon the details of the case. Athletes who do not meet all criteria for a classification are labeled as having an eating disorder not otherwise specified (ED-NOS).[6]

There are some common warning signs that could indicate either eating disorder. These symptoms include: (a) complaining frequently of constipation or stomach aches; (b) mood swings; (c) social withdrawal; (d) relentless, excessive exercise; (e) excessive concern about weight; (f) strict dieting followed by binges; (g) increasing criticism of one's body; and (h) strong denial that a problem exists even when there is evidence.[6] Attempts to control eating disorders should not be performed by the strength and conditioning coach through monitoring food intake or periodic weigh-ins. This can sometimes compound the issue. Referring the student-athlete to medical professionals (i.e. athletic trainer, team physician, counselor, etc.) to better understand and manage these issues is usually best. Due to the psychological component of the issue, this is the most appropriate route to diagnosis and management.

Iron Deficiency (Anemia)

Iron loss within the female body occurs through menstruation as well as intense physical training. Iron loss (30-60 mL of blood; 15-30 mg of Iron) during a menstrual cycle requires the female athlete to increase iron intake by 5 mg per day, or 150 mg per month to synthesize red blood cells properly and maintain adequate iron levels.[2] Anemia occurs when the hemoglobin levels within the blood reach 12 g·dL^{-1}. In theory, iron is lost during physical activity in three ways: (1) loss of iron during perspiration (sweat); (2) loss of hemoglobin in urine due to increased body temperature, increased involvement of the spleen (thermoregulatory), and foot-strike hemolysis (pounding feet on hard surface, which affects circulation rates in major organs); and (3) gastrointestinal bleeding due to endurance (distance) running.[2] The symptoms of iron deficiency anemia include: (a) sluggishness/dizziness; (b) loss of appetite; (c) pale skin; (d) sore tongue; (e) brittle nails; (f) frontal headaches; and (g) over time, the reduced ability to perform mild exercise.[2]

While regular bloodwork from a physician or hospital could help to monitor iron levels, it can become time-consuming and expensive. Most athletes receive yearly physicals which include blood sample analysis. The SCP should be aware of all symptoms related to iron deficiency and should refer the athlete to medical professionals if symptoms become chronic in nature and begin to influence physical performance.

Conclusion

With appropriate instruction and education in the weight room along with adherence to the considerations presented in this chapter, female athletes can expect similar improvements from baseline testing as a result of resistance training as do their male counterparts. While there undoubtedly sex-related differences between genders, the response from a strength and conditioning program can highly benefit female athletes not only in sport, but in other areas of health and fitness, as well.

References

1. Curry E, Logan C, Ackerman K, McInnis K, Matzkin E. Female athlete triad awareness among multispecialty physicians. *Sports Medicine-Open.* 2015;1(38):1-7.

2. McArdle W, Katch F, Katch V. *Exercise Physiology: Nutrition, Energy, and Human Performance.* Baltimore, MD: Lippincott Williams & Wilkins; 2010.

3. American Council of Sports Medicine. *ACSMs Guidelines for Exercise Testing and Prescription.* 9th ed. Philadelphia, PA: Lippincott Williams & Wilkins; 2014.

4. Rockwell M. Body composition: What are athletes made of? 2015; http://www.ncaa.org/health-and-safety/sport-science-institute/body-composition-what-are-athletes-made. Accessed March 15, 2017.

5. Haff G, Triplett N. *Essentials of Strength Training and Conditioning.* 4th ed. Champaign, IL: Human Kinetics; 2016.

6. Nattiv A, Loucks A, Manore M, Sanborn C, Sundgot-Borgen J, Warren M. American College of Sports Medicine position stand. The female athlete triad. *Medicine and Sports Science.* 2007;39(10):1867-1882.

7. Schneider J, Wade G. Inhibition of Reproduction in Service of Energy Balance. In: Wallen K, Schneider J, eds. *Reproduction in Context: Social and Environmental Influences on Reproductive Physiology and Behavior.* Cambridge, MA: MIT Press; 2000:35-82.

8. Hewett T, Zazulak B, Myer G. Effects of the menstrual cycle on atherior cruciate ligament injury risk: A systematic review. *American Journal of Sports Medicine.* 2007;35(4):659-668.

9. Emami M, Ghahramani M, Abdinegad F, Namazi H. Q-angle: An invaluable parameter for evaluation of anterior knee pain. *Archives of Iranian Medicine.* 2007;10(1):24-26.

10. Tillman M, Bauer J, Cauraugh J, MH T. Differences in lower extremity alignment between males and females. Potential predisposing factors for knee injury. *Journal of Sports Medicine & Physical Fitness.* 2005;45(3):355-359.

PRINCIPLES of ATHLETIC
Strength & Conditioning

The Foundations of Success in
Training and Developing
the Complete Athlete

CHAPTER 13

Spotting Fundamentals

Mark Naylor

Objectives

- Understand the fundamentals behind proper spotting techniques, including which lifts to spot, proper posture/positioning, and etiquette for spotting the training athlete

- Be able to safely and effectively spot selected specific lifts using proper form and posture

Introduction

With participation in competitive sports at historic levels, the use of weight training as a means of improving overall athletic performance and individual sport skills is similarly increasing. The value of learning perfect weightlifting technique is at a premium. Unfortunately, the ability to implement a correct and appropriate spot or assistance to a lift, at times, gets overlooked. For the strength and conditioning professional (SCP), ensuring athlete safety demands the knowledge and skill necessary to provide a safe and effective spot in a variety of training situations.

While a personal knowledge of spotting principles and practice is essential, many SCPs work in environments where large groups are the norm. While it would certainly be nice for the SCP to spot every athlete, this simply is not realistic in most team training situations. To make these settings work, it is often necessary to have athletes spot each other on certain exercises.

Unfortunately, athletes are often told to "go spot each other" with no instruction or knowledge of how to spot and assist those lifting correctly. Correct spotting needs to be taught to everyone involved in the weight training program, but the SCP should be cautious about allowing inexperienced trainees to spot each other. Anyone who is charged with spotting another person in the weight room should be given instruction and should be able to demonstrate focus and attention to detail. This chapter will outline proper spotting technique and provides a framework for the SCP to use when teaching athletes how to properly spot each other.

General Spotting Guidelines

A good spotter provides the lifter a safe environment to complete each rep. The spotter can also play a significant role in providing feedback and encouragement to improve each set. There are some general guidelines to follow when spotting regardless of the exercise being performed. These guidelines have more to do with the overall lifting environment and the safety of both the lifter and spotter.

First, the spotter should actively coach. This means that everyone in the role of a spotter (coach or athlete) needs to be engaged with the lifter. Coaching during the lift means to **instruct** on proper technique and provide **encouragement** to the lifter. A basic rule of thumb is to not allow more than two reps to be performed without any feedback.

Next, the spotter should check for proper weight. If a free weight exercise is being performed, the spotter should double check that the weight is appropriate and loaded evenly on both side of the bar. Also, the spotter should check for collars that are properly tightened on each side of the bar and help ensure that the appropriate weight is selected for each exercise.

The spotter should also know how many reps the lifter is attempting before the beginning of the set. He or she should check the surroundings for any obstructions, including other lifters who may be in the way and pay attention to the lifter during the set. The spotter should be in the proper position to spot and know the appropriate hand placement to administer the spot before the lifter commences the set. The spotter should also assume a stable and balanced stance in which to perform the spot. This means standing with a rigid torso and the knees slightly flexed. This will help to avoid any injury if a heavy load suddenly needs to be handled.

The spotter should be familiar with the lift and know what constitutes the difference between sound form and faulty technique on each repetition. The spotter should verbalize the lifter to "rack it" at the first site of faulty technique and to know where assistance should be given when racking the weight.

The responsibility of performing good reps is always on the lifter. The spotter should be viewed as a secondary resort for safety measures. Once a spot is required, the set is done and the weight should be racked correctly. When spotting a barbell into a rack, the spotter should keep his or her hands firmly on the bar until it is resting securely in the racking hooks.

Spotting Specific Lifts

The remainder of this section will outline the specific spotting techniques of common lifts including the barbell bench and incline press, the barbell back squat, the dumbbell press, pull-up/chin-ups, and machine and bodyweight lifts done to muscular failure. Learning how to spot these common lifts will give spotters enough knowledge to carry over to spotting just about any lift performed in the weight room. It is also relevant to discuss exercises that should not be spotted to ensure the safety of both the lifter and spotter.

Barbell Bench Press / Incline

Before the lift, the spotter should check to ensure the lifter is in a good position with hands evenly spaced, eyes under the bar, and feet firmly on the ground. At lift-off, the spotter should stand over the lifter with a balanced stance to gain leverage and employ a mixed grip on the bar. The spotter should allow the lifter to determine the take-off or un-racking of the bar. There is often a countdown or verbal cue given for this such as "3-2-1." The spotter should assist in bringing the bar to a balanced position over the lifter's chest and help only as much as is needed. Giving too much assistance can take the lifter out of proper position. Once the lifter is balanced, the spotter should slowly let go of the bar and allow the lifter to perform the exercise.

Figure 13.1: Spotting the bench press

When the lifter can no longer move the weight, the spotter should use the mixed grip to assist with the completion of the rep. Following the path of the bar while maintaining the mixed grip, the spotter should maintain a strong, stable body position and assist just enough to keep the bar moving. If the lifter is performing a test on the bench press, the spotter should take and rack the weight immediately as soon as assistance is necessary. If the spotter is not capable of lifting the bar off the lifter's chest as in the case of heavy lifting, additional spotters should be placed on each side of the bar to take the weight upon momentary muscular failure. Once a spot is necessary, the spotter should never let go of the bar until it is secured safely inside the catches of the rack.

Barbell Back Squat

While a spotter should always be present for emergencies, the SCP should typically avoid situations where a spot is necessary for the barbell back squat and its variations for day-to-day training. A spot is usually only necessary when an athlete is using an inappropriate weight or has reached momentary muscular failure. Both of these situations should be avoided, particularly in a young athlete, as they can be very dangerous. The lifter should only use a weight that can be lifted with proper technique, and reaching muscular failure during any squatting lift often leads to a breakdown in technique that can be harmful.

Before the lift, the spotter should check the rack for proper set up. Safety catches and bar height should be adjusted specifically for the lifter, and the lifter should never have to come up to the toes to un-rack the bar. Once the lifter is ready to initiate the exercise, the spotter should check alignment of

bar on shoulders to ensure that the weight is balanced evenly. The lifter should be allowed to take the bar off the rack and step back into a lifting stance. This is usually accomplished with a single step backward and requires no interference from the spotter.

When spotting a male athlete, the spotter should stand behind the lifter with a strong stance and posture as outlined

Figure 13.2: Spotting the barbell back squat

previously. The spotter's hands and arms should be ready near the lifter's torso and under the chest or armpits. For the female lifter, the spotter should place the hands under the bar outside the lifter's shoulders. If unable to lift of reach the bar in this position, the spotter should move the hands under the arm pits, being extremely cautious of hand placement, as it is near the breasts.

The spotter should then maintain proper squatting mechanics, following the lifter's range of motion without touching them. The spotter should be prepared to provide assistance as soon as it seems like the movement is about to stop. The spotter should try to apply assistance before movement has fully stopped, as this is the point where technique breaks down quickly.

Once a spot is given, the set is over. The athlete should not attempt to perform another rep. When re-racking the weight, the lifter should walk the bar back into the rack as the spotter uses an overhand grip to guide the bar back into the rack. The spotter should not release the bar until it is securely placed in the racking hooks.

DB Pressing

Before the lift, the spotter should ensure that the lifter understands how to bring the weight into proper lifting position. The spotter should also be sure that the lifter's space is clear before and during the set. It is common for a dumbbell to roll into the lifter's space, which may lead to an accident when the lifter completes the set.

When spotting the lift, the spotter should stand with a strong stance and posture as outlined previously, keeping the hands close to the wrists and fully ready to provide assistance. The spotter should follow the path of the lifter without touching. When (or if) a spot is needed, the spotter should firmly grab the lifter's wrists and provide assistance. This lift should never be spotted by pushing the elbows of the lifter.

Once a spot has been provided at the wrists, the set is over. Dumbbells should always be promptly returned to the rack. Proper training space etiquette dictates that dumbbells not in use should never be left on the floor, as this could pose a hazard to other lifters.

Figure 13.3: Spotting the dumbbell bench press

Chin-Up/Pull-Up

Once the lifter needs a spot to finish the set, the spotter should be directly behind the athlete. The spotter should then place both hands on the low to mid-back of the lifter and push up in the direction of the proper path of the exercise. The spotter should help only enough to get the athlete to the top of the range while allowing the athlete to continue to work and give effort to reach the top range.

It is important to note that spotting at the athlete's feet should only be done if the athlete is too heavy to spot at the lower back and feels as though his or her grip is very secure. In this case, one hand would go under the lifters ankles and the other at the lower back as seen in the photo. It can be very dangerous if the lifter loses grip while the spotter is holding his/her feet, so encourage the lifter to communicate if he/she feels the grip giving way. Once the

Figure 13.4: Spotting the pull-up

athlete is at the top of the ROM, the spotter can then move back and allow the athlete to complete the eccentric portion of the rep. The eccentric, or lowering, of the lift rarely needs any assistance.

Lifts Done to Momentary Muscular Failure

It is not recommended to take barbell lifts to muscular failure. Lifts to muscular failure work well with bodyweight exercises such as push-ups and pull-ups, as well as most upper-body pulling exercises such as the chest-supported row or pulldowns. In most cases, the spotter should simply step back and allow the lifter to work, providing verbal encouragement and technique cueing to maintain proper lifting position. The spotter should only spot enough to slightly keep the weight moving in the concentric direction while allowing the lifter to do most of the work. When a spot becomes necessary, the spotter should only provide assistance on the concentric portion of the lift, as the lifter will still be strong enough to control the eccentric portion.

Closing Thoughts

Spotting every lift is not always necessary. Power movements and lifts commonly performed on a platform are not to be spotted. This includes all deadlift variations as well as the Olympic lifts and their derivatives. Applying a spot to these lifts can be very dangerous for both the lifter and spotter. Instead, athletes should be taught how to "bail" on a failed attempt or stop a lift when technique breaks down. With the speed of movement and/or the high degree of technical difficulty present in these lifts, a lifting partner can help to coach proper lifting technique and check the area for anything that might be in the way of performing a safe lift.

CHAPTER 14

Incorporating Speed & Agility Training into Programming

Jim Kielbaso

Objectives

- Identify the key mechanical principles associated with proper speed and agility training

- Understand the difference between open-loop and closed-loop skills and when to apply each concept when training speed and agility

- Describe and discuss the four key factors of an effective speed and agility development program

- Be able to effectively incorporate speed and agility training into an existing strength & conditioning program for maximum effectiveness and efficiency

Introduction

Speed development can be very complex, but the Strength & Conditioning Professional (SCP) can take some very simple steps to incorporate speed training into an overall strength & conditioning program. There are a variety of reasons that many SCPs do not include speed & agility training in their program including lack of time, lack of space, and a lack of proficiency in teaching mechanics. Additionally, some choose to forego speed and agility as a component of programming because it is not perceived as a priority or a belief that it really is not important compared to other aspects of training.

Rather than allowing these things to stop the SCP from incorporating speed training altogether, it is important to understand that almost any obstacle can be circumvented. To that end, rather than focusing on the intricacies of speed development, and getting overwhelmed with details, this chapter will give you a plan for incorporating a quality speed program as a small part of an overall physical development program.

Foundations of Speed & Agility Development

To fully understand the science behind these training methods would require a great deal of time studying anatomy, physiology, biomechanics, and motor learning. Other materials provide much greater detail on these areas. Instead, most of the science involved in speed & agility development boils down to these five basic training concepts:

1. Learn/teach optimal movement mechanics and practice them until they are second nature

2. The athlete should perform movements with maximum intensity, resting long enough between repetitions to ensure maximum intensity on every rep

3. The athlete should develop strength in order to increase force production potential, correct limiting factors, and reduce the risk of injury

4. The SCP should use plyometrics and other explosive methods to optimize the nervous system for power

5. The athlete should be conditioned appropriately for sport so that the newly developed speed and athleticism can be fully utilized during competition.

While the latter three concepts (strength, plyometrics, and conditioning) are typically cornerstones of most comprehensive programming, the concepts of movement mechanics and maximum intensity with appropriate rest intervals are absolute essentials to speed and agility training and will be the main focus of this chapter. These two components of speed development include both coaching (teaching mechanics) and programming (prescribing the right number of repetitions with adequate rest in order to elicit a positive training adaptation).

The two main constituents of enhanced speed and agility performance are nervous and the muscular systems. The basic purpose of strength training is to force the involved musculature to adapt by increasing the size or strength of the tissue. Adding strength and power to the available musculature allows the body to execute movements with increased force. Increasing the potential muscular force will create greater velocity and more powerful movement in any direction.

Similarly, the nervous system can also be trained to improve speed and agility. When the athlete wants to perform a specific movement, the nervous system responds by sending impulses to the appropriate muscles. The nervous system sends impulses to control the speed, strength, and sequence of contraction to create the desired movement pattern. Once the basic pattern is established, the nervous system will adapt to additional practice by adjusting the number of motor units recruited, the sequence in which they need to fire, etc. Simply put, the more an athlete practices a movement, the better and more efficient the movement typically gets. However, practice doesn't always make perfect. Perfect practice is necessary if the athlete is looking for meaningful results.

It is of vital importance to make sure that all movement training is done with impeccable technique so the nervous system has the opportunity to create the most effective motor patterns possible. The motor learning literature suggests that several weeks of purposeful training can create what is known as a motor engram, a neural pathway that is so strong that it no longer requires cognitive effort to properly execute. Some erroneously refer to this phenomena as muscle memory (even though this is not really an accurate name) because the body learns to perform the movement without thought. With this in mind, it is absolutely critical that a speed development program begin well before the season when coaches usually want to see the new-found speed in competition.

Mechanics

In the late 1990s, a number of collegiate strength coaches worked to determine which physical tests had the highest correlation to the ability to play the game of football. Athletes were run through a large battery of tests including the 40-yard dash, pro-agility shuttle, vertical jump, several strength tests, and numerous other drills.

Next, they had the football coaches rate each player's on-field ability. The hope was to find out which athletes were the most effective on the field. A statistical analysis was run on all data to determine which tests had the highest correlation to on-field success. They SCPs surmised that if any of the tests correlated highly to on-field success, programming could be designed to improve performance on those tests. The test that had the highest correlation to on-field ability was the 10-yard sprint. In other words, the ability to accelerate allowed the athletes investigated to perform at a higher level on the field.

Even in the absence of such testing, logic dictates that the ability to accelerate likely correlates favorably with the ability to play many sports. Soccer, basketball, baseball, softball, lacrosse, field hockey, track sprints, etc. are all heavily dependent on the athlete's ability to accelerate over and over again. The ability to cover ground faster than the opponent will put the athlete in position to make plays throughout a game, and having just one step on that opponent can be the difference between making a play or not. As a result, when training athletes, the SCP must keep in mind what's important and be sure to spend plenty of time addressing the ability to accelerate.

To truly improve acceleration, mechanics MUST be addressed early and often. The athlete must learn how to produce horizontal force, and this does not always feel natural. We know from several other studies that mechanics seem to be the most important factor in running faster.[1,2]

Morin et. al (2011) demonstrated that force application technique (aka mechanics) and orientation of the force (the direction in which it is applied to the ground) were more important to running speed than the total amount of force applied.[1] Investigators discovered that horizontal force was correlated to running speed but vertical and total force were not. This was a breakthrough study because up until that point, many SCPs and exercise scientists believed that the total amount of force applied to the ground was the determining factor in speed.

Another investigation in 2014 demonstrated that force orientation (mechanics) was the most important determinant to running speed.[2] This investigation demonstrated that competitive sprinters actually run differently and have different force orientation than non-elite sprinters people. Specifically, elite sprinters produced relatively little additional force than non-elite sprinters (30% more) but were able to run 80% faster, demonstrating the importance of mechanics.[2]

Speed work requires adequate rest between sets in order to maintain a high level of intensity. Acceleration work should occur relatively early in a workout, and athletes should usually be held to distances under 20 yards. Further training of the nervous system helps with both speed and magnitude of neuromuscular recruitment, creating more explosive movements.

Many coaches claim that you cannot coach speed, but this is an untrue statement. Of course, there is a genetic limit to the amount of improvement that any individual can make, but great improvements can certainly be made in most athletes. As a person nears his or her genetic potential, improvements will become smaller and more difficult to elicit, but hard work and proper training will certainly benefit any athlete. Initiating training at a young age and focusing on challenging the nervous system can raise the potential abilities of an athlete. This training should focus on body awareness, control and the proper execution of specific movement patterns such as sprinting and directional change mechanics.

It also seems that there is more room for improvement in acceleration and agility than in top-end speed for many athletes. While conclusive scientific evidence supporting this notion is currently lacking, many athletes seem to have the potential to improve these areas to a greater extent than maximal sprint speed. Fortunately, improving these traits seems to be a more important factor in many competitive situations than improving top-end speed.

More research needs to be done in this area to both validate training methods and help coaches create optimal programs. Until then, the application of the basic science behind speed and agility training seems pretty clear: the SCP should have the athlete practice specific movement patterns in order to enhance function, and it is important to incorporate strength and power training in an effort to increase the potential force that can be created in any movement.

Three Fundamental Aspects of Sports Training

When analyzing the science behind training, it is also important to understand the three basic components of sports performance: physical ability, technical skills, and tactical understanding. First, physical ability is related to quantifiable aspects such as speed, agility, conditioning, strength, power, flexibility, etc. Secondly, technical skills involve more sport-related components of performance such as catching, throwing, shooting, passing, dribbling, trapping, play execution, etc. Lastly, tactical understanding involves aspects of performance such as game awareness, reading plays, recognizing opponents' tendencies, decision making, etc.

Technical and tactical skills are crucial for success in athletics, but there are numerous resources that concentrate on specific technical and tactical aspects of each sport. Each of these components will be addressed briefly, but the focus of this chapter is on improving the physical abilities involved in sports.

The ability to stop, start, and change directions is commonly referred to as agility. It is important to note that agility is not as straightforward as sprint mechanics because the multi-directional movements seen in sports are typically performed in reaction to an external stimulus (i.e. an opponent). It must be understood, then, that agility movements can be broken into two categories: closed loop skills and open loop skills.

Closed-Loop Skills

Closed-loop movements are performed with a pre-determined starting point and finish. Sometimes referred to as volitional or voluntary skills, such patterns do not require the Central Nervous System (CNS) processing in order to respond or react to external stimuli in order to properly perform the movement. In other words, closed-loop skills do not require the athlete to react to an opponent or environmental change. Examples of closed skills include the golf swing, a basketball free throw, all gymnastics events, track & field events, weightlifting or powerlifting events, combine tests such as the 40-yard dash, pro-shuttle, vertical jump, etc., diving, figure skating, and the tennis serve.

Essentially, these skills can be practiced over and over until the motor engram has been effectively learned and is able to be expressed on demand. There will always be external pressures such as a noisy crowd or competing against a rival, but these pressures do not affect the actual skill being performed. For example, the athlete does not need to adjust his or her gymnastics floor routine to another competitor; the flooring is always the same (to a certain degree), the music and skills are pre-determined, and the entire routine can be practiced exactly as it will be performed in competition.

Similarly, the mechanics of a basketball free throw do not need to change because the basket is moving; the hoop is always the same height and the foul line is always the same distance from the hoop. The high jumper does not need to react to or evade a defender before take-off; the obstacle is stationary and the athlete can pace-off the distance from the line in which he/she begins the approach.

In closed-skill events, the athlete is essentially competing with him or herself to perform a sports skill in competition. The skill can be started and finished whenever the athlete chooses (to a certain degree; there are generally time limits on these events) without any external interference. Once the movement is initiated, the body can react to internal feedback. For example, in the middle of a dive, a diver may realize he needs to rotate faster to properly complete the required number of rotations before he hits the water. He can then adjust his body accordingly to increase rotational speed, but it is not necessary to react to external factors such as moving targets in the water or opponents crossing his path in mid-flight.

It almost seems humorous to think of external factors being involved in traditionally closed-skill performances. Closed-skill sports are already so incredibly technical that they are difficult enough without having to deal with external feedback. Just think how difficult it would be to perform a balance beam routine with opponents throwing balls at the gymnast. Or imagine how interesting it would be if the 4 x 100 relay race were a full contact event. (Hmmm, perhaps we're on to something here.)

Open-Loop Skills

Open-loop skills require the athlete to process information from external stimuli and react accordingly. The athlete must take external information, such as the positioning of opponents, process it through the CNS, then produce movement patterns that appropriately deal with this information.

Examples of open skills include a tennis player moving across the court to retrieve an opponent's shot, a football running back evading an oncoming defender, or a soccer goalie diving for a shot. While all of these skills require practice, but all of these athletes must process external information in order to execute the appropriate movements. There is no pre-determined beginning or end of each movement, as this is determined in response to external cues.

Interestingly, if an athlete takes too long to "think about" the reaction to the external stimuli, he or she will generally appear very slow on the field or court. This is a where reaction time and response time need to be addressed.

Reaction Time vs. Response Time

Reaction time is the amount of time it takes an athlete to process the external stimuli and initiate a physical response. Response time, on the other hand, is the amount of time it takes to process the external stimuli, decide on the appropriate response, and actually complete the physical response. Reaction time is dependent on cognitive ability and neural efficiency, while response time is heavily dependent on those aspects as well as physical ability. Response time is basically reaction time plus the physical response. This can be very confusing, but in order to maximize individual potential and play a game as effectively as possible, both of these aspects must be taken into consideration.

Practicing speed and agility drills can improve response time but will not necessarily improve reaction time. Reaction time can be improved through external recognition drills and practicing pre-determined responses to external cues. First, it is important to note that most agility drills are practiced in closed environments. Cones are set up in varying patterns, ladder drills are performed with a stationary apparatus, shuttles are timed to impress coaches, etc. In all of these situations, the athlete does not need to react to an oppositional stimuli or opponent. This is a completely acceptable part of agility practice as long the limitations of these drills are recognized.

Far too often, athletes perform agility drills just to get through the drill. Later when performing improper technique during a game, the athlete then wonders why the drills are not improving performance. Athletes must understand that practicing agility drills in closed environments is done to learn to properly execute the skills during competition. The proper execution of these basic movement patterns needs to be practiced over and over until they can be properly performed without thought during a competition. If an athlete is thinking about his foot placement (internal feedback) during a directional change in the middle of a football game, there is a good chance that the external stimulus is not receiving the attention it deserves. To simplify this, if a running back is worried about sprinting mechanics as he comes through a hole, he's probably not going to notice the linebacker who is about to put him on his back.

Agility mechanics must be properly practiced in a repetitive fashion the same way sprinting mechanics are practiced over and over again. Unfortunately, many coaches do not pay attention to the biomechanics involved in directional changes and agility drills are used as conditioning drills. Make no mistake: many agility drills can be used to efficiently condition athletes, but learning and executing proper technique during these drills is of paramount importance.

Once the neural pathways involved in a specific movement are solidified through closed skill practice, they may be utilized in an open-loop environment such as competition. If the motor pathways are not strong, however, that skill will probably not be performed correctly in the heat of a competition. When an athlete can properly execute directional changes, it can greatly decrease response time because more efficient movement patterns are being utilized. This will allow the athlete to get into position faster with a decreased likelihood of injury.

On the other hand, in order to improve reaction time, a great deal of time and effort must be spent understanding the intricacies of the game being played, i.e. tactical skills. Athletes with limited physical abilities can excel if they can anticipate and put themselves in proper position to make a play. Many athletes excel in physical tests such as the 40-yard dash or pro agility shuttle, yet appear quite slow on the field. Other athletes are average at those tests, but look amazing on the field. Such athletes are able to read the play so well that they can initiate appropriate movements well before their opponents. In such situations, the athlete's reaction time is quicker because of superior visual and cognitive processing abilities.

Coaches can help improve reaction time by teaching athletes what to look for in specific situations to have better "field vision." To really make improvements, coaches should give these athletes a limited number of responses to each external cue. For example, soccer defensemen should be taught to recognize when an opponent is making a run toward the goal. Or, a quarterback should be taught how to read a defense at the line so he can anticipate how the called play is going to work after the snap. When this can be picked up, the athlete should be given one or two responses to the external cue. Such athletes should be instructed exactly how to defend the attack or which options to look for and should be given the opportunity to practice the recognition and reaction pattern over and over again until it can be performed with limited cognitive processing. It should be more of an instinct than a conscious decision.

Simple "reactionary agility" drills can also be incorporated into a training program. These can be as simple as having the coach point in the direction an athlete should travel. You can make the drills more complex by having athletes react to each other. Ultimately, athletes must learn how to "read" an opponent, so introducing these drills helps athletes learn what to look for and how to react. Keep in mind that offensive and defensive players will move differently and need to practice different reactionary skills. Put them in positions to practice both offensive and defensive movements to maximize their movement vocabulary.

Through practice, athletes can significantly improve reaction time by learning how to read an opponent's movements. This is very important because it means the SCP should incorporate "recognize & react" drills into training programs to help bridge the gap between agility drills and sports competition. When athletes can easily recognize external cues, they may have the feeling of everything happening in slow motion. Conversely, without the ability to recognize external cues, an athlete will always be late in responding and will have to rely on superior physical ability in order to make plays.

Finally, superior athletic performance will never be achieved without excellent technical skills. It does not matter how fast a receiver can run if he cannot catch a ball. A soccer player must be able to trap, pass, and dribble the ball efficiently if success is expected. Basketball players must be able to dribble and shoot if they expect to make an impact on the game. As such, devoting more time on technical skills can be particularly beneficial, particularly for younger athletes.

For example, if a basketball team has five great athletes who are not able to dribble or shoot, success is going to be limited. On the other hand, if five average athletes are skilled ball handlers and good shooters, success is more likely. Obviously, having athletes with great physical, technical, and tactical skills is the optimal situation, but technical skills must be the foundation.

An amazingly large number of basketball and soccer players claim that they need "first step explosiveness," but upon closer examination, it is their fundamental ball-handling skills that need work.

Take a lightning-quick basketball player and put a soccer ball at his feet and see how explosive his first step looks. Conversely, put a basketball in a skilled soccer player's hands and it is likely he or she will move far more slowly. If an athlete lacks great technical skills, improving physical abilities will be of limited value.

If the SCP's goal is to improve speed, agility, and quickness, it is essential that practice occurs from both the "neck up" and the "neck down." Most every professional athlete has exceptional physical and technical abilities, yet such individuals still watch game films and practice situational drills for hours at a time in an effort to improve cognitive ability to recognize external tactical cues and decrease reaction time.

Sound coaching and situational practice is extremely important, but this needs to be addressed differently for each sport and position. Including detailed information for each and every sport and position is way beyond the scope of this resource. Response time, on the other hand, is what this book and the drills involved will help you improve.

Four Factors of an Effective Speed Training Program

An effective program has to take important pieces from several areas of science: physiology, neurology, biomechanics, and motor learning.

Biomechanics & Motor Learning

The first thing that needs to be addressed in any quality speed program is the quality of movement. Athletes must learn how to put force into the ground in a way that will help them move more efficiently. While not everyone needs to run, cut, and accelerate the exact same way, there are certainly ways that are more effective than others. These techniques need to be understood and taught to young athletes so they aren't making gross errors in their movement.

Drills should be selected that teach athletes the best way to apply force into the ground. These drills also need to be taught in a way that creates real movement changes. Many times, speed programs appear to address mechanics on the surface, but upon closer examination, much of this lacks real substance. Things like ladder drills and mini-hurdle drills as typically performed do nothing to address movement quality, yet we see them passed off as "speed & agility" all the time.

Each drill should have a purpose and the coaching cues used in the drill should lead to a positive change in the way an athlete moves. Wall drills, for example, can be used to teach the mechanics of a forward lean, high knees, and forceful backward push during acceleration. But, if the SCP is only having athletes performing the drill because it was seen on YouTube, it is likely a waste of time. Motor learning is very specific to the skill being practiced. In other words, performing skips and ladder drills will help the athlete get better at skips and ladder drills, while practicing sprinting and acceleration will get the athlete better at sprinting and acceleration. The question becomes what does the athlete want to get better at?

Physiology

Once mechanics are addressed, athletes should work on producing more force. Strength training improves the force production capabilities of an athlete. If greater force is put into the ground with good mechanics, the athlete will move faster. If the mechanics are not efficient, the force will not be used as effectively as possible and the results will be sub-par. Simply working hard is a great start, but carefully planning each workout, documenting progress and constantly overloading each movement is a much more efficient way to develop strength. The human body takes time to adapt to a stimulus like a strength program, so be patient and sti

Neurology

The ability to produce force quickly is often referred to as power. In speed and agility, power is important because the athlete needs to put force into the ground as quickly as possible in order to move fast. Strength training will help make this happen, but explosive training will make it happen more efficiently. Explosive training is all about optimizing the nervous system so that the muscles contract quickly and in a coordinated fashion that produces maximal power. This can be accomplished through training methods such as plyometrics, weighted sleds, resisted movement, or explosive strength exercises.

The key to enhancing neurology is to perform the exercises with precision, maximum speed, and maximum effort. This means that the athlete will be performing relatively low reps (less than 10 reps per set) with maximal effort and attention to detail. The athlete will also need to perform these exercises when fresh and take adequate rest breaks between sets. This allows the athlete to give maximal effort on every rep.

Keys to Enhancing Speed

Some athletes spend years working on speed development, and there are so many factors that influence the development of speed that it can be difficult to identify which are most important. That said, the following are three simple ways to run faster, including proper foot strike, enhanced strength, and improved explosiveness.

Foot Strike

The first simple tip is to cue the athlete to get off the heels and strike the ground through the ball of the foot (metatarsal heads). Faulty mechanics can take numerous forms, including arm swing, knee drive, foot placement, body lean, and other such mistakes. However, the most common mistake in slow athletes is that they tend run on their heels. It sounds very simple to run on the ball of the foot, but it is not always an easy correction to make. Patience and coaching are required here because it will likely take some time to adjust to this new style of running.

Many athletes start running on their toes when they hear this coaching cue, so the SCP must be very clear on what part of the foot to land on. The heel will only be a couple of millimeters off the ground, so the weight is on the ball of the foot, not the toes. In this position, the ankle should be "locked" or "cocked and loaded" so that it is rigid instead of loose. If the ankle is rigid, all of the force produced by the hips can be transferred to the ground. If the ankle is not stable, much of that force will dissipate through the foot and ankle before it goes into the ground.

The reason this is usually the best correction is that running on the ball of the foot usually forces a better knee drive as well. The knee drive allows the athlete to travel further on each step, thereby increasing stride length. It also allows the athlete to take advantage of the strength that will be gained in tip #2.

The SCP should teach the athlete to have an exaggerated forward lean without breaking at the hips. Knee drive should be exaggerated for the first 2-4 steps. Athletes need to be taught to apply force backward into the ground through the balls of their feet.

Acceleration mechanics should be addressed very early in the training program and should be kept as simple as possible so athletes are concentrating on a few, basic cues rather than intricate instructions that bog them down.

Training for speed also requires a lot of rest between sets in order to maintain a high level of intensity. Acceleration work should occur relatively early in a workout, and should be performed with relatively short distances (i.e. under 20 yards).

Enhanced Strength

This does not mean that the strongest person in the world is the fastest. However, most people who ask how to run faster are weak, especially in the gluteals and hamstrings. Hitting the weight room is usually a great place to start if the goal is to increase speed. While a tremendously aggressive strength and conditioning program is not necessary for the athlete who is most interested in enhancing speed, a solid total-body workout only requires 45 minutes, 2-3 days a week. If the goal is to run faster, then the athlete should do what it takes to get stronger without taking away from other aspects of training. Specifically, posterior chain development (glutes, hamstrings, calves, low back) through exercises like the glute/ham raise, Nordic hamstrings, back extensions, RDLs, hip thrusts/bridges, etc. in addition to more traditional lifts like a squat or Bulgarian split squat are particularly beneficial.

Improved Explosiveness

If the athlete wants to run faster, then it is necessary to run fast. Oftentimes, when an athlete is asked what they do to improve speed, they describe training consisting mainly of technique drills. Technique is a huge component of speed, but the athlete is going to have to regularly run as fast as possible if the plan is to improve speed. The athlete will typically want to run at top speed 2-3 days a week with long rest periods between sets. Quantity need not be excessive, with 5-10 shorts sprints coupled with long rest periods being sufficient as long as intensity is high. Most athletes can get away with 10-20 sprints if conditioning is relatively high. The goal is to perform all sprints at high speeds. Once the athlete begins to show signs of fatigue and begins to slow down, it is time to shut that portion of the workout down for the day.

These are simply some basic tips on how to run faster, and they are a good starting point when planning a training program. Once the SCP has these three components covered, more advanced programming considerations can be explored. However, it is important not to rush training. Everyone seems to want to get faster immediately, but it is well worth the time to take a couple of steps back to ensure proper form and maximal effort. In the end, the athlete will enjoy great benefits and be significantly faster.

How to Incorporate Speed Training Into a Strength & Conditioning Program

Once instruction has been given, it is time to give athletes the opportunity to train the movements. In this case, training means giving athletes the opportunity to practice the skill of acceleration repetitively. In other words, athletes need plenty of reps to perfect the movement.

Taking 15 minutes twice a week is a great way to start working on acceleration and give athletes the reps they need to develop the skill. When speed is going to be addressed, it should be placed early in the workout when the athlete is most fresh. Speed work should never be performed after lower body strength work.

The athlete should begin with a brief warm-up that includes some mechanics instruction or reinforcement such as high knee runs, arm swings, and hops on the balls of the feet. After this brief warm-up, the SCP can utilize one of the following workouts to incorporate a small amount of speed work to the overall program multiple times a week:

Option #1

- 6 x 10-yard sprints
- 6 x 10-yard sprint – 2 steps backward – 10-yard sprint
- 3 x 5 squat jumps

Option #2

- Line hops (perform each drill for 10 seconds as fast as possible with :30-:60 seconds rest)
  - Forward/backward
  - Side-to-side
  - 1-foot forward/backward
  - 1-foot side-to-side
- 2 x 5 vertical jumps
- 2 x 15 tuck jumps
- 2 x 20-yard sprints
- 3 x 60-yard shuttles

Option #3

- 6 x 10-yard sprints, start from various positions
- 6 x 10-yard sprint – 2 shuffles back – 10-yard sprint
- 3 x 5 Long Jumps

Option #4

- 4 x 10-yard sprints with resistance (sleds or bands)
- 4 x 10-yard sprints
- 4 x pro-agility shuttle

These workouts are NOT intended to be an all-inclusive speed development program. Instead, these are very brief workouts intended to give the SCP the opportunity to insert a small amount of speed training into a jam-packed, all-around sports performance program when time is limited.

Each of these workouts give athletes several repetitions in a short amount of time, and they allow the SCP to provide feedback to certain athletes will the others continue the routine. These workouts would generally be used in a situation where time is limited and many different needs must be met concurrently.

At points in the training year when more time can be dedicated to speed training, the programs can be much longer, more in-depth and incorporate many other aspects of speed such as top-end mechanics, speed-endurance, multi-directional agility, conditioning, sports specific movements and more. It is important for the SCP to understand when to use these brief workouts, and when a more expansive program can be used.

When incorporating speed training into an all-around strength & conditioning program, the SCP must understand both the needs and time constraints of the athlete or team. Including a small amount of speed training consistently throughout the year will give athletes the reps, instruction and feedback needed to make great progress. When strength, conditioning and sport skills are added to the overall program, excellent all-around results can be seen.

References

1.   Morin J, Edouard P, Samozino P. Technical ability of force application as a determinant factor of sprint performance. *Med Sci Sports Exerc.* 2011;43(9):1680-1688.

2.   Clark K, Ryan L, Weyand P. Foot speed, foot-strike, and footwear: linking gait mechanics and running ground reaction forces. *J Exp Biol.* 2014;217(Pt 12):2037-2040.

CHAPTER 15

Coaching & Supervision in the Weight Training Program for Sports

Aaron Hillmann

Objectives

- Identify and discuss the fundamental questions to be considered before implementing a comprehensive, multi-sport strength & conditioning program

- Describe and discuss the common principles of successful strength & conditioning programs

- Examine the various ways to schedule a common facility shared among multiple teams to best benefit all parties involved

- Be able to implement an effective scheduling strategy to best utilize shared facilities

Introduction

It has been said numerous times that "success leaves tracks." One of the common denominators in successful strength and conditioning programs is expert coaching, supervision, and organization. The implementation and execution of the program are of paramount importance. The methods and means chosen are only as good as the manner in which they are performed, both in the training session and over the course of weeks, months, and years. Group training is a reality and necessity in the strength and conditioning field today and this chapter will outline the steps taken to ensure safety and productivity in training. In coaching, you will get what you tolerate and improve what you emphasize. The strength and conditioning program is no different.

Fundamental Questions to be Answered Before Implementing a Program

Who is Coaching the Athlete in the Weight Room?

The Strength and Conditioning Professional (SCP) is the individual charged with planning and implementing the strength and conditioning program. The selection of this qualified and highly motivated professional is the first and most important step the institution or club can take in making a serious commitment to prioritizing the strength and conditioning program. The SCP who possesses a certification from a nationally accredited organization is a must and a degree in a related field is highly encouraged to establish a strong foundation of knowledge. The SCP also preferably has some level of experience in training athletes—especially in group settings. Updated CPR/AED/First Aid training should also be required. The highly effective SCP develops further than these base certifications. He or she is a master of their craft.

The duty of training and developing young athletes is a passion for the true professional and such individuals continue to research, learn, and evaluate the program being implemented. Programming must meet the needs and fit into the uniqueness of the situation. Oftentimes, priority is placed on the physical facility first and coaching or supervision second. This approach is misguided, since the effectiveness of the training program is a direct reflection of a properly designed and expertly coached program. A school or institution should invest in the right personnel first, since great gains can be made with even the most remedial of equipment.

Who is Training?

Most likely, athletes who are training in the middle school, high school, or collegiate setting are, at best, novice to intermediate lifters. A formal assessment of strength and mobility should be incorporated into the first few training sessions to give the SCP a good idea of how best to program. The training program should be fluid, as a skilled SCP continually assesses and evaluates the program and trainees.

Novice lifters have little to no experience with proper training and are still learning consistent and proper technique. These individuals are not yet accomplished in the nuances of the exercises and typically respond well to both basic exercises and set/repetition schemes. Although such athletes will usually respond to most any stimulus, an excess of variety in training will actually stunt progress since consistency is essential in order to improve skill level in the exercises. Once repetitions become consistent, then true overload training can occur. The novice is not skilled enough to strain with proper form or effectively train to volitional muscular failure, so sub-maximal sets performed with proper technique are most effective. The novice will also need enough volume to stimulate strength gains since efforts are sub-maximal. Lastly, the novice will get stronger each workout and should be placed on a system of linear progression for as long as it is working.

The intermediate trainee has demonstrated consistent form of the basic exercises and has progressed linearly and consistently for an extended period of time. The duration of time spent in the novice phase will depend upon the individual and the ebb and flow of their training and sport play. The intermediate trainee will respond well to a bit more variety in exercises and loading/progressing patterns. Since the intermediate trainee is skilled at the exercises, more intensity-driven protocols can be implemented.

Lastly, the coach must consider the training population in terms of interest in weight training and any prejudices or misconceptions that the trainees' might have. Communication, listening, and teaching are valuable skills the coach must have in order to make a connection with the athlete and the team. Many tools can be used to get the job done and make progress and the good coach is open-minded enough to be adaptable. This does not insinuate that the athletes should be coddled and certain exercises avoided because of prejudices and misconceptions. Rather, effective teaching will help athletes embrace productive training methods and means.

What Are the Goals of Training?

This chapter is not written in the context of training athletes involved in the barbell sports. Weight training for other athletes is always used as secondary means of preparation for sport play. The primary means of development for sport is always practice and play of the actual sport. Nonetheless, proper weight training is arguably the most effective and efficient means of general preparation for sport. Proper weight training will increase the strength of the structures trained and improve functional mobility. When an athlete gains strength, both injury resistance and peak force production are enhanced. This is especially true for the novice or intermediate athlete. An effective weight training program can easily be integrated into the weekly training schedule for an athlete and need not take much time or energy reserves. During times of the year when sport practice is reduced, more emphasis can be placed on the weight training program in order to accelerate progress.

Principles of Successful Weight Training Programs

Safety

Safety comes in many forms. Administratively, safety will begin with a well-thought-out Policy and Procedure Manual. This manual should include qualifications for weight room supervisors, hours of operation, pre-participation screening and medical clearance for all students using the facility, maintenance and equipment upkeep and cleaning checklist, maximum occupancy standards, supervisor-to-athlete ratios, the facility's Emergency Action Plan, and athlete Informed Consent documents. Detailed work on the front end will save a lot of headaches on the back end if problems occur. It is the duty of athletic and scholastic administration to mitigate risk through policy and ensuring that these policies are followed.

The program, facility, and groups must also be organized to maximize safety. The weight room is arguably one of the most dangerous places in a scholastic setting. Accidents and injuries can and will occur if safety and adequate supervision is not a priority. Horseplay by the trainees, equipment that is in ill repair, training stations that are placed too close together, and a poor traffic flow through the facility can all be areas of safety concern. Safety should also take the form of proper exercise technique and appropriate loading and progressions. A systematic program with accurate record keeping will go a long way here.

Proper warm-up in both a general and exercise-specific sense will also prepare the trainee and reduce the chance of injury during training. Safety is also a factor in choosing specific exercises for the trainee population to perform. Advanced exercises are for advanced trainees and the novice or intermediate athlete should be programmed as such. As a general rule, if it looks unsafe, it probably is.

Lastly, safety of the athletes should be of concern as the SCP prepares individuals for the rigors and demands of sport competition. Identifying the areas of the body that are vulnerable to injury (either acute or chronic) due to sport participation and determining where can risk be mitigated by developing strength and hypertrophy in the athlete are critical questions to address. These areas of training must be a priority for the coach and athlete.

Consistency

All the best, most cutting-edge programming and training techniques are rendered useless without consistency. Development of the young athlete is a long-term process, and although amazing progress can be made in a few short weeks, the real value comes through months and years of proper training. Accepting this fact will dictate organizational factors in the program. Training sessions should be reasonable, repeatable, and enjoyable. The coach needs the trainee to be ready, willing, and able to return for training physically and psychologically prepared. "Slow cooking" the program with slow, steady linear progressions will result in positive adaptation and engaged trainees.

Progressive Design

For the novice or intermediate weight trainee, linear progressive overload is a game changer. Such athletes literally get stronger with each training session. A recording system that accurately tracks performance will be an incredibly valuable administrative tool. As mentioned previously, such tracking is also important for safety reasons, as well. There is a wide variety of systems that can be implemented for such purposes and have proven beneficial, including computerized programs, Excel worksheets at racks/stations, and workout cards filled in by trainees/coaches, etc. The specific system chosen is not nearly as important as how consistently it is implemented. Training data must be valid in order to be effective, and it is the job of the SCP to ensure it is accurate.

Comprehensive Approach

An effective weight training program for any athlete is intended to provide comprehensive development in order to minimize the risk of injury and increase physical capabilities to improve performance. This should not be a bodybuilding, powerlifting, or Olympic weight lifting program. The SCP should focus on the basics and strive for balanced development in all structures. Again, specific emphasis can—and should—be placed on areas of the body vulnerable to injury. Incorporating un-structured free time at the end of any particular session to allow athletes to perform additional work is acceptable, but the focus should be on fundamental movements and injury minimization.

Time Efficiency

Training in the scholastic setting (high school or college) is a race against time. Academic and sport requirements will necessitate a training program that is efficient and quite frankly does not take much time. The SCP is advised to strip the programming to its most basic and fundamental elements. Focusing on proper performance, accurate record keeping, and structured rest periods helps maxi-mize efficiency. Time left over is a bonus, but the SCP must be certain include all the most important aspects of training. Warm-up included, an effective training session should rarely last longer that 60-90 minutes and can frequently be cut to 30-45 minutes when necessary.

Flexibility

Successful weight training programs for athletes are not rigid in programming or exercise selection. The old saying "Many roads lead to Rome" applies. The focus should be on quality move-ment and repetition performance. The basic movements must be emphasized, yet the tool used (barbell, dumbbell, machine, bodyweight, etc.) is less important as long as progression is present. Sturdy and standard equipment is necessary: barbells, racks, dumbbells, and benches, with enough to accommodate the largest groups. Athletes will frequently need to train around injuries, so a com-prehensively outfitted training facility will have a variety of tools available. Examples would be 4-way neck machines to document progress in neck strength or "no hands" or "no feet" equipment to train athletes with specific injuries. Without proper tools and a flexible SCP, the athlete will easily become de-trained.

Program Goals

The SCP must clearly communicate the goals of the training program to all involved. Although goals can—and should—vary from coach to coach and site to site, several are relatively universal and applicable regardless of personal philosophy or situation specifics. First, the program should be designed to reduce risk of injury both in training and on the field. The SCP should identify areas or mechanisms of injury in sport that are vulnerable and require specific attention. Next, the program should increase the maximum outputs and capacities of the trainees. Strength, power, speed, aerobic capacity, and sport-specific energy system capacity are all measurable and should be improved over time. Additionally, programming should improve—or at least maintain—functional mobility in joints and structures, reducing risk of injury and enhancing sport performance. Furthermore, the program should improve athlete body composition through the increase in lean body mass and reduction of fat mass. Lastly, it should help the athlete develop and nurture the intangibles such as attention to detail, work ethic, teamwork, and leadership.

Program Synergy

It is essential that all areas of a sport program share a common vision and consistent message. The core values and beliefs of a program must be emphasized throughout. The success of the program hinges on all involved parties, including the administration, sport staff, medical staff, parents, and the athletes being on the same page. Frequent meetings, newsletters, and email updates can all serve to enhance communication. The absence of ego and the development of genuine respect and deference to individual's areas of expertise is critical to the process. Too often, the sport coach or administrator will attempt to dictate the program to the SCP. Only possessing "dangerous knowledge" can lead to resentment and a program that lacks synergy and flow. The SCP was hired to bring their expertise to the program. As such, those individuals must be empowered to do so and supported to get the job done. Communication is the lifeblood of any successful organization, and all parties are responsible for maintaining clear lines of communication.

The weight training program itself must also have synergy and consistency for all athletes. Especially at the novice or intermediate levels of sport, there is no such thing as a "sport-specific" weight training program as it pertains to performance. As stated previously, weight training is not a primary means of development for sport but rather general physical preparation. This does not mean that all athletes need to perform the same exercises; however, the training templates should be similar. The sport-specific aspect of the weight training program should be reflected in the injury prevention aspect and whether that particular sport is in-season or off-season. This will allow the SCP to effectively implement programs for various sport participants simultaneously. Sport-specificity will be seen more during conditioning, movement work, and actual sport practice.

Consistent Obligations and Expectations

The program will be able to run smoothly when administrative issues are handled appropriately. Most athletes thrive in a consistent environment with consistent standards, expectations, and consequences. There must be clear and consistent obligations and expectations from both athletes and sport coaches. While a number of principles could suffice here, issues such as promptness, attire, rest periods, spotting, and overall demeanor are critical components to a winning (or a losing) culture.

First, athletes should be prompt and on time for scheduled training sessions. If unable to attend the session on time, the athlete should contact the SCP beforehand so that necessary arrangements can be made. Next, having a dress code will go a long way towards eliminating issues beforehand. Shirts with sleeves (not cut-offs, tank tops, etc.), gym shorts of appropriate length, training sneakers tied up (no sandals, cleats), a no hats or other headgear, earphones, and no cell phones policy should be strictly enforced. Thirdly, everyone in the training environment should have a responsibility: coach, lift, spot, load. There should be no sitting down in the weight room unless the exercise calls for it. Keeping athletes on task will eliminate excessive socializing and horseplay that will get in the way of productive training. "Resting strong" connotes being ready and not leaning on or sitting on equipment during the session. Furthermore, the jobs of spotters and repetition counters are just as important as performing the actual lift. Getting the athletes to work together and to be accountable to each other will safeguard against missed reps and sets. Athletes need to be held to consistent standards. Lastly, attitude precedes performance. Creating a culture and community where athletes look at training as something they "get to do" versus something they have "got to do" will increase effectiveness. This is where the art of coaching comes into play. The training environment, although structured, should not be a place that the athletes dread coming into. The SCP's job is to create an atmosphere and program that is nurturing and enjoyable, yet safe and productive.

Training Readiness

Weight training will stimulate positive adaptation to occur as a response to the overload stimulus. Gains occur during the recovery time between training sessions. Frequent education on proper sleep, nutrition, and hydration can be an effective means of changing behaviors. It is not enough to train hard—the "24-hour athlete" who is committed away from the weight room will show the most progress. Set aside time daily to educate athletes about recovery.

Depending upon training time of day, the SCP should consider providing a light snack and fluids before the session. This is a great way to get the booster or parent clubs involved. Fruit, snack bars, hard pretzels, and peanut butter and jelly sandwiches are all inexpensive ways to pre-fuel athletes. Getting a donation of water bottles so that athletes can monitor their hydration daily is also effective. An athlete-centered model will prioritize things like this.

Athletes perform better when they have a daily routine. It serves to prepare not only the body but the mind for training. Consistent obligation to time, dress, and demeanor should all be involved in the daily routine.

Scheduling

In order to make training safe and effective, the weight training facility must adhere to a strict schedule. This will allow the SCP to be organized with both workouts and staff. Training groups before school, after school, and in weight training-specific classes will help avoid the over-crowded and under-staffed weight training facility. Groups can also be run on Saturday mornings if necessary. The SCP should have a scheduling policy to help avoid conflicts. Since schedules for in-season teams are usually already tight, scheduling priority should go to the in-season teams with the largest numbers of participants.

The weight training schedule should be completed as far ahead of time as possible to allow for planning. The SCP must also be flexible enough to adapt to schedule changes and the fluidity of the academic year. Once a schedule is in place, the SCP will be able to anticipate how many trainees must be accommodated at a time. Weekly schedules should be posted and distributed so that sport coaching staffs, athletes, and parents can be informed and reminded through whatever communication channel has been established (text, e-mail, team apps, etc.).

Schedule Example

Date: February 6-11, 2017

	M	T	W	R	F	Sa
6:45 AM	*Off-season football athletes not enrolled in weight training class. Speed training & lift: 2-3 non-consecutive days/week. Before school or Saturday @ 9:00 AM. Pre- and post-training fueling station.*					
8:00 AM	Weight training class. In or off-season athletes.					
9:00 AM	Weight training class. In or off-season athletes.					
10:00 AM	Weight training class. In or off-season athletes.					
11:00 AM	Planning period					
12:00 PM	Lunch room supervision					
1:00 PM	Weight training class. In or off-season athletes.					
2:00 PM	Weight training class. In or off-season athletes.					
3:00 PM	In-season sport practice. *Off-season non-football athletes not enrolled in weight training class. Speed training & lift: 2-3 non-consecutive days/week or Saturday @ 10:00 AM*					
4:30 PM	Post-practice lift, in-season athletes not enrolled in weight training class.					

Coaching Assistants

Ideally, coach-to-athlete ratios in the weight training program should be as small as possible. Unfortunately, this is not a common reality in most scholastic weight rooms. It is imperative that the SCP train the coaches assisting in the weight training program so that standards of repetition performance, rest periods, and data tracking be consistent. All supervisors involved must share a common vision, standards, and use similar coaching cues. This will maintain consistency with the trainees.

In an ideal setting, the SCP would hire other trained and qualified individuals to assist him or her either on a full-time or part-time basis. Unfortunately, in many high school and small college environments, this is simply not feasible. As an alternative to hiring more SCPs to assist in group settings, the SCP should recruit volunteer assistance. Sport coaches can and should be involved with their team's weight training program.

Another avenue for increasing the number of supervisors on the floor would be to recruit students from universities who desire a career in the strength and conditioning profession. These experiences could account for practicum or internship requirements for a college degree. All coaches and supervisors who will be on the floor for a training session should be well versed in the training script for that day. A short staff meeting is highly beneficial preceding a session. It is also wise to have a debriefing session after the workout to review and make any individual adjustments that will be necessary for the next training session. Regardless of the process, it is clear that a successful weight training program will have a number of motivated and qualified individuals to assist in the implementation.

Facility

The weight training facility should be designed and organized according to how the SCP will be conducting group training sessions. Equipment should be arranged to maximize coaching efficiency and training flow. As time and efficiency are factors, the SCP should eliminate any equipment that is unnecessary for training groups. Some equipment may be in storage and pulled out during times of the year that it will be put to use. Every piece of equipment in the weight room must have a purpose. Novelty items may be interesting, but functionality should overrule entertainment. The SCP should continually evaluate the equipment used and functionality of the facility. Yearly budgets should cover repairs and consumable equipment such as bands, balls, and jump ropes. A facility that is cared for with great pride will last longer and be less costly over time. Regular daily cleaning and maintenance will ensure a healthy and safe facility that will last.

Coaching on the Floor

With the facility organized and arranged to maximize training efficiency, considerations should be made to optimally position coaches and supervisors. The SCP should be the manager of the training session with assistants and sport coaches serving supervisory roles. A well-organized session will begin with the SCP going over the workout and expectations in front of the group. This is a great time to hit the group with master coaching cues. Each session may have a different emphasis: depth on squats, full extension on chin-ups, tempo on neck exercises, etc. A group warm-up or mobility session can follow assigning athletes to areas/stations. This will eliminate wandering around to start the session or attempting to organize athletes in the middle of training.

Ideally, each coach should be assigned to no more than 8-12 athletes at a time, and less is almost always better. Coaches must position themselves so that athletes are in front of them. It is impossible to coach a technique or skill that one cannot see. It is advisable for the coach to jump in, give some coaching cues, and get back out so that all athletes under their care can be seen.

Keeping the athletes training in a proper sequence is another responsibility of the SCP. For example, in a four-person rotation in a squat rack, athlete #1 will be lifting, athlete #2 will be spotting and athletes #3 & #4 will be responsible for changing the weight for next athlete. They will then rotate through these roles in a prescribed order. This will provide consistency to rest periods and keep traffic flow consistent. Accountability to all aspects of the program (repetition performance, recording, etc.) can now be maintained.

The system that works best for each SCP will be individualized, but the key is structure and order. Some coaches may have athletes rotate on a whistle, while others allow the athletes to work at their own pace. Still other coaches may prefer the use of timed stations where a certain number of sets and reps must be performed in a given amount of time. Coachable moments are everywhere and organization can ensure that they are not missed.

Coaching Instructions and Cues

As mentioned earlier, all coaches must share common standards for both repetition performance and load or intensity parameters. The coaching staff must also use common instructions and cues on the weight room floor in order to ensure consistency and aide in corrections. A staff who frequently meets with one another and discusses athlete training can share instructions and cues that work best with the group. As with learning any other skill, hammering the athletes with a consistent message, expectations, and standards will eventually result in safe, consistent, and productive training. It is helpful if each coach can perform and demonstrate each exercise for the athlete. If a coach is not comfortable teaching a particular exercise, the SCP either needs to thoroughly train that coach, change that coach's station, or eliminate the exercise from the training session. The SCP should put coaches and supervisors in stations and groups that fit their skill set.

Each movement taught should also have consistent progressions and regressions for coaches to use. For example, a progression on the squat exercise may look like this:

A. Body weight squat with dowel: held in front of the body, held on the back of the shoulders, held overhead

B. Front loaded squat with dumbbell

C. Front loaded squat with barbell

D. Back loaded squat with barbell

Each coach can progress the athletes from stage to stage once mastered and regress when there is a need to take a step back in terms of difficulty or load. As the coach becomes highly skilled, he or she will know what to look for, how things can be corrected, and any individual nuances that may present themselves. The better the coach, the better the quality of the training.

Daily Script and Template

Organizing a daily training script and template is a way for the SCP to organize training multiple groups at one time. Below is an example of how one may organize an after-school training group made up of off-season athletes from a variety of sports. Time, staffing, equipment, and training are organized to optimize both personnel and equipment. The SCP is essentially the manager of the training session and is able to coach and administer the workout. The assistants, interns, and sport coaches ensure that each athlete is getting adequate coaching. The methods and means chosen are based upon the space and equipment available. Two sample scripts are given. Script #1 is an example of a program that is getting adequate support from sport coaches and administration, while Script #2 may be more applicable (but far from ideal) in a program that is still developing full support but does have an SCP on staff.

Sample Script # 1

Date:	M 2/6/17		
Time:	3:00 PM, after school		
Groups:	Off-season athletes		Coaches assigned:
A	Var. football (20#)		SCP- 1
B	Fr. football (12#)		FB Coach- 1
C	Track/cross country (8#)		Volleyball Coach- 1
D	Volleyball (6#)		
	Total:	46	3

3:00 PM Fieldhouse

Equipment: 8# MBs (11), 12# MBs (5), Hurdles (4 high, 4 low), QF Ladder (2)

Warm-up- group

	Start	Coach	
1. Mobility: quadruped series (5:00)	Start all	Coach SCP	
2. Prepatory Stations (3 x 5:00 ea.)	Start	Coach	
A. Extensive MB Routine: 2 x 15 ea.	A	SCP	*rotate on whistle
B. Hurdles/Crawl	B	FB	
C. OF Ladder Hops	C/D	VB	

3:20 PM

A/B Groups: Speed/Power- Fieldhouse			C & D Groups: Core Lifts- Weight Room			
Equipment: 12# MBs (6), 20# MBs (5), Speed Sleds (6) w/ 10 & 25# plate			Equipment: Racks w/ benches (8)			
	Start	**Coach**	*Pace- 4, rest- 2:00*	**Start**	**Coach**	**AREA**
						RACK-
A. C.O.D. Progression	A & B	SCP	A.BP- BB	C & D	VB	3
B. MB THROW: 2 X 6	A	FB	5 X 5 CHART			
C. Sled Sprints X 6 (1:30)	B	FB	B. FT SQT- BB		SCP	
			5 x 5 chart			

3:40 PM	A/B Groups: Core Lifts- Weight Room				C/D/E Groups: Aux. Lifts- Weight Room			
	Equipment: Racks W/ BP (8)				Equipment: DB stations (4), TRX (6), GHR (4), Ankle Boards			
	Pace- 4, rest- 2:00	**Start**	**Coach**	**AREA**	*Pace- 2, rest-1:00*	**Start**	**Coach**	**AREA**
	A. BP- BB	A & B	FB	RACK-8	C. BK.RAISE. GHR	C	SCP	GHR
	5 x 5 chart				3 x 8			
	B. FT SQT- BB		SCP		D. SA TRX ROW	D	VB	TRX
	5 x 5 chart				3 x 8			
					E. ANKE PROGRAM			WALL

4:00 PM	A/B Groups: Core Lifts- Weight Room				C/D/E Groups: Speed/Power- Fieldhouse			
	Equipment: DB stations (6), TRX (6), GHR (6), Neck Machine (4)				Equipment: 12# MBs (6), 20# MBs (5), Speed Sleds (6) w/ 10 & 25# plate			
	Pace- 2, rest-1:00	**Start**	**Coach**	**AREA**			**Start**	**Coach**
	C. BK.RAISE. GHR	A	FB	GHR	A. C.O.D. Progression		A & B	SCP
	3 x 8				A. MB THROW: 2 X 6		A	VB
	D. SA TRX ROW	B	FB	RACK-5	B. Sled Sprints X 6 (1:30)		B	VB
	3 x 8							
	E1. FT/BK NECK X 12-10 EA.		FB	NECK				
	E2. SA DB SHRUG X 12-10 EA.		FB	DB				

4:20 PM	Fieldhouse- Post Stretch	SCP

Sample Script # 2

Date:	M 2-6-17	
Time:	3:00 PM, after school	
Groups:	**Off-season athletes**	**Coaches assigned:**
A	Var. football (20#)	SCP- 1
B	Fr. football (12#)	
C	Track/cross country (8#)	
D	Volleyball (6#)	
	Total: 46	1

3:00 PM Fieldhouse

Equipment: 8# MBs (11), 12# MBs (5), Hurdles (4 high, 4 low), QF Ladder (2)

Warm-up- group

		Start	Coach	
1. Mobility: quadruped series (5:00)		all	SCP	
2. Prepatory Stations (3 x 5:00 ea.)		Start	Coach	
A. Extensive MB Routine: 2 x 15 ea.		A	SCP	*rotate on whistle
B. Hurdles/Crawl		B	SCP	
C. OF Ladder Hops		C/D	SCP	

3:20 PM Speed/Power- Fieldhouse

Equipment: 12 cones, 12 mini-hurdles, 8# MBs (11), 12# MBs (5)

	Start	Coach
	all	SCP

1. C.OD. Progression- 4 cone drill x 4

2. Mini-Hurdle Hop to Sprint 10 x 4

3. MB Throw to Sprint x 4

3:40 PM Strength- Weight Room

Equipment: Racks W/ BP (5), DB stations (4), TRX stations- wall mounted (4), Bands (12)

*rotate as group when completed, down then back to top

EXERCISE	SETS/REPS	Start	Coach	AREA
A. BP- BB	5 x 5 chart	A	SCP	RACKS
Pace- 4, rest- 2:00				
B. DB FT SQT	5 X 10	B	SCP	DB
Pace- 2, rest- 1:00				
C. SA TRX ROW	3 X 8	C	SCP	WALL
Pace- 2, rest- 1:00				
D. CORE- BIRD-DOG & DEAD BUG	3 X 10 EA.	D	SCP	BAND
Pace- 1, no rest				
E. A & B GROUPS- NECK/TRAPS, C & D GROUPS- ANKLE			SCP	

NECK/TRAPS: DB AREA   ANKLE: BAND AREA

A. M.R. FT & BK NECK X :90 EA.   A. BAND 4 WAY ANKLE X 10 EA.

Summary

The ultimate success of a strength and conditioning program will lie in the results obtained. Properly trained athletes will be more resistant to injury and continue to develop on a year-to-year basis toward their full potential. It is frequently the SCP's attention to the details of administration, organization, and implementation of the program that determines success or failure. Selecting qualified professionals, providing adequate resources, and supporting the program are crucial factors. The program will also be most successful when prescribed training is executed with precision, passion, and a hint of individualization. This requires expert coaching and training of additional weight room supervisors. Facilities and training sessions should be organized for safety, maximum supervision, and efficient flow through the workout. When the strength and conditioning program is running with this attention to detail, positive results are all but assured.

CHAPTER 16

Motivation and Leadership Through Coaching

Ron McKeefery

Objectives

- Describe the construct of motivation and discuss the ways through which one person can motivate another

- Examine the unique features of intrinsic, extrinsic, and self-motivation and identify ways to leverage each to best benefit the athlete

- Describe and discuss the five keys to motivation

Introduction

Most Exercise Science programs do not offer a course in motivation or leadership. As an aspiring strength and conditioning professional (SCP), most students spend the majority of their time learning the technical side of the profession and often come out with an educational understanding of scientific principles and how they apply to the field of Strength and Conditioning. However, most any SCP will tell you that such is simply the first step. The old adage is true: "You can write the best strength and conditioning program on paper, but unless you can get them to do it, the program might as well be the worse."

Speak to any veteran coach and they will tell you that athletes today demonstrate a greater sense of entitlement. There is a decline in player leadership and athlete motivation is at an all-time low. Each generation probably says that about the one before, but data seems to support this notion. Tim Elmore in his book Generation IY states, "This generation is the smartest generation of all time, but they are the most socially disconnected as well."[1] How many times have you walked into a locker room and seen multiple players sitting in their locker starring at their phones rather than conversing with one another? Pair that with those same phones streaming tons of information, and it creates a tough shell to crack.

What is Motivation?

Simply put, motivation is a desire to achieve a goal or the ability to commit to a goal and go after it with enthusiasm. It is sometimes described as an inner drive, impulse, or intention that causes a person to do something or act in a certain way. Maximizing that motivation leads to the greatest improvements in any pursuit.

Why Should We Worry About Motivation?

We should back up and first ask why we even need to worry about motivation. If we put the most talented and physically gifted athletes on the field, we should win, right? There are three things that affect how well you perform, including ability, difficulty of competition, and motivation. Ability is composed of those attributes an individual is born with such as physical, technical, tactical, and mental capabilities. As a coach, the SCP has the ability to contribute to those capabilities; however, there is a genetic ceiling. Plus, how many times has a more gifted athlete lost to an inferior opponent? It is one of the things people love most about sport: rooting for the underdog.

Athletes and coaches have little to no control over the difficulty of the competition. Each season will start with coaches telling their teams that there is only one champion. Only one team will win it all. Even then, sometimes those athletes or teams have been beaten at some point in the regular season. There is always someone more talented, and athletes would do well to understand that there is little they can do to control that. The athlete must also understand that he or she cannot control the away game crowd, the officials, or the weather, all of which can influence an outcome.

The one attribute of performance that the athlete has direct control over is the ability to put in the time and effort to improve performance and realize it on game day. In fact, it is the only contributor to sports performance that is directly controllable. Motivation is the foundation of all athletic effort and accomplishment. Without the ability to motivate him or herself or the team, an athlete's competition and ability are meaningless. If both teams are equally skilled, the more motivated team will typically determine the outcome of the game.

Can One Person Motivate Another?

Most coaches were typically former athletes who have chosen the profession of coaching for the rest of their life. They are typically Type A, intrinsically motivated individuals. The thought of not being motivated to play or train for a sport they love is difficult for them to comprehend. Tommy Moffitt, Head Strength & Conditioning Coach at Louisiana State University, states that "the athletes you work with each and every day will never love the weight room as much as you do, because you chose to do this for the rest of your life." So the question becomes, can one person really motivate another? Motivating anyone can be difficult, dynamic, and frustrating. To be effective takes insight and patience.

Types of Motivation

Intrinsic Motivation

Remember when you were a kid out in the backyard playing football? When your mom called you home for dinner, you did not want the game to stop. Even though you wanted to win, you did not really care who won, either. You just loved to play. That is best way to describe intrinsic motivation. When you participated in sports for internal reasons, you found sport enjoyable and satisfying without being preoccupied with external rewards. The building blocks, or psychological needs, that underlie intrinsic motivation are the need to determine one's behavior. This self-determination is the need to feel competent and to have meaningful relationships with other people.

To help an athlete find motivation intrinsically, you must help them change the way he or she thinks about their roles, their reasons for coming to practice, their influence on teammates, their membership on the team, and their reasons for playing and competing. You must provide an environment that is conducive to personal growth and is highly encouraging. It is a significant time investment, but this is most effective for long-term motivation. Having intrinsic motivation helps the athlete navigate emotional dry patches and helps keep the emphasis on having fun. Intrinsic motivation comes with a complete absence of any internal or external pressure to perform well.

Intrinsic Behaviors

- **Better task-relevant focus**
- **Fewer changes (ups/downs) motivation**
- **Less distraction**
- **Less stress when mistakes are made**
- **Increased confidence and self-efficacy**
- **Greater satisfaction**

Why Do Athletes Play The Game?

- **To be with friends or make friends.**
- **Be part of a group**
- **Competition**
- **Support from others**
- **Parental pressure**
- **Want to find something to be identified with.**

Extrinsic Motivation

Extrinsic motivation focuses on the competitive or performance outcome. Extrinsically-motivated athletes typically have less interest, value, and effort toward achievement. They are usually more anxious and have more difficulty coping with failure than their intrinsically-motivated peers. Coaches who use extrinsic motivation tactics use often use social incentives and/or fear as motivators for athletic performance. Social methods will include not wanting to disappoint a parent, teammate, and friends.

Fear is simple to use and can be effective; however, it can easily breed resentment and disloyalty. Athletes who are motivated by fear are not working toward achieving something, but rather trying to avoid negative consequences. They become focused on what *not* to do rather than what *to* do.

When used correctly, incentives can benefit athletes. Dangling the carrot (playing time, awards, money, etc.) is effective in the short term, however these items must be increased or made more appealing over time to continue to have the same effect. Highly competitive athletes may experience decreases in their intrinsic motivation because of the increasing use of extrinsic rewards offered by the media, coaches, and parents. Extrinsic reward controls the behaviors of the athlete, rewards negative information about the athlete's ability, is not directly connected to a specific behavior or performance level, and is provided for a behavior that is should already be intrinsically rewarding.

As coaches, we need to continue to promote the idea of personal satisfaction from physical activity. Being driven solely by extrinsic motives is not psychologically healthy. The lack of intrinsic rewards can lead an athlete to quit or question their involvement, while an athlete who is predominately extrinsically motivated tends to become discouraged when performance fails to meet expectations. Conversely, an athlete who is predominately intrinsically motivated often does not have the competitive drive to become a champion. This is because this athlete tends to enjoy mastering the tasks that comprise their chosen discipline but lacks a strong competitive streak that can fuel a relentless work ethic. The goal is to combine intrinsic with extrinsic motivation. Experiencing competence and success due to their own actions and skills, the greater their intrinsic motivation. Even with extrinsic rewards, athletes who feel like they are in control of their behaviors will be more satisfied and more likely to continue participating. Extrinsic motivation is most effective when intrinsic motivation is high.

Self-Motivation

A self-motivated athlete possesses an internal pressure to perform well, maintains a positive attitude, and develops an unflinching concentration that is mediated by both intrinsic and extrinsic factors. Pro Football Hall of Fame wide receiver Jerry Rice is a great example of a self-motivated athlete. Rice, one of eight children, was the son of a hardworking bricklayer who employed him and his brothers each summer. Rice went on to play football at Mississippi Valley State, a small NCAA I-AA (now FCS) school two hours west of his hometown of Crawford, Mississippi. From there, he worked his way to All-American honors to become a first-round pick in the 1985 NFL draft. It would have been easy for him to end the story right there. He never was the fastest runner, highest jumper, or strongest lifter but became legendary for his tireless work ethic to become the best he could be. That effort and attitude propelled him to a 20-year career in the NFL, multiple Super Bowl rings, and first-ballot enshrinement into the Pro Football Hall of Fame in 2010.[2]

Most people will refer to a self-motivated athlete who has a balance of intrinsic and extrinsic factors as being "in the zone" or "flow." Flow is the complete immersion in an activity to the point that nothing else seems to matter. It is a perfect blend between the perceived demands of an activity, and the perceived ability to meet those demands.

Different athletes are motivated by different situations and feedback. As coaches, we must surround them with a healthy balance of both in order to maintain a high level of motivation. An effective coach will have the ability to identify signs of low motivation in an athlete and provide what is needed to enhance their mental state and effectiveness.

Self-Motivated Behaviors

- **Internal control of behaviors**
- **Choice to participate even with extrinsic rewards**
- **Greater interest enjoyment and effort towards achievement**
- **Desire to learn new skills or strategies**
- **Positive coping styles**

Signs of low motivation include a lack of desire to practice as much as you should, less than 100% effort in training, a tendency to skip or shorten training, and effort that is inconsistent with the scope of expressed goals. Having a balance of intrinsic and extrinsic motivation will not only help in good times, but also in bad. It takes a self-motivated athlete to be able to effectively push through the "grind" of training and competition. Human nature will force you to arrive at a point at which it is no longer fun. It gets tiring, painful, and tedious. It takes a motivated athlete to push past it. Despite popular motivational websites and memes to the contrary, very few people actually love the grind. However, many athletes can come to accept and enjoy the outcome of seeing hard work pay off with success.

Motivation in sports is important because an athlete must be willing to work hard in the face of fatigue, boredom, pain, and the desire to do uncommon things. Motivation will impact everything that influences an individual's sports performance: physical conditioning, technical and tactical training, mental preparation, and general lifestyle including sleep, diet, school or work, and personal relationships.

Five Ways to Motivate

Reinforcement

Reinforcement is one of the most effective ways to motivate. Think of this as the foundation of the motivation pyramid. Much like the foundation of a house or building, the concrete slab is reinforced by rebar. If that metal is strong and supportive it will lead to a sturdy foundation. If it weak and negative the whole house can come down.

As a coach, reinforcement will provide an indication of knowledge. It can be both positive and negative. Negative criticism will detrimentally influence motivation 100% of the time. Athletes will become angry, confused, and/or hurt. Positive feedback is very effective but can also become negative if only used as a reward. The SCP's job is to provide the athlete with both internal and external techniques that can be used for motivation and support. Internally, there are three ways, including self-talk, immersion effect, and daily self-questions.

Self-Talk

Self-talk is one of the most tried and true strategies among sports psychologists, coaches, and athletes. One of the most notable athletes to use this technique was Mohammad Ali. He would use it to maintain concentration and to induce optimal arousal.

There are three types of self-talk, including task-relevant, mood-related, and positive self-affirmation. Task-relevant techniques are common among fighters, many of whom are well known for reciting coaching cues throughout practice and matches to maintain proper technique. "Guard up. Chin down," helps the athlete be sure to maintain the proper posture to move, take, and deliver a blow. This technique must be used consistently and often in a fatigued state to have a positive effect.

Mood-related self-talk can be seen in most any locker room before a competition. Chants, sayings, songs, etc. heard and/or repeated aloud is a form of mood-related self-talk. This technique triggers the athlete's psyche and raises the emotional state. For what is being asked of an athlete's body in competition, it often takes altering conventional wisdom.

Lastly, positive self-affirmation is yet another approach. "I am the greatest" would be heard in most of Ali's press interviews. No one and no thing has more power to elevate or break down an athlete's mental state than his or her own voice. Ali knew this, and made sure that the voice in his head was his own with a very positive message.

Immersion Effect

Immersion effect is another form of intrinsic reinforcement. It requires the athlete to find a quiet place where they can focus. There the athlete will recall a time that they were performing at the very peak of their ability when everything seemed to work flawlessly, then diving deeply into everything that characterized it. This can be beneficial in recreating a time or place when performance was ideal, but may be difficult for an athlete who has experienced limited success.

Daily Self-Questions

It is hard for an individual to look into the mirror and lie. Asking a question in the mirror in the morning such as "What can I do today to be the best athlete I can be?" then returning at night to that same mirror to ask, "Did I do everything I could today to be the best athlete I can be?" is an example of this approach. The technique of asking daily self-questions can be a very effective form of intrinsic reinforcement.

Externally, it is very important to provide reinforcement both individually and within the group. As coaches, we must recognize the attention to social influence and actively seek opportunities to recognize specific contributions by the athlete to practice and to the team. For this to be most effective you must research and identify their support system. Those individuals could be their family, previous coaches, teammates, etc. Providing positive reinforcement to the athlete in front of those individuals will build a strong, trusting relationship that can be used as a solid foundation for some of the following motivational strategies.

Feedback

Knowledge of results is similar to reinforcement, but provides much more relevant information to the athlete. Objective, accurate, and meaningful feedback is essential for proper skill acquisition. Athletes love feedback, especially when it is enriched with accurate and objective information. When feedback is given with encouragement, significant improvements in motivation occur, and self-perception of ability rises.

Athletes learn in primarily three distinct ways: through verbal, visual, or kinesthetic means. As such, it is important that the SCP and the sport coach provide instruction and feedback in all three ways. When introducing a new skill, the SCP should make sure to provide clear verbal instructions complete with coaching cues and common mistakes. Visually demonstrating the skill to the athlete either personally or through the use of a highly skilled team member is beneficial. With many of the younger generation increasingly dependent on visual learning styles, this approach is typically far more effective than verbal instructions alone. The SCP can then observe the athlete's efforts and subsequently provide feedback and ways for the athlete to perform the movement or skill correctly.

Feedback also involves keeping the athlete informed. The athlete will benefit from knowing the when, where, how, and why of sport performance—with the "why" being the most important. Athletes are not generally motivated to start or finish a task that is not clearly defined by those terms. As an SCP, it is essential to take away any questions or doubts the athlete may have by clearly and consistently communicating the desired expectations and intentions.

Goal Setting

Goal setting can be the best motivator of all the techniques. It provides a step-by-step approach to the athlete to help reach their desired outcome. Goals should not become expectations that weigh down an athlete. Instead, proper goals are clearly defined and include some over-reaching, some mid-term, and some short-term process goals.

For goals to be most effective, they should be both intrinsically and extrinsically-based. Extrinsic goals are best established by getting input from coaches, teammates, sports medicine staff, etc. on how the athlete may best improve. Intrinsically, this is best accomplished in the goal-setting meeting as the athlete sits down and meets with the SCP and sport coach to express exactly what they intend to accomplish.

The SCP should steer this discussion and make sure there is an understanding of perceived reality. Oftentimes, athletes need feedback in order to develop an accurate understanding of their abilities. The SCP should first define what is good. Most athletes want to be the best where they are or are motivated by going to the next level (high school to college, college to professional, etc.). The SCP should establish and reiterate standards for what it would take to go to the next level of their sport.

It is important to note that the SCP's job is not to be a dream killer but rather a dream lifter. Just because an athlete is far from their desired goal or standard does not mean any coach has an obligation to make that individual come to that harsh reality. Instead, the SCP's job is to define what is good and then work to get the athlete as close to that aspirational goal as possible. Once this has been done, the athlete must be reminded that the imposed expectations are in pursuit of the goals the athlete themselves established and in pursuit of dreams that they want. Often, this can be done through the use of a signed commitment contract. A commitment contract is a written statement or series of statements that the athlete promises to follow. Both athlete and coach should commit to evaluating and changing goals as needed.

Environment

Different athletes are motivated by different situations and feedback. Administration, coaches, parents, and teammates should all work together to promote a motivational climate for the athletes. Consider four ways to make your environment more motivating.

1. Competition – Athletes love to compete, as it brings out their natural instincts. It is a free source to provide a motivating environment and should be used often. The SCP should find ways for athletes to compete against themselves, a standard, or others.

2. Multi-sensory images – Sight, sound, and touch are very powerful motivators. Using music, inspirational messages, and photographs can raise an athlete's emotional energy.

3. Recognition – The SCP must create an environment that allows for challenge, accountability, recognition, appreciation, and quality. Recognizing athletes before and after training, in the locker room, and around campus generates feelings of inspiration and pride.

4. Variety –Athletes get bored easily, and want training that is fun, different, and always challenging.

Care

The SCP must give his or her athletes a reason to want to work hard. It is essential for the SCP to take the time to develop genuine, honest, caring, and trusting relationships with the athletes under his or her care. This begins with modeling desired behaviors. Simply put, if you want someone to work hard for you, then you better work hard for them and for others. If the intention is for athletes to put in the extra time, that behavior should be demonstrated by the SCP. Most coaches want to appear like they have all the answers and do not like showing vulnerability, but vulnerability is endearing. Demonstrating that the SCP is putting extra work and time for his or her athletes can be highly motivating.

As an SCP, you typically have your athletes for one or two hours a day. For that time to be most effective, you have to be involved with the remainder that occurs outside of the walls of your facility. Find time to get outside of the weight room or the boundaries of the practice field/court to interact with your athletes. The author has found creating life experiences, bonding opportunities, one-on-one interactions, special or variety workouts, and involving his family to be most effective in demonstrating a caring heart.

The Bottom Line

If two teams are equal in skill, the motivated team will typically win. As such, it is easy to understand why coaches must learn to harness and develop the concept motivation. However, it must be a two-way street. The SCP can give the reinforcement, feedback, goals, environment, and show genuine care, but if athletes do not reciprocate, we will find ourselves in the losing column. Most every athlete wants to win and has big goals. However, how many are doing everything they can to achieve those goals? While it is easy to say you *want* success, it is much harder to actually work for it. As a coach, the SCP has two choices: lower goals to match poor effort or raise effort to match stated goals. Prime motivation means putting 100% of your time, effort, energy, and focus into all aspects of success. As coaches, SCPs have an obligation to hold a team to that high standard.

When faced with obstacles, focus on the 3 D's: direction, decision, and dedication. First, consider the different directions you can go, stop, stay, or strive. Next, decide on a direction. And lastly, dedicate to that direction and decision. Leadership does not just mean finding the ways to motivate. It means establishing a culture and standard for the organization to strive for, then refocusing when the natural tendency to settle for less takes over. Those who can do that the best will provide a phenomenal experience for their athletes and often find themselves on the positive end of the win/loss column.

References

1.   Elmore T. *Generation iY: Our Last Chance to Save Their Future.* Atlanta, GA: Poet Gardener Publishing; 2010.

2.   Wikipedia. Jerry Rice. 2017; https://en.wikipedia.org/wiki/Jerry_Rice. Accessed March 19, 2017.

CHAPTER 17

25 Ways to Make an Impact

Robert Taylor, Jr.
with contributions from Mike Whitman and Alex Walsh

Objectives

- Examine, consider, and discuss the multiple ways through which the strength & conditioning professional can make an impact within and among athletes, coaches, and co-workers

Introduction

Coaches have the opportunity to be incredible influencers in the lives of athletes, parents, staff members, and within a community. Many former athletes consider their coaches growing up as role models, life coaches, and even outstanding life-long friends. The level or sport has nothing to do with the quality of the coach or the influence he/she can have. Rather, the true measure of a coach is the positive impact he/she makes on the people he or she is privileged to work with.

The typical path of a strength and conditioning professional (SCP) starts with an individual spending countless hours studying the human body, searching for the best program possible, gaining hands-on experience with equipment ranging from dumbbells/barbells to machines and manual resistance, and learning how to integrate technology into a strength program. But it takes a coach years, if not decades, to realize that learning how to make a positive impact isn't found in a book or on the internet. Once a coach recognizes this, he/she often begins a lifelong journey to discover exactly how to make a difference in people's lives. This long-lasting effect is what the remainder of this chapter will explore.

This is Not Taught in School

Many sport coaches played their sport at a high level or spent countless hours learning the sport in an effort to share the passion of athletics with their team. In many cases, there are no degrees from institutions of higher learning specific to coaching. Only a few sports offer a coaching curriculum, annual conference, or certification process to encourage continued learning, and very few colleges have quality programs that teach the art of coaching.

SCPs often pursue a degree and certification in the field of kinesiology, exercise science or physical education. Some put in vast amounts of time, while others seem to be in the right place at the right time. No matter the path, it is common to hear SCPs pontificate on topics like program design, injury prevention, recovery, identifying a need to integrate plyometrics, whether or not to use Olympic lifts, and many more that may never have a concrete answer. We spend our lives searching for answers to questions that may never be answered and debating topics that will never be settled.

Whether you are a sport or strength coach, it is conceivable that you have never taken a course or even had a conversation about how to create an environment that will positively impact the lives around you. We are more concerned with offenses, defenses, fad strength programs, new uniforms, pictures for the website, and more that take our focus away from the most important part of coaching. At some point you have to ask yourself if any of these really offer an opportunity to truly make a positive impact on the lives of others, or are we steering the boat in the wrong direction?

Separating

We are often told that success cannot be achieved without perseverance, diligence, and hard work. Coaches often push athletes out of their comfort zone. Parents can provide structure and instill beliefs. Friends and other family can be a great support system to help achieve greatness. However, the discipline, attitude, toughness, and effort that is needed to separate yourself from those around you must come from *within*. There has to be an internal passion to achieve success in any facet of life. No one can be great if they do not have the desire to become great. Coaches who push an individual against their desires will often see adverse effects such as burn-out and athletes losing their love for their sport. A coach that truly wants to make a positive impact will find an individual's inner desire to be different—be better—than the average athlete. He or she will help them discover a path toward separating from the pack and being the best they can be.

Environment

The atmosphere you create will have an incredible impact on the mindset, performance, and outcome of your entire program. Coaches, teammates, administrators, parents, support staff, boosters, and even fans all play a major role in the experience of an athlete. Athletes will adapt to the environment that is created, fostered, and encouraged.

When creating your ideal training environment, it is important to recognize the nuances that breed success. If you have never been in a highly successful environment, take whatever steps are necessary to experience this. Take note of the music, cleanliness, fragrances, technology, colors, branding, logos, wall wrapping, written messages, flooring, ceiling, flow of the room, and even the entrance and exits. All of these small things play a role in decreasing stress, maximizing productivity, and enhancing the experience of the athlete. Make training an event that athletes look forward to.

Make a point to take an annual trip to observe other programs. Learn about equipment being used by others, the programs that have worked for them, and experience the culture that a video, or Instagram post just cannot provide. Notice the small things and think about what you can do to enhance your environment. It all matters.

Messaging

With the current state of smartphones, tablets, and computers, we need to embrace technology to stay in touch with our athletes, clients, coaches, and more. The speed at which a typed message, picture, or video can spread virally can positively or negatively impact a player's game day decision-making ability, recruiting, or even life. Taking the time to help your players, coaches, and staff focus on daily tasks is important to the overall success of a program or business.

Sending an email, posting a video, tagging on social media, or even using a text message to brighten someone's day can give them confidence, direction, and a goal. Help set the tone each day with a message in the locker room, stopping by a class, or even sending a quick video that shows your athletes you care about them as people, players, teammates, and future leaders.

Repetition

Repetition plays a huge role in the development of young athletes. Doing the same motions over and over helps their neuromuscular system learn movement patterns and can help them respond when it is most important. Similarly, having a message that is memorable and repeatable is a key to successfully getting it through to athletes. Simple motivational sayings or messages can become a team mantra when repeated consistently. A message that is repeatable can unify and have a lasting impact at all levels of sport.

Touch. Give. Ask.

Great coaches have a way of letting athletes know they care. There are many ways to achieve this, but perhaps the simplest involves three words: "Touch. Give. Ask."

This is useful in more than just the athlete/coach relationship, as it can be applied to just about any relationship. Any interaction with an athlete should begin with a 'positive touch' in the form of a high-five, handshake, hug, etc. The SCP will need to decide what is appropriate for that individual. A fist bump has become one of the most popular and safe ways to do this. This touch is a great way to immediately connect with someone early in the interaction and channel some positive energy through intentional, physical contact.

The second step is to 'give.' This could be a towel for the workout, water bottle, or even a gift on occasion. Coaches should give people something to show that they care. This obviously will not happen every time a coach interacts with an athlete, but the SCP should look for opportunities to take advantage of this concept. Even handing an athlete the workout card for the day can work, and it should not be the same thing every day. Change what is given to keep them guessing and looking forward to each interaction.

The final, and most important step is to 'ask.' Instead of telling athletes about your life, ask athletes about theirs. Ask how they felt after the last workout, or how they performed at the weekend tournament. Every human being wants to be heard, and asking questions shows that the SCP is interested in the athlete.

Perhaps the most important part of this concept is that the SCP needs to actively LISTEN when an athlete responds to a question. Being interested in what someone has to say is one of the most effective ways to build rapport.

Two-Second Rule

Actively listening to someone talking is a skill that can take a long time to acquire but will pay invaluable dividends. A simple way to implement this is to always wait two seconds after an athlete has finished talking before replying. This has an effect on both the player and the coach. The athlete will be reassured that the coach is paying attention, processing what he/she is saying, and most importantly, is interested in what he/she has to say. This is also a great mental tool for coaches to utilize as it keeps one from interjecting too early in an interaction. Often times, people latch onto the first thing a person says and they begin to formulate their response instead of listening. Disciplining one's self to wait until someone is completely finished speaking is a skill that will improve any interaction.

The Power of a Handshake

Today's young athletes can become immersed in the electronic world that surrounds them. Making positive human interactions engaging and rewarding is helpful to their growth as players, teammates, people, and future leaders. When an athlete is being recruited, a confident handshake is one of many things that is discussed by the coaches and scouts. A proper handshake, with appropriate pressure and eye contact, can help the athlete make a memorable impression. At the end of each practice, training session, and game, establish an expectation that encourages each player and coach to shake hands with eye contact. Take it a step further and ask that they say a few simple words such as:

"Great effort today."

"Good defense at practice." and/or

"I saw you using your non-dominant hand during the game."

This helps develop interpersonal relationship skills that are necessary in a winning culture and simply aren't practiced enough by young athletes.

Unconditional Support

Coaches everywhere can agree that being supportive of their players, teams and fellow coaches is incredibly important, but not nearly as many are unconditionally supportive. Supporting unconditionally is one of the most difficult things to do because it may require sacrificing one's own interests or comfort for the good of another. Regardless of the outcome, each person on your team wants to know that their efforts are appreciated, worthy of your attention, and have been noticed by their peers. The SCP has the opportunity to demonstrate unconditional support by always encouraging athletes and praising small improvements. When athletes feel appreciated and noticed, they will often put even more effort into an activity.

Post-game Communication

There are times to be critical and there are times to praise. What is said and the tone that is used to deliver what is said during the game, at half time, and especially after the game has a huge impact on the motivation and attitude of a team. As a coach or leader of a team, the SCP must be sure to think first, control emotions, and share a positive message whenever possible after a game.

The best time to analyze, critique and provide feedback is during practice. While under the stress of game action, it is important to "stay present" and consider what is important at that time. Beating a player down with negatives, "could-haves" and "should-haves" does not change what just happened, but could have a negative impact on what will happen in the future. Explaining what is expected the next time a predictable moment occurs is helpful in the learning process of an athlete. Remember to provide positive, enthusiastic praise in public, while critiquing in private where an open and comfortable dialogue can occur to ensure development and ownership. There is little to gain from a post-game message that insults, berates, or focuses on negative plays. Allow the emotion to pass. Allow the individual the opportunity to go through their own learning process. Remind your players and teammates how much you enjoyed playing with them, how much you enjoy watching them play, and how lucky we all are to have experienced this moment as a team. Be positive, and stay positive while providing instructions and feedback.

Eye Color

Always make a point to know the color of somebody's eyes when addressing them. This is most commonly applied in a setting where a coach addresses a group of players at practice, during team strength training, or even before a game. Eye contact is the only way one can truly tell if he or she has the attention of the person or people being addressed. Coaches should use this to remember to always be in close enough proximity of athletes before giving an important message. Addressing athletes from close range—close enough so that each can see the color of the others' eyes—is one simple tool coaches can use to ensure the message is being heard. Similarly, coaches should ask athletes the color of their coaches' eyes to ensure they are fully engaged and focused. Speaking to a team who is looking at the ground, their teammates, or watching the other team warm-up is not an effective environment for communication.

Someone is Always Watching

Joe DiMaggio once said "Every time I play, some kid is watching me for either the first or last time. I owe him my best." This concept is easily understood in the case of professional athletes such as DiMaggio or any other public figure who is constantly in the spotlight, but this really applies to all people—especially coaches.

Coaches need to be careful what they say and do and how they live their lives because someone is always listening or watching. Coaches are surrounded by children who can be incredibly impressionable. Kids often look up to their coaches, listening intently to their words and using their actions as a model for how to behave. This is why it is so important for coaches to model positive behaviors. The moment a person decides to be a sport coach or SCP, he or she also becomes a role model. A SCP's words and actions can have a major impact on a young athlete, so always assume that kids are watching.

Praise What is Valued

Many coaches focus on what athletes are doing wrong and falsely assume that telling them NOT to do something will help athletes correct the mistakes. Unfortunately, the human brain operates quite differently than this. For the most part, humans think in pictures and images. For example, when someone is told "Do _not_ think about a red corvette," the first mental picture he/she will get is a red corvette. Our brains operate with positive cues, and coaches can take advantage of that by adapting their instructions and feedback.

Rather than trying to correct what is *wrong*, the SCP should praise and reinforce what is being done *correctly*. Focus on reinforcing the behaviors you desire and want athletes to exhibit. This even helps the athletes who are not receiving the praise. When athletes hear a coach praise another athlete for a certain behavior, they subconsciously want to receive praise. This motivates them to exhibit the behavior they heard praised. The SCP should paint mental pictures for an athlete to help them see what the desired outcome. Athletes will have a much easier time processing and performing the actions you want to see.

Avoid Being Consumed by Problems

There will always be athletes who require more work than others. Some kids seem to do everything right all the time. They pay attention, are positive role models, and give great effort. Some have a few of these qualities. Still others have none.

The "difficult" athletes—those who require constant monitoring—can take up a lot of the SCP's time. They seem to constantly find themselves in the coach's office, whether for behavior issues or because they need to be reminded to be part of the team. This can be exhausting and it often feels like these individuals consume all of your time.

A good coach will not allow him or herself to be consumed by dealing with problems. Coaches should intentionally seek out players that make good choices and do not require much attention. Be sure to invest in those players just as much as those who require constant monitoring. The "easy kids" who always bring positive energy can sometimes fly under the radar and get less attention.

"Don't" and "Can't" are Four-letter Words

Speaking carelessly is something that happens way too often. People speak before they think, use language others don't understand, or repeat words over and over again unnecessarily. This happens in all environments and at all levels of interaction. Coaches should carefully monitor the words they choose when talking to athletes and parents. One easy recommendation is to avoid using words like "don't" or "can't" that have negative connotations and can bring down team morale. These words can have a dramatic effect on athletes who struggle to stay positive. They can also be misunderstood by parents, which can cause problems the SCP may not even know about.

As coaches, we are always looking for the correct message to help guide and inspire those around us. But how many practice, pre-game, half-time, or post-game speeches do you really remember? By adding creativity to our message, we may be surprised as to what our athletes retain. Using acronyms to share a common team phrase or emphasis can be helpful for athletes. Try using one of the following at your next practice:

- WIN: What's Important Now
- FEAR: Forget Everything And Repeat
- YET: Your Energy Talks
- RACE: Response After Critical Error
- FAMILY: Forget About Me. I Love You.
- TEAM: Together Everyone Achieves More

Collaboration is Key

In many atmospheres, asking for help or even admitting the need for assistance is considered a sign of weakness. This attitude can be especially common in male-dominated environments. A lot of males subconsciously think that independence and confidence defines their manliness. While modern society may back this concept up and tell young people that they need to strive to be independent individuals, quite the opposite is true of a successful team.

No matter the age, gender, sport, position, level of play, or experience of an athlete, he/she will always be stronger alongside teammates with a common goal. Old adages like "two heads are better than one" or "a cord of three strands is not easily broken" could not be more appropriate for such a situation. A team of people who are striving toward a goal together develop a bond that is not found in many other settings.

There is another level to the concept of collaboration that is not easily achieved. This step requires people to openly *acknowledge* their need for help. This recognition that one is needed by others reaches into a person's soul and creates motivation unlike anything else. Athletes should recognize their strength in numbers and rally behind their cause, and coaches should encourage this behavior and positively reward it when demonstrated.

Take Risks

There are two Teddy Roosevelt quotes that should be posted in every facility: "It is hard to fail. It is worse to never have tried to succeed." "The only man who never makes a mistake, is the man who never does anything."

In 2007-08 the New England Patriots went 18-1, only losing in the Super Bowl because of a once-in-a-lifetime catch by David Tyree. At the end of the year, they did not accomplish their goal. Their goal was to win the Super Bowl, and while they had a terrific season, they felt as though they did not succeed. They failed to reach their goal, and they failed to become the only team in history to go 19-0. Despite all of this perceived "failure," that team is considered one of the greatest of all time.

No athlete wants to fail. No coach wants to fail. And, at the end of the season, every team wants to achieve their goals. However, complacency can accompany a goal if the bar is not set high enough.

Special things can happen when you shoot for the moon.

If the standard is set too low, it is easy to meet expectations and there is little risk of failure. Without risk of failure, the reward is rarely satisfying. When a massive goal is set, great things can happen even if the goal is never actually realized. The value of setting large goals is an important lesson that coaches can teach young athletes. This lesson can have a profound impact in all areas of a person's life, so the SCP should not miss out on the opportunity to give this gift.

Appreciate the Process

Athletes, coaches, and parents alike tend to focus on making the playoffs, winning championship games, getting into a good college for their sport, or other outcome-based achievements. One of the most valuable lessons a SCP can teach is the concept of focusing on the process. Like many things in life, the process of strength development takes a long time and progress is only made when effort is given consistently. Teaching young athletes to focus on the process helps them learn that many small actions can create large results over time.

Championships are not won by a single play, so young athletes need to understand the importance of working a plan one day at a time.

Relationships Win

Successful teams and businesses have one thing in common; they have more positive relationships than others. Players who want to be on winning teams need to develop relationships with their teammates, coaches, and support staff. In the traditional preparation for sport, coaches focus most of their time and energy on the X's and O's of execution, but it is important to set aside time to allow athletes to get to know one another. Coaches usually invest emotionally well before their athletes, so it is up to the coach to create an atmosphere that fosters teamwork and relationships.

For example, the SCP can organize activities outside of standard training such as a canoe trip, challenging hike, or special workouts done outside of the normal environment. Develop a team challenge that tests the team's knowledge of each player's middle name, elementary or middle school attended, favorite foods and movies, other family members, musical preferences, other sports they play, countries they have visited, etc. Have them meet outside of practice for a scavenger hunt where they can share photos on a team social media site of them at different places. The SCP must create opportunities for athletes to interact with their teammates so they begin to feel more comfortable around each other. The more we can learn about each other, the better the overall athletic experience will be.

Keep Them Engaged

Young athletes often feel that running the same sprints, shuttles and drills can become monotonous. Many express distaste in doing exercises or drills they find boring and this negative energy can infect a team. If one athlete hangs his/her head or complains, teammates will follow suit, and the energy is quickly sucked out of the practice. It can be difficult to counteract this effect, so the SCP should strive to create an environment that is positive and engaging, and minimizes negativity before it even begins.

While we know that repetition is a key to skill acquisition and physical development, the SCP must find ways to vary things enough to keep athletes engaged. This does not mean that the entire workout needs to be totally different every day. Rather, the SCP should bring positive energy to every session and change the routine just enough that athletes don't know exactly what to expect.

Simply changing the order of your warm-up routine each day is one way to keep athletes interested. Another idea is to change the last two exercises in the workout and only announce them when it is time to perform them. It can be as simple as changing the music selection to create "Metal Monday," "Techno Tuesday," or "Throw-back Thursday." Of course, the workouts will remain fairly consistent, but one or two small changes can make a big difference.

Although drills and practice can feel repetitive or boring sometimes, it is the SCP's attitude and energy that determines the atmosphere. Any activity can be more enjoyable and beneficial with positive energy.

Give Back

There are many coaches whose only goal is to win championships. While this is a goal every team should strive toward, it is only a small part of sports. A coach's success should not only be judged on their win/loss record. Rather, a coach should be evaluated by the impact he/she has on the players, coaches, and parents involved in the program. Additionally, coaches and players should always strive to make a positive impact on people outside of their program such as opponents, other teams in the community, families of players, etc. Teaching young athletes the value of community service is a lesson that can have a ripple effect in a community. When young athletes are thinking outside of their own lives, great things can happen, and coaches have the ability to put these wheels in motion. Show young athletes how to give back, and they will learn through your actions.

Embrace Technology/Social Media

The fastest way to interact with young athletes is through social media, smartphones, and other electronic technology. There are still coaches that believe that this is just a fad, but this is how young athletes communicate. Young people use their phones for just about everything today, so we need to meet them where they are to make the biggest impact in their lives.

Of course, the SCP should always encourage personal interaction, but the use of text messages, images, and videos can help the team stay connected. While we must be very careful with technology and social media, we should not let fear stop us from utilizing these resources. Keep all interactions very professional, and focus on spreading positive messages. Take a moment to post a positive message on the team's social media account or post a video highlighting the team's accomplishments.

Be sure to include each player and their family in the process of sharing on the team's platform. Finding "team communication" or "strength training" apps is easier than ever, and this technology can help you disseminate positive information to your athletes.

Invest

When investors put money into a business or project, they do not simply write a check and forget about it. They typically follow along with the progress and check in regularly to see if there is anything they can do to increase the value of their investment.

This attitude should be adopted by the SCP who wants to see their athletes grow into well-adjusted, successful adults. Rather than focusing strictly on the development of strength or speed, the SCP must remember that we are part of a team that is investing in the life of a younger person. In order to get the most out of our investment, we need to be cognizant of how we can help this person grow. This may come in the form of attending sporting events, talking about homework, or teaching a lesson when something goes wrong. Of course, we always need to get results through training, but finding other ways to make a difference will show athletes that you care about them as human beings.

Know Your Role

The SCP plays a role in the overall success of an athlete or team, and it is important to fully understand and accept that role. Successful teams can be compared to a Hollywood movie production: each actor and behind-the-scenes contributor plays a role in the overall production. When everyone does their part, the production turns out well. When anyone fails to perform, the entire production may be adversely affected.

In this analogy, the SCP plays a small, behind-the-scenes role in the overall production. People do not come to a sporting event to watch the SCP perform any more than they pay attention to the sound quality of a movie. While sound quality is absolutely critical to a Hollywood production, in most cases, the audience only notices it when something has gone terribly wrong. Similarly, the SCP has a very important role in a sports program, but he or she should never be the center of attention. Instead, the work of the SCP is usually only known to people inside the program.

Unfortunately, the SCP may feel compelled to perform roles outside of his/her job description. Sometimes, taking on additional responsibilities is very helpful to the overall success of the program. Other times, it can be seen as "stepping on toes" and can create internal conflict. Before the SCP performs a duty outside of the scope of the job, he or she should be 100% sure that it will not cause problems or resentments from other members of the team. For example, helping load equipment onto the bus will probably be viewed as very helpful. On the other hand, talking to athletes about a defensive formation may not be as well-received. The coach responsible for this may feel as though you are confusing the athletes or teaching them something they don't use in their system. At no point in the SCP's job description does it say "correct pitching mechanics" or "teach athletes how to play cover 2." Understand your role in the overall program, and do it as well as possible.

Give Thanks

In the fast-paced world we live in, taking the time to appreciate what has been accomplished is often overlooked. SCPs should make time to show respect and appreciation by writing an email, sending a text, putting pen to paper, or even speaking face to face to let others know how much they mean. This may be the most important life lesson a SCP can teach. It is amazing how hard people will work, play, and train when they realize that their efforts are appreciated. The support of one another will go a long way in creating an environment that develops championship qualities one day at a time.

About the Editors

Jim Kielbaso

Jim Kielbaso is the President & CEO of the International Youth Conditioning Association and the Director of the Total Performance Training Center in Wixom, MI. He is a former college strength & conditioning coach and the author of Ultimate Speed & Agility. He has produced several educational products for coaches/trainers and has written articles for many magazines, journals and websites. Jim runs a popular NFL Combine training program and is hired by the University of Michigan Football Program to prepare their graduating seniors for the combine. Jim lives in Plymouth, MI with his wife Elaina and their three sons Cameron, Drew, and Jack.

Toby Brooks

Dr. Toby Brooks serves as an Associate Professor and Clinical Coordinator in the Master of Athletic Training Program at Texas Tech University Health Sciences Center in Lubbock, Texas. After completing both a Master's and PhD at the University of Arizona where he worked as an athletic trainer with the women's gymnastics and football program, Brooks has worked as a certified athletic trainer and/or strength coach with numerous professional, collegiate, and high school athletics programs, including the Oakland Raiders, USA Baseball, the University of Texas El Paso, Liberty University, the Florida Firecats, Shawnee Community College, the Southern Illinois Miners, and 10 high schools across three states. He has has published nine books, more than 20 articles and studies, and is a regular presenter at national and international conferences. He and his wife Christi live just outside of Lubbock along with daughter Brynnan and son Taye.

About the Authors

Mark Naylor is an assistant strength & conditioning coach with the University of Michigan football program. He previously served as director of Ball State University's football strength and conditioning program and his career includes stops as a strength and conditioning assistant with the Baltimore Ravens and as a graduate assistant with both Ball State and Missouri Southern. Naylor earned his undergraduate degree from Missouri Southern and his master's at Ball State in 2006. A native of Broken Arrow, Oklahoma, he and his wife, the former Melissa Obermann, have three children, daughter Macy and sons Matthew and Mason.

Mark Naylor

Darl Bauer is the Associate Director of the football strength and conditioning program at West Virginia University. Bauer came to West Virginia after serving as a strength and conditioning intern at Eastern Michigan for the 2007 summer. Bauer was a sports performance specialist at the Total Performance Center in Wixom, Michigan for two years and also served as a strength and conditioning coach at Detroit Country Day School and Fairmont Senior High setting up training programs for their varsity programs. Coach Bauer was a four-year letter-winner at Hillsdale College in Hillsdale, Michigan where he graduated with a bachelor's degree in education. He received a master's of science degree in athletic coaching education from West Virginia. He and his wife Carly, and daughter, Gigi, live in Morgantown, WV.

Darl Bauer

Blair Wagner

Blair Wagner is a strength & conditioning coach with the Los Angeles Rams of the National Football League. Before that, he spent two years with the University of Washington Olympic Sports Strength and Conditioning Department and as the Head Strength Coach for the WNBA's Seattle Storm during the 2016 season. Prior to his arrival at the UW, he spent 9 months training the 1st Special Forces Group, Green Berets, in Tacoma, WA. Before arriving in the Pacific Northwest, Wagner was the Head Sports Performance Coach at Eastern Michigan University an assistant strength and conditioning coach at The Citadel and did stints at the College of Charleston and the University of Nebraska Kearney. Wagner completed his master's degree in Exercise & Sport Science from The Citadel Graduate College and his BS in Kinesiology and Health Promotion from the University of Wyoming. Blair holds certifications from the Collegiate Strength and Conditioning Coaches Association, National Strength and Conditioning Association, USA Weightlifting, National Academy of Sports Medicine, Precision Nutrition and the International Youth and Conditioning Association. A native of Cheyenne, Wyoming, Wagner is the proud husband to Cam, and father to their son, Bremer.

Freddie Walker

Freddie Walker is an assistant strength & conditioning coach at the University of Pittsburgh. He received his BS in Exercise Science from Bowling Green State University where he also played football. He spent time training at the Total Performance Training Center in Wixom, MI before accepting a Graduate Assistant position with the Michigan State strength & conditioning program. After finishing his Masters Degree at MSU, Coach Walker worked as a strength coach at the University of Illinois. Freddie is certified through the IYCA, CSCCa, and NSCA.

Joe Powell

Joe Powell is an assistant strength & conditioning coach and adjunct faculty member at Central Michigan University. Powell received both his BS in Exercise Science and MS in Exercise Physiology from CMU. Coach Powell spent two years working at the Total Performance Training Center in Wixom, MI and one summer interning with the University of Michigan football program before heading back to Central Michigan to teach and coach.

Bill Burghardt is an assistant strength and conditioning coach at Michigan State University where he assists with the football team and is in charge of the wrestling strength & conditioning program. He spent two seasons as a strength and conditioning graduate assistant at Michigan State and had a brief stint as an assistant strength and conditioning coach at the United States Military Academy in West Point, N.Y. Burghardt is a certified strength and conditioning specialist with the Collegiate Strength and Conditioning Coaches Association (CSCCa) and the National Strength and Conditioning Association (NSCA). After earning his bachelor's degree from Michigan State University in Kinesiology, Burghardt worked as a graduate student volunteer on the Spartan strength and conditioning staff in 2009-10. He also received his Master's degree in Kinesiology from MSU. Burghardt and his wife, Alaina, were married in May 2012 and have a daughter, Annabelle.

Bill Burghardt

Brian Clarke is the head strength & conditioning coordinator and chairman of the Wellness Department at Noblesville High School in Indiana where he sees over 600 hundred student-athletes every day. Coach Clarke earned his BS from Butler University and his career includes highly successful stops at Warren Central and Pike High School. Brian leads one of the most efficient high school strength & conditioning programs in the country, and he has become a leader in the field for his ability to engage large groups of students with diverse backgrounds and goals.

Brian Clarke

Rob Taylor is the founder and owner of SMARTER Team Training in Baltimore, MD and the former strength & conditioning coach at Loyola University Maryland. Rob was a strength and conditioning consultant for athletes on the Women's Lacrosse World Cup Champions Team Australia in 2005, and was the Head Strength Coach for Team Australia's 2009 World Cup team. He has worked with professional organizations such as the Anaheim Angels, Tampa Bay Buccaneers, Tampa Bay Mutiny, and San Antonio Silver Stars.

Coach Taylor has also been the Head Strength and Conditioning Coach at UNC Greensboro. He left to pursue a graduate degree in Exercise Physiology from the University of Delaware, while working as an Assistant Strength and Conditioning Coach. Rob has also worked with the athletic departments at Cincinnati, Princeton, and Villanova. Taylor is certified through numerous national and international organizations. Coach Taylor has been part of the Advisory Boards for Polar, Zephyr, and several other businesses throughout his career. Most recently he has become an Advisory Board Member for the International Youth Conditioning Association.

Rob Taylor

Ron McKeefery

Nationally recognized as a leader in the area of sports development, Ron McKeefery has twice been named Collegiate Strength and Conditioning Coach of the Year. First by the Professional Football Strength and Conditioning Society (2008 Under Armour Collegiate Strength and Conditioning Coach of the Year), and next by the National Strength and Conditioning Association (2016 Collegiate Strength and Conditioning Coach of the Year). In 2013, Coach McKeefery was honored as a Master Strength and Conditioning Coach by the Collegiate Strength and Conditioning Coaches Association (CSCCa). The Master Strength and Conditioning Coach certification is the highest honor that can be achieved as a strength and conditioning coach, representing professionalism, knowledge, experience, expertise and longevity in the field. Prior to becoming the Vice President of Performance and Education for PLAE, Coach McKeefery served as a strength and conditioning coach at both the Professional and Collegiate level. Working with such professional organizations as the: Cincinnati Bengals (NFL), Kansas City Royals (MLB), Tampa Bay Buccaneers (NFL), and the Berlin Thunder (NFL Europe), and collegiate programs including Eastern Michigan University, the University of Tennessee, and the University of South Florida.

Greg Pyszczynski

Greg Pyszczynski is an assistant strength and conditioning coach at Iowa State. A native of West Seneca, N.Y., and graduate of St. John Fisher (N.Y.) College, Pyszczynski was the head strength and conditioning coach at Buffalo for two seasons. Before that, Pyszczynski was an assistant strength and conditioning coach at Illinois after serving on the strength and conditioning staff at Eastern Michigan from (2009-12). Pyszczynski was also a graduate assistant at Utica (N.Y.) College in 2008-09, assisting with its strength and conditioning programs for football, men's lacrosse, women's ice hockey and field hockey.

Kristin Shuman

Kristin Shuman is an Associate Professor of Exercise Science at Concordia University (MI) and the former Athletic Director of Strength and Conditioning at Idaho State University. After receiving her master's degree in athletic administration from ISU, Shuman became the Human Performance Lab Coordinator in the Sport Science and Physical Education department. She went on to complete her PhD in Educational Leadership-Higher Education Administration from Idaho State before being named the Director of Strength & Conditioning. Before being named as the director of the ISU program, Shuman also worked with the women's soccer program, women's basketball program, softball program, and the Dept of Law Enforcement. Shuman served as a strength and conditioning coach at the University of Detroit Mercy and graduated with her bachelor's degree in Sports

Medicine/Exercise Science in 2008 from Eastern Michigan. Shuman and her husband Berrett reside in Michigan with their son Hudson and daughter Ivy.

Aaron Hillmann has over 20 years of experience as a strength & conditioning coach and is currently the Director of Player Development for the Iowa State football program. He was the head S & C coach at the University of Illinois, Bowling Green State University, the University of Connecticut, and spent time as an assistant S & C coach at the University of Michigan, Cincinnati, Ball State, and Notre Dame. Hillmann is a Master Strength & Conditioning Coach through the CSCCa and holds multiple certifications in addition to his bachelor and master degrees. He and his wife, Dina, have two sons, Jacob and Jonah, and a daughter, Skylar.

Aaron Hillmann

Fred Eaves is the Director of Athletics at Battle Ground Academy in Franklin, Tennessee and was named the 2015 NSCA High School Strength & Conditioning Coach of the Year. Fred has nearly 20 years of coaching experience at places like LSU, the University of Tennessee, the University of Tennessee-Chattanooga, and Battle Ground Academy. He holds degrees in Administration and Supervision, Educational Counseling and Sports Psychology.

Fred Eaves

Adam Feit is the Business Manager for Reach Your Potential Training (RYPT) and an active speaker for Precision Nutrition. Before that, Adam served as the Assistant Strength and Conditioning Coach and Nutrition Coordinator for the NFL's Carolina Panthers and the Head Sports Performance Coach for Eastern Michigan University. Coach Feit also served as an Assistant Strength and Conditioning Coach for the University of Louisville's football team and as a Graduate Assistant Strength and Conditioning Coach for The Citadel in Charleston, SC. He also performed strength and conditioning internships with Arizona State University, the US Olympic Training Center, the University of Connecticut, and Springfield College. Adam played football for Springfield College in Springfield, MA. He earned an M.S. from the University of California Pennsylvania and holds certifications from multiple organizations. He is married to Mary Kate Feit (Jones), also a sports performance coach and competitive lifter, and have a son (Cody) and daughter (Macy).

Adam Feit

Bobby Smith

Bobby Smith is the co-owner of Reach Your Potential Training in New Jersey. He played both football and threw the javelin at Monmouth University in New Jersey and won the U.S. Olympic Trials for javelin in 2008. He holds certifications from multiple organizations and his energetic and positive attitude has made him one of the most popular strength coaches on the east coast.

Selena Budge

Selena Budge received her doctorate in physical therapy from Ohio State University and the founder of Stability Enhancement Systems (SES). The SES program has been used by major colleges and professional teams throughout America as well as many high schools and club sport athletes. Selena played basketball at the University of Miami-Florida and she has received national grant funding for her work on ACL injury prevention.

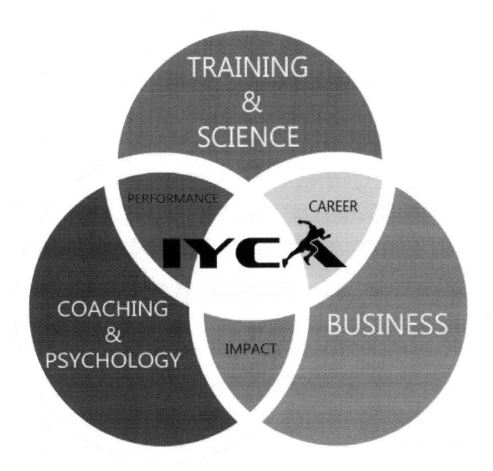

The International Youth Conditioning Association (IYCA) is the only organization that stands at the intersection of scientific training principles, coaching/psychological methods that help make a positive impact on young people, and sound business development education. We tackle these important areas through courses, certifications, free information, lives events, mentorships, and personal interactions with our membership.

This book is part of the High School Strength & Conditioning Specialist course and certification material.

For more information about IYCA courses, certifications, products and programs, visit us at IYCA.org